P9-DEH-232

The Tyndale New Testament Commentaries

General Editor:
THE REV. CANON LEON MORRIS, M.Sc., M.Th., Ph.D.

2 PETER AND JUDE

THE SECOND EPISTLE GENERAL OF PETER AND THE GENERAL EPISTLE OF JUDE

AN INTRODUCTION AND COMMENTARY

by

MICHAEL GREEN, M.A., B.D.

Professor of Evangelism and New Testament at Regent College, Vancouver, and formerly Rector of St Aldate's Church, Oxford, and Principal of St John's College, Nottingham

Inter-Varsity Press
Leicester, England

William B. Eerdmans Publishing Company
Grand Rapids, Michigan

Inter-Varsity Press
38 De Montfort Street, Leicester LE1 7GP, England

Wm. B. Eerdmans Publishing Company
255 Jefferson S.E., Grand Rapids, MI 49503

Published and sold only in the USA and Canada by Wm. B. Eerdmans Publishing Co.

First edition 1968
Second edition 1987

Reprinted 2000

Unless otherwise stated, quotations from the Bible are taken from the HOLY BIBLE: NEW INTERNATIONAL VERSION. Copyright © 1978 by the International Bible Society, New York. Published in Great Britain by Hodder and Stoughton Ltd, and used by permission of Zondervan Bible Publishers, Grand Rapids, Michigan.

British Library Cataloguing in Publication Data

Green, Michael, *1930–*
  The Second Epistle General of Peter and the
  General Epistle of Jude.—2nd ed.—(The Tyndale
  New Testament commentaries)
  1. Bible. N.T. Peter 2nd—Commentaries
  2. Bible. N.T. Jude—Commentaries
  I. Title   II. Series
  227'.9307   BS2795.3

IVP EDITION 0-85111-887-9

Library of Congress Cataloging in Publication Data

Green, Michael, 1930-
The second epistle general of Peter, and the general
epistle of Jude.

(The Tyndale New Testament commentaries)
  1. Bible.   N.T.   Peter, 2nd — Commentaries.
2. Bible.   N.T.   Jude — Commentaries.   I. Title.   II. Series.
  BS2795.3.G7   1987   277'.9307   87-26058

ISBN 0-8028-0078-5

Set in Palatino
Typeset in Great Britain by Parker Typesetting Service, Leicester
Printed in USA by Eerdmans Printing Company, Grand Rapids, Michigan

Inter-Varsity Press is the publishing division of the Universities and Colleges Christian Fellowship (formerly the Inter-Varsity Fellowship), a student movement linking Christian Unions in universities and colleges throughout the United Kingdom and the Republic of Ireland, and a member movement of the International Fellowship of Evangelical Students. For information about local and national activities write to UCCF, 38 De Montfort Street, Leicester LE1 7GP.

GENERAL PREFACE

The original *Tyndale Commentaries* aimed at providing help for the general reader of the Bible. They concentrated on the meaning of the text without going into scholarly technicalities. They sought to avoid 'the extremes of being unduly technical or unhelpfully brief'. Most who have used the books agree that there has been a fair measure of success in reaching that aim.

Times, however, change. A series that has served so well for so long is perhaps not quite as relevant as when it was first launched. New knowledge has come to light. The discussion of critical questions has moved on. Bible-reading habits have changed. When the original series was commenced it could be presumed that most readers used the Authorized Version and one could make one's comments accordingly, but this situation no longer obtains.

The decision to revise and update the whole series was not reached lightly, but in the end it was thought that this is what is required in the present situation. There are new needs, and they will be better served by new books or by a thorough updating of the old books. The aims of the original series remain. The new commentaries are neither minuscule nor unduly long. They are exegetical rather than homiletic. They do not discuss all the critical questions, but none is written without an awareness of the problems that engage the attention of New Testament scholars. Where it is felt that formal consideration should be given to such questions, they are discussed in the Introduction and sometimes in Additional Notes.

But the main thrust of these commentaries is not critical. These books are written to help the non-technical reader to understand his Bible better. They do not presume a knowledge of Greek, and all Greek words discussed are transliterated; but the authors have the Greek text before them and their comments are made on the basis of the originals. The authors are free to choose their own modern translation, but are asked to bear in mind the variety of translations in current use.

The new series of *Tyndale Commentaries* goes forth, as the former series did, in the hope that God will graciously use these books to help the general reader to understand as fully and clearly as possible the meaning of the New Testament.

LEON MORRIS

5

CONTENTS

AUTHOR'S PREFACE TO THE FIRST EDITION

2 Peter and Jude are a very obscure corner of the New Testament. They are hardly ever preached upon; commentaries and articles in learned journals rarely deal with them. There are not wanting voices, such as those of Professors Käsemann and Aland, urging their deletion from the Canon. The question may well be asked, have they any relevance for today?

The commentary that follows is written in the conviction that these two Epistles carry a very important message for our times. We live in days when the contents of the Christian faith are widely questioned, when new and speculative theologies are widely disseminated, and when a new morality is being advocated which is capable of being misunderstood as 'the old immorality writ large'. Christianity is presented to us in terms of love, with the content of the faith and the hope for the future both strangely muted in deference to the contemporary intellectual climate. There is, moreover, an intellectualism about much of our Christianity which is not, perhaps, so far removed from that attacked in these letters – the knowledge that has little relation to holy living, growing spirituality and deepening love. We can hardly maintain that 2 Peter and Jude, written as they were to meet problems very like our own, have nothing to teach us. So long as sin needs to be exposed, so long as man needs to be reminded that persistent wrongdoing ends in ruin, that lust is self-defeating, that intellectualism devoid of love is a barren thing, and that Christian theology has no right to outrun the 'faith once delivered to the saints', these Epistles will remain uncomfortably, burningly relevant.

This commentary sprang out of my Tyndale Monograph, *2 Peter Reconsidered*, from which its introductory matter should be supplemented, since lack of space has prevented me from dealing as fully as I would have liked with textual problems. I would like to express my gratitude to Professor C. F. D. Moule who first interested me in this part of the New Testament by inviting me to read a paper on 2 Peter to his Cambridge New Testament Seminar; to Professor R. V. G. Tasker, the former General Editor of the series, and Dr I. H. Marshall of Aberdeen University, both of whom read the manuscript in its first draft and made many helpful suggestions.

E. M. B. GREEN

7

PREFACE TO THE SECOND EDITION

This Commentary, first published in 1968, and based on the AV, is here reissued, based on the text of the *New International Version* of the Bible. While adhering to the broad positions adopted in the first edition, I have taken the opportunity afforded by this revision to make a thorough reappraisal of the text of the Epistles and the commentary in the light of modern writing. There is a resurgence of interest in this long-neglected corner of the New Testatment, and a willingness to consider fresh possibilities. Many of the commentaries on 2 Peter and Jude which emerged since 1968, such as those of Sidebottom, Kelly and Fuller, have added little to the discussion and have disappointed. But Spicq, Fornberg, Neyrey, and J. A. T. Robinson have done much to break new ground and I wish to express my indebtedness to them.

As will be apparent from the following pages, my biggest debt is to Dr R. J. Bauckham, who has not only written the fullest and incomparably the best commentary on 2 Peter and Jude to appear in English, but has made available to me a detailed supplementary bibliography on these letters, an account of recent research, and a great deal of personal interest and help to one who has exchanged academic life for the parish. Dr Carsten Thiede has been particularly helpful as I have set out to revise the commentary. My thanks are also due to Dr Leon Morris, the present General Editor, for his careful comments on the manuscript of the revised edition, and to Dr David Stone who did a superb job on the proofs.

I am more than ever convinced that these letters have much to teach the modern church, and that they stress areas (such as sexual permissiveness, toleration of false teaching, adherence to New Testament Christianity, and a proper basis for Christian hope together with an appropriate lifestyle) which greatly need our attention.

MICHAEL GREEN

CHIEF ABBREVIATIONS

AV	Authorized Version of the Bible (King James), 1611.
BAC	*Biblioteca de Autores Cristianos*
BJRL	*Bulletin of the John Rylands Library*, Manchester.
E.T.	English translation.
JBL	*Journal of Biblical Literature.*
JETS	*Journal of the Evangelical Theological Society.*
JTS	*Journal of Theological Studies.*
LXX	Septuagint (pre-Christian Greek version of the Old Testament).
NEB	New English Bible: New Testament, 1970.
NTS	*New Testament Studies.*
NIV	New International Version of the Bible, 1980.
RSV	Revised Standard Version of the Bible, 1952.
RV	Revised Version of the Bible, 1881.
ZNTW	*Zeitschrift für die neutestamentliche Wissenschaft.*

SELECT BIBLIOGRAPHY

Alford, H., *The Greek Testament*, 1880.

Barclay, W., *The Letters of Peter* and *The Letters of John and Jude* (*Daily Study Bible*), 1958.

Barnett, A. E. and Homrighausen, E. G., *The Second Epistle of Peter and the Epistle of Jude* (Interpreter's Bible), 1957.

Bauckham, R. J., *2 Peter and Jude* (Word Biblical Commentary), 1983.

Bengel, J. A., *Gnomon Novi Testamenti*, 1773.

Bigg, C., *The Epistles of St Peter and St Jude* (*International Critical Commentaries*), 1901.

Boobyer, G. H., Contributions in *Peake's Commentary*, rev. ed., 1963, and in *New Testament Essays*, 1959.

Brox, N. ed., *Pseudepigraphie in der heidnischen und judischchristlichen Antike*, 1977.

Caffin, B. C., *The Pulpit Commentary*, 1908.

Calvin, J., *The Epistles of Peter*, edited by D. W. and T. F. Torrance (*Calvin's Commentaries*), 1963 and *The Epistle of Jude*, edited by John Owen, 1855.

Chaine, J., *La Seconde Épître de Saint Pierre, L'Épître de Saint Jude*, 1973.

Charlesworth, J. H., *The Pseudepigrapha and Modern Research*, 1976.

Cranfield, C. E. B., *1 and 2 Peter and Jude* (*Torch Bible Commentaries*), 1960.

Fornberg, T., *An Early Church in a Pluralistic Society*, a Study in 2 Peter, 1977.

Fucks, Wilhelm., *Nach allen Regeln der Kunst*, 1968.

James, M. R., *2 Peter and Jude*, 1912.

Grundmann, W., *Der Brief des Judas und der zweite Brief des Petrus*, 1974.

Käsemann, E., 'An Apologia for Primitive Christian Eschatology' in *Essays on New Testament Themes*, 1964.

Kelly, J. N. D., *The Epistles of Peter and Jude*, 1969.

Lumby, J. R., *The Epistles of St Peter* (Expositor's Bible), 1893.

Leaney, A. R. C., *The Letters of Peter and Jude*, 1967.

Mayor, J. B., *The Second Epistle of St Peter and the Epistle of St Jude*, 1907.

Moffatt, J., *The General Epistles, James, Peter and Jude* (Moffatt New Testament Commentary), 1947.

Mounce, R. H., *A Living hope: a commentary on 1 & 2 Peter*, 1982.

Neyrey, J. H., *The Form and Background of the Polemic in 2 Peter*, in *JBL*, 1980, pp. 407–431.

Plummer, A., *The General Epistles of St James and St Jude* (*Expositor's Bible*), 1891.

Plumptre, E. H., *The General Epistles of St Peter and St Jude* (*Cambridge Bible for Schools*), 1903.

Reicke, B., *The Epistles of James, Peter and Jude*, 1964.

Reisner, R., 'Der zweite Petrus-Brief und die Eschatologie' in *Zukunftserwartung in biblischer Sicht*, hrsg. von Gerhard Maier, 1984.

Robinson, J. A. T., *Redating the New Testament*, 1976.

Robson, E. I., *Studies in the Second Epistle of Peter*, 1915.

Schelkle, K. H., *Die Petrusbriefe und der Judasbrief (Herder Kommentar)*, 1961.

Schlatter, A., *Die Briefe des Petrus, Judas, Jacobus, der Brief an die Hebräer*, 1964.

Sidebottom, E. M., *James, Jude and 2 Peter*, 1967.

Spicq, C., *Les Epîtres de Saint Pierre*, 1966.

Spitta, F., *Der zweite Brief des Petrus und der Brief des Judas*, 1885.

Strachan, R. M., *Expositor's Greek Testament*, 1900.

von Soden, H., *Briefe des Petrus (Holtzmann's Handkommentar zum Neuen Testament)*, 1892.

Wand, J. W. C., *The General Epistles of St Peter and St Jude* (Westminster Commentaries), 1934.

Zahn, T., *Introduction to the New Testament*, E.T. 1909.

For a supplementary bibliography, see Bauckham, R., '2 Peter: a supplementary bibliography' in *JETS*, March 1982, pp. 91–93, together with his Bibliography in his Commentary.

INTRODUCTION

I. THE AUTHORSHIP OF 2 PETER

This Epistle has had a very rough passage down the centuries. Its entry into the Canon was precarious in the extreme. At the Reformation it was deemed second-class Scripture by Luther, rejected by Erasmus, and regarded with hesitancy by Calvin. The critical questions which it raises are most perplexing. I have considered them in some detail in my monograph 2 *Peter Reconsidered.*[1] Because of lack of space, I do not propose to adduce again all the evidence from patristic and other sources for Petrine authorship which is set out in the earlier work. All I shall attempt to do here is to indicate the argument in broad outline.

a. The evidence of the Ancient Church

The external evidence is inconclusive. No book in the Canon is so poorly attested among the Fathers, yet 2 Peter has incomparably better support for its inclusion than the best attested of the excluded books. It is not cited by name until Origen, at the beginning of the third century, who six times quotes it as Scripture. In short 'Peter blows on the twin trumpets of his own Epistles'.[2] Yet it was used in Egypt long before this.[3] Not only

---

[1]Tyndale Press, 1961.   [2]*Homily on Joshua 7:1.*
[3]The discovery of the early third-century Papyrus 72, including both Epistles of Peter and Jude, sheds light on the early use of this letter in Egypt. The Coptic mother tongue of the scribes concerned, together with the variant text types embodied in this MS (Alexandrian for 1 Peter and a 'wild' text for Jude) indicate a considerable history of the use of these letters in Egypt before the third-century papyrus in which they are embodied.

was it contained in the Sahidic and Bohairic versions of the New Testament, dating from (?) the late second and fourth centuries respectively, but we are told[1] that Clement of Alexandria had it in his Bible and wrote a commentary on it. This takes us back at least to the middle of the second century. The *Apocalypse of Peter*, written somewhere between AD 110–140, makes much use of 2 Peter,[2] which throws the date of our Epistle back further still.

Furthermore, there are possible or probable traces of 2 Peter in 1 Clement (AD 95), 2 Clement (AD 150), Aristides (AD 130), Hermas (AD 120), Valentinus (AD 130) and Hippolytus (AD 180). Why, then, was it suspect in the ancient world?

Eusebius and Jerome give the reasons.[3] Eusebius, who places the Epistle in his category of 'contested' books, along with James, Jude, 2 and 3 John, seems to have been struck by the lack of ancient testimony to it, as it was not quoted (sc. by name) by any of the 'ancient presbyters'. He recognizes, however, that it has approved itself to many who have studied it enthusiastically along with the other Scriptures, and classes 2 Peter with James, Jude, 2 and 3 John as 'disputed, but reckoned authentic by most people'. He then goes on to speak of the uncanonical books, such as Hermas, Barnabas and 1 Clement. Jerome records the doubt, explains it as resting on the divergence of style from 1 Peter, and suggests the hypothesis of a different amanuensis, a view which has subsequently often been held by those who uphold the authenticity of the Epistle. Two additional reasons for hesitation in the ancient church were probably the extent to which Peter's name was used to gain currency for unorthodox literature, mostly of a Gnostic nature, and also the fact that this Epistle was known

[1]By Eusebius (*H.E.* vi:14. 1) and Photius (*Cod.* 109). Traces of 2 Peter exist in Clement's surviving works, and his recently discovered *Letter to Theodorus* (if authentic) includes a very probable allusion to 2 Peter 2:19.

[2]When the *Apocalypse* was discovered in 1887, Harnack claimed that it was one of the sources of 2 Peter. This view has not been held by any responsible critic for many years now, since the articles of A. E. Simms (*Expositor*, 1898, pp.460–471) and F. Spitta (*ZNTW*, 1911, pp.237 ff.) convincingly demonstrated the priority of 2 Peter. See E. Hennecke, *New Testament Apocrypha* (E.T. 1965), vol. II, p.664.

[3]Eusebius, *H.E.* iii. 3. 1, 4 and iii.25. 3, 4, Jerome, *Script. Eccl.* 1, *Ep. ad Hedib. cxx, ad Paul. liii.*

only in limited areas in the first two centuries.[1]

It was in Syria that the greatest doubts about 2 Peter existed. It was not included in the Peshitta (AD 411), which contained only 1 Peter, James and 1 John of the Catholic Epistles. It was not until the Philoxenian recension (AD 508) that the remainder of the Catholic Epistles, including 2 Peter, found a secure place. It must be remembered that the early Syrian Canon was much more restricted than that of the Western church; the *Diatessaron* was used instead of the four Gospels, and originally, it seems, neither the Catholic Epistles nor the Apocalypse were regarded as Scripture. There was a particular reason why 2 Peter and Jude should have been treated with reserve in Syria, where the extravagances of Jewish angelology were so notorious: Jude explicitly, and 2 Peter implicitly, quote the *Assumption of Moses* and the *Book of Enoch*, two apocryphal books which were steeped in speculation about angels. However, 2 Peter and Jude won their way on merit even in Syria, and not only were they included in the Philoxenian recension of the Bible, but there is evidence that men like Ephraem Syrus in the fourth century (see on 2 Pet. 2:18, note 1) and Theophilus of Antioch[2] (died AD 183) used them freely as Scripture.

By the fourth century, then, 2 Peter was accepted throughout most of the world. Its absence from the Muratorian Canon (*c.* AD 180) is no more remarkable than that of 1 Peter, which was universally accepted. Perhaps the mutilated text of that Canon is the reason for the omissions. 2 Peter was recognized as canonical by the Councils of Hippo and Carthage in the fourth century, and this is the more significant because these Councils rejected the *Epistle of Barnabas* and *1 Clement* (long read alongside Scripture in the churches), because they were not of apostolic origin. Thereafter its position was unchallenged until the Reformation.

Such, broadly speaking,[3] is the external attestation. We have

---

[1] Its restricted attestation and the bad state of the text led Vansittart to assume that for a time it existed in a single copy only (*Journal of Philology*, III, pp.357 ff.). This, if true, would explain its poor attestation among the 'ancient presbyters'.

[2] *Ad Autol.* ii:13 quotes 2 Pet. 1:19 as the Word of God.

[3] Other early attestation could be adduced. Irenaeus (*A.H.* iii:1. 1, v. 23. 2), Justin (*Dial:* lxxxi, Barnabas (*Ep.* xv.4), Polycarp (*Phil.* iii), and Hermas (*Vis.* iii.8), all allude to 2 Peter. Indeed its affinities to Hermas and 1 and 2 Clement are marked.

no positive evidence that it was ever rejected as spurious anywhere in the church;[1] though unknown in many places, the recognition it enjoyed was considerable and primitive. It is significant that so careful a critic as Mayor (who himself rejects Petrine authorship on grounds of dependence on Jude and incompatibility with 1 Peter) should conclude his examination of the external evidence with the admission that, if we had nothing else to go on, we should be inclined, like the ancients, to accept it.

Indeed, it may be that we shall be forced to do so. That depends on the final evaluation of a fascinating discovery in Cave 7 at Qumran. The papyrus fragment 7Q5, discovered in this cave which was sealed in AD 68, appears to be a part of St Mark's Gospel, comprising verses 52–53 of chapter 6.[2] Papyrologists, including C. H. Roberts, have dated this fragment to around AD 50. But 7Q10, found in the same cave, (a tiny scrap of only 2 centimetres), has on it six letters (belonging to two lines) which could come only from 2 Peter 1:15 if they derive from the New Testament at all.[3] The evidence is highly precarious at this stage, but if 7Q5 is indeed part of Mark's Gospel, as it may well be, there is no good reason why 7Q10 should not also be a New Testament fragment, and why it should not come from 2 Peter. The community at Qumran was voracious for religious literature of all kinds, and C. P. Thiede has argued, in a fully documented monograph on Simon Peter, that if this is indeed a fragment of 2 Peter, it was sent probably as a covering document to Mark's Gospel to the Qumran community shortly before the Jewish War in AD 68 when the cave was closed.[4]

---

[1] This holds good despite the fact that Dionysius of Alexandria (d. AD 395) regarded it as spurious (though not only did he attest its widespread use; he even wrote a commentary on it!). Its place in the Alexandrian Canon was so secure that it could appear in Athanasius's Festal Letter, written in AD 367, which contains the Canon of the New Testament exactly as we have it today and which marks the close of controversy about the Canon in Catholic Christendom.

[2] See *JBL*, 91, Supplement, 1972; *Biblica*, vol.65, 1984, pp.538–59.

[3] It is not certain that this is a fragment of 2 Peter. However, preliminary textual comparisons so far demonstrate that if it comes anywhere in the New Testament, this fragment can be a part only of 2 Peter 1:15. Details are published by José O'Callaghan 'Los papiros griegos de la cueva 7 de Qumran', Madrid, BAC, 1974, pp.74–75, and plate v.

[4] *Simon Peter – From Galilee to Rome*, Exeter, 1986, pp.18–19 and 180, no.320. Cf. also C. P. Thiede, *Die älteste Evangelien-Handschrift?*, Wuppertal, 1986, p.58, and his paper in *Biblica*, *op. cit.*, p.533.

If this can be substantiated, there will be unimpeachable and very early evidence for the origin of 2 Peter before AD 68.

b. The contrast with 1 Peter

Is it conceivable that these two Epistles, 1 Peter and 2 Peter, should have come from the same hand? The language is different (strikingly so in the original), and the thought is also very different. Let us examine them in turn.

1. *The language.* There is a very great stylistic difference between these two letters. The Greek of 1 Peter is polished, cultured, dignified; it is among the best in the New Testament. The Greek of 2 Peter is grandiose; it is rather like baroque art, almost vulgar in its pretentiousness and effusiveness. Pedantic words (such as *rhoizēdon*) and cumbersome phrases (such as *hyperonka . . . mataiotētos phthengomenoi, 2:18*) abound. The rich variety of connecting particles, a feature of 1 Peter, have almost disappeared. Many of 1 Peter's favourite words (such as *hagiazō, elpis, klēronomia*) are also missing, while others (as *epakoloutheō, martus*) are replaced by synonyms in 2 Peter. When we find that a number of words in 2 Peter occur elsewhere only in Homer, and that the author has a curious tendency to fall into an iambic rhythm (*e.g.* 2:1, 3–4), and to use language redolent of the pagan mystery cults (such as *sōtēr, epignōsis, theia phusis, aretē,* to look no further than the first few verses), then it is not hard to sympathize with Jerome's reluctance to ascribe both Epistles to the same hand.

Of course, something of the force of these objections can be met by supposing, with Jerome, that Peter used a different secretary, and that he allowed him a large say in the form of the composition. This appears to have been the case with 1 Peter, where the stylistic polish may well be due to Silvanus.[1] We are specifically told[2] that not only Mark but also one Glaucias[3] were among Peter's other secretarial assistants, so there is nothing

[1]See 1 Pet. 5:12, where the *dia* means nothing short of joint authorship, according to E. G. Selwyn, *The First Epistle of St. Peter,* 1946, pp.9 ff.
[2]By Papias in Eusebius, *H.E.* iii. 39, Irenaeus, *A.H. iii.* 1, Tertullian, *Adv. Marc. iv.* 5.
[3]Clement of Alexandria, *Strom.* vii. 17.

improper in arguing that much of the stylistic difference may well be due to a change in scribe. This view is strengthened by several stylistic resemblances between the Epistles which, in their way, are as remarkable as the differences. There are strong Hebraisms and the striking habit of verbal repetition in both,[1] and these are features likely to have survived through the employment of different secretaries. Peculiar, striking words are a feature of both letters.[2] It is hardly surprising, therefore, to find even an opponent of Petrine authorship like Mayor confessing 'there is not that chasm between 1 and 2 Peter which some would try to make out'.[3] B. Weiss's judgment that 'the Second Epistle of Peter is allied to no New Testament writing more closely than to his First'[4] is justified on a purely linguistic analysis. But we can go further. Holzmeister[5] showed that 1 and 2 Peter are as close linguistically as 1 and 2 Corinthians, while in a fascinating article in the *Expositor*[6] A. E. Simms has shown that 1 and 2 Peter stand as close on the score of words used as 1 Timothy and Titus, where nobody is inclined to doubt the unity of authorship. Finally, A. Q. Morton has shown from cumulative sum analysis on the computer, that 1 and 2 Peter are indistinguishable linguistically.[7] And yet the conclusion of a common authorship for the Petrines is most commonly resisted on linguistic grounds!

One further point must be made on the subject of style. Commentators on 2 Peter tend to castigate the author for his 'artificial rhetoric' and his attempt to write 'in a style which is beyond his literary power'.[8] Few criticisms could be more beside the point, as some little-known German researches have made

---

[1]See Bigg, pp.224–232; Mayor, pp. lxviii-cv.

[2]Of the words which appear in no other Greek author except later ecclesiastical writers, there are nine in 1 Peter and five in 2 Peter. Twenty-seven words in 1 Peter, twenty-four in 2 Peter are not to be found in any classical author. 1 Peter has thirty-three rare words in common with the LXX, 2 Peter twenty-four. Of the 543 words in 1 Peter, sixty-three are New Testament *hapax legomena*; of the 399 words in 2 Peter there are fifty-seven *hapax legomena*.

[3]Mayor, p. civ.   [4]*Introduction to the New Testament*, 1887, ii, p.165.

[5]*Biblica*, 30, 1949.

[6]*Expositor*, 1898, pp.460 ff.

[7]*The Authorship and Integrity of the New Testament*, S.P.C.K. Theological Collection no. 4, 1965, chapter 3. Since then, he tells me, he has shown that 2 Peter is distinguishable from any New Testament book that is longer, with the sole exception of 1 Peter.

[8]E.g. Chase, *Hastings' Dictionary of the Bible*, vol.3, p.809, s.v. 2 Peter.

clear. So far from being a hopeless farrago of bad Greek, both the style and the diction of 2 Peter belong to a quite deliberate pattern. It is now clear that there was a definite Asiatic style of writing, with a florid, verbose type of diction verging on the bizarre, which was a far cry from the canons of classical simplicity. Two examples of this style come from the Decree of Stratonicea in Caria, Asia Minor,[1] and the grandiose inscription[2] of Antiochus the First of Commagene in central Asia Minor. Bo Reicke, who has acutely seen the significance of this inscription for the whole question of the language of 2 Peter, gives the following extract: 'It was as being of all things good not only a most reliable acquisition, but also – for human beings – a most pleasant enjoyment that I considered piety; and the same conviction I held to be the reason for a most successful authority as well as for a most blessed employment thereof; furthermore, during my entire lifetime I appeared to all in my monarchy as one who regarded holiness as both a most trustworthy safeguard and an inimitable satisfaction.'

Judged by this sort of literary standard, the style of 2 Peter no longer seems so remarkable. Indeed, it fits very well the varied emotional thoughts that lie behind this stirring Epistle. Furthermore, it seems possible[3] that this letter, if genuine, was intended by Peter to be a sort of last will and testament; the great man says farewell to his associates, and reminds them of important truths (1:12–15; 3:1–2), gives them salutary warnings (1:9f.; 2:1–22; 3:17) and offers them earnest exhortations (1:5ff., 19–21; 3:11, 14). Ever since this pattern emerged in Deuteronomy, where Moses gave his last directions, warnings and encouragements to Israel, this had become a literary genre. We find it in the *Testaments of the Twelve Patriarchs*, and in the New Testament itself 2 Timothy has something of this character.

When, in addition to all this, it is remembered that part of the difficulties in the diction of this Epistle arise from the Aramaic

---

[1]Text in *Corpus Inscriptionarum Graecarum*, ii, 2715; comment in A. Deissmann, *Bible Studies*, 1901, pp.360 ff. It dates from the first century AD.

[2]E. Norden, *Die antike Kunstprosa*, 1909, pp.126–152 and J. Waldis, *Sprache und Stil der grossen Inschrift vom Nemrud-Dagh*, 1920, pp.57–59. It dates from the first century BC.

[3]Bauckham believes this to be one of the crucial factors in determining the literary genre of 2 Peter. See below.

thought[1] which lies behind it, and the possibility that it may be dependent upon traditional oral or written material for use against heretics (see section IX below), the language of 2 Peter need no longer be a serious stumbling-block to accepting the authenticity of the letter if it should commend itself on other grounds.

2. *The thought*. Another objection to the authenticity of the Epistle has been raised in modern, though not in ancient times. It is that the thought of 2 Peter is too different from that of 1 Peter for them both to have come from the same mind. Naturally the subject-matter of 1 and 2 Peter is quite different, for these Epistles are written to two entirely different situations. 'It is too often forgotten that these early Christian Epistles are missionary letters written to meet what was often a very urgent need, and not theological treatises penned with meticulous care in the quiet of the study'.[2] 1 Peter envisages Christians facing persecution, 2 Peter Christians facing false teaching of a Gnostic flavour. The key-note of 1 Peter, is, accordingly, hope; of 2 Peter, true knowledge. 1 Peter directs the thoughts of the recipients to the great events of the life of Christ for their emulation and comfort; 2 Peter dwells on the great hope of the return of Christ, so as to warn the false teachers and challenge the waverers. The difference in tone may, perhaps, be reflected in the use of different words for the return of Christ, which is a prominent theme in both Epistles. In 1 Peter *apokalupsis* is used, the removal of the veil which hides from the sight of the faithful the Lord who is with them all the time. In 2 Peter *parousia* is used, the sudden appearance of the absent king among his disobedient servants. The one word breathes comfort for the afflicted; the other, warning for the scoffers. 1 Peter has much to say about the cross (not least as a principle to be followed by his hard-pressed readers); 2 Peter has much less, for his readers do

[1]Chaine gives a whole page on the Semitisms of 2 Peter (Chaine, p.18). Indeed, so marked are they that it has been suggested by G. Wohlenberg that the letter might originally have been written in Aramaic and later translated into Greek! (*Der erste und der zweite Petrusbriefe und der Judasbrief*, 1923, p.xxxvi.) The example of *Symeōn Petros* (1:1) may be helpful to include here – *cf. 2 Peter Reconsidered*, p.14.
[2]*2 Pet. Rec.*, p.17.

not need the gentle encouragement to follow Jesus obediently, even, if need be, to martyrdom; they need the warning that Christ will come to judge those who deny the Lord who bought them (2:1). Thus in the Second Epistle the past judgment of God in Old Testament days and his future judgment at the parousia support the strong moral challenge of the letter, where the *imitatio Christi* theme of 1 Peter would have been out of place and ineffective. The writer's mind is full of the dangers of false teaching.[1] The full knowledge of Jesus Christ is the best safeguard against these dangers, and it is this, therefore, which is stressed, in contrast to the hope which pervades 1 Peter. Both letters are determined, as far as subject-matter goes, by the pastoral needs which evoked them, and herein lies the difference in doctrinal emphasis between them.[2]

Another point at which 2 Peter is unfavourably contrasted with 1 Peter is in references to the life of Jesus and of Peter himself, so prominent in the First Epistle. This is very surprising in view of the following allusions:

The reference to the transfiguration (1:16).
The prophecy of Peter's own death (1:14; *cf.* Jn 21:21–23).
Denial of the Lord (2:1).
The invasion of false prophets (2:1ff.; *cf.* Mk. 13:22).
The last state worse than the first (2:20; *cf.* Mt. 12:45).
The day of the Lord like a thief in the night (3:10; *cf.* Mt. 24:43).
The predictions of the parousia (see below).
The reference to *establishing* (*stērizō*) (3:17; 1:12; *cf.* 1 Pet. 5:10) which seems to go back to the poignant incident culminating in Lk.22:32) and to *fishing* (*deleazō*, 2:14, 18, means to 'catch by a lure' and could be an allusion to his trade).

Equally beside the point is the argument that, because 1 Peter spoke of the resurrection of Jesus (1:3; 5:1), 2 Peter cannot be genuine because it neglects this and stresses instead the transfiguration. The fact of the matter is that the resurrection was

---

[1]Hence the emphasis on *aretē*, 'virtue', and *eusebeia*, 'godliness'.
[2]For a detailed examination of the doctrinal affinities between the two Epistles, see my *2 Peter Reconsidered*, pp.14–23.

being 'demythologized' as early as AD 50 (see 1 Cor. 15) not only in Europe but in Asia (2 Tim. 2:17–18). The transfiguration, falling as it did within the incarnate life of Jesus, could not be thus gainsaid by the scoffers. Peter insists upon it to back up his claim to a personal knowledge of the Lord Jesus, whom the false teachers wrongly claim to know. Further, the transfiguration would have been particularly significant for Jewish readers who would be reminded by 'the sacred mountain' (1:18) of the revelation on Sinai, and this fits far better into the context (stressing the solidarity between Old and New Testaments) than the resurrection possibly could.

Finally, the eschatological teaching is urged as cause for separating the authorship of the two Epistles. Both speak of it a great deal. Both teach that it will mean judgment for the wicked (1 Pet. 4:5, 17; 2 Pet. 3:7), and joy for the faithful (1 Pet. 4:13; 2 Pet. 3:13f.). In both the parousia is made the sanction for holy living (1 Pet. 4:7; 2 Pet. 3:11, 14), but whereas it is hinted in 1 Peter that the coming may be soon (1 Pet. 1:4–8; 4:7), it is delayed in 2 Peter (3:4). But this is, surely, natural. When encouraging the persecuted, it is obviously sensible to remind them that their vindicator is near; when dealing with those who are sceptical about the parousia it is proper to remind them that, though delayed, it will certainly come. It is astonishing that so simple a solution should have escaped that otherwise shrewd critic J. Chaine, who, on almost this point alone, abandons the Petrine authorship of this Epistle.

But, it may be objected, there is nothing about the destruction of the world by fire in 1 Peter. True. But then there is nothing about 1 Peter's story of Jesus preaching to the spirits in prison to be found either in 2 Peter or anywhere else in the New Testament. That is no sufficient reason for rejecting the First Epistle. In this case, it can be shown both that the doctrine of the destruction of the world in 2 Peter 3:10–13 is consonant with the rest of Scripture,[1] and also that this passage is rooted in the

[1]This is in striking contrast to the macabre and, in places, obscene obsession displayed by the *Apocalypse of Peter* (c. AD 130) with the tortures of the damned and the nature of their transgressions. By this time the content of the judgment is stressed to the exclusion of the New Testament emphasis (so strong in 2 Peter) that what is important is the personal return of Jesus and man's relationship to him. Whereas 2 Peter is indebted to the eschatological

eschatological discourse of Jesus. Thus, apart from the thief metaphor, the dissolution of the heavens (3:12; cf. Mk. 13:31 and parallels), the falling of the stars (implied in 3:10f.; cf. Mk. 13:24–25), the permanence of the divine promise (3:9; cf. Mk. 13:31), the prevalence of unbelief (3:4; cf. Mt. 24:11–12), and the need for evangelism (3:12; cf. Mt. 24:14) and watchfulness (3:12–13; cf. Mk. 13:9, 33, 35; see also Mt. 24:45–51) are features in common. And, although expressed in the apocalyptic language of Isaiah 65:17; 66:22 (cf. Enoch 91:16; Rev. 21:1), the promise of Jesus about the cosmic regeneration (Mt. 19:28) appears to lie behind 3:13.

It would seem, in view of all this, that the ancients were not unreasonable in their failure to discern any fatal difference of thought and teaching between the First and Second Epistles of Peter.

It is unfortunate to find in many commentaries on 2 Peter a virtual abandonment of the normal criteria used for establishing the authenticity of any other ancient document – for example, the Letters of Plato. There is a clear methodology among literary critics, and that is to allow the text to speak for itself. It is then considered whether the grammar, style, contents, what the letter claims and what the author says or implies about himself contradict the putative authorship. If not, the claim is allowed to stand. Nothing has been demonstrated in the language, style or content of 2 Peter which falsifies the claim that it is a mid-first-century AD letter, deriving from Simon Peter.

c. The relationship with Jude

This is a third factor relevant to the authorship of our Epistle. That there is a dependence either of 2 Peter on Jude or of Jude on 2 Peter, of both on some lost document, or that both share a common author, is certain. For of the twenty-five verses in Jude no less than fifteen appear, in whole or in part, in 2 Peter. Furthermore, many of the identical ideas, words and phrases occur in parallel in the two writings, and leave us in no doubt

discourse of Jesus, the *Apocalypse* is dependent on Virgil's description of Hades and the speculation of Orphic-Pythagorean mystery cults.

that there is some sort of literary relationship between them. Which way the dependence lies will be discussed in section IX below. The only problem which concerns us here is whether apostolic authorship of 2 Peter must be ruled out if Jude was written first.

The answer must be in the negative. It is very widely held that baptismal catechesis, even perhaps a baptismal homily, underlies a good deal of 1 Peter. It is equally plain that some primitive Christian household rules are incorporated in that letter. Carrington would suppose that there is other traditional catechetical material behind 2 Peter, and Selwyn postulates, in addition, a tract composed to encourage the faithful in the face of persecution.[1] If Peter thus took over and used in his First Epistle a good deal of material composed by others, why should he not have done so in his Second? It is, as we shall see in section IX, very possible that both Jude and 2 Peter are indebted to a tract against false teachers, which would, from the nature of the case, have proved a necessity to the infant church before very long. But whether Peter drew from this type of 'fly-sheet' or directly from Jude makes no difference to the argument. If Paul was not averse to adapting to his own purposes the writings of heathen poets, lists of Stoic virtues, fragments of hymns, or the dubious war-cries of his opponents,[2] is there any reason to suppose that Peter would have been unwilling to draw from the work of a brother of his Master, should it prove to be the case that the Epistle of Jude was written first? It is simply naive to say, with Kümmel, 'Petrine authorship is forbidden by the literary relationship with Jude.'[3] Peter could well have taken up and used either a traditional sermon or tract devised by the early church to meet the ravages of false teaching, or alternatively the short fiery letter of 'Jude the brother of James', had he deemed it appropriate to his purpose. The ancients had no law of copyright. In short, the question of the relationship of 2 Peter to Jude

[1]See P. Carrington's *The Primitive Christian Catechism*, 1940, and Essay 2 in E. G. Selwyn's *The First Epistle of St. Peter*, 1946, H. Preisker in Windisch's *Die katholischen Briefe*, 1951, pp.156 ff., and M. E. Boismard in his monograph *Quatre Hymnes Baptismales dans la Première Epître de Pierre*, 1961.

[2]See, *e.g.*, 1 Cor. 15:33; 8:1; 6:12a and 13a. Phil. 2:6–11; 1 Tim. 3:16; 1 Cor. 15:3–5 are further examples of his use of traditional material.

[3]*Introduction to the New Testament* (E.T. 1966), p.303.

has no bearing whatever on the authenticity of 2 Peter. This has been highlighted, albeit paradoxically, by J. A. T. Robinson in *Redating the New Testament*, pp. 169–99. He argues that if Silvanus was Peter's amanuensis for 1 Peter, Jude penned 2 Peter for him. Thus Peter, from Rome, writes (through Jude) to Asian Christians where the heresy was breaking out. But while preparing the letter the situation becomes so acute that Jude writes a quick warning letter in his own name (to which 2 Peter 3:1 refers). This is stylistically attractive and historically plausible (Peter and the Lord's brothers are frequently linked in antiquity) but if Jude wrote 2 Peter to Petrine churches for the apostle, why did he write his epistle under his own name? Robinson's view has not won adherents, but it does at least show that the literary relation between 2 Peter and Jude need not affect authenticity either way.

d. Three indications of a subapostolic date

Let us look at these one by one.

1. *The 'Hellenistic' cast of 2 Peter.* Kümmel advances the following points under this head which, he thinks, point to a late date.[1] First, the attribution of 'goodness' to God (1:3). But the same thing is done in 1 Peter 2:9, the only other place in the New Testament. Furthermore, both 'goodness' and 'glory' are qualities of God in Isaiah 42:8, 12 (LXX). What Peter is doing is to take this phrase predicated of Yahweh in the Old Testament and apply it also to Jesus; that is why God and Jesus are combined under a single article in 1:1.

Secondly, Kümmel complains of the emphasis on knowledge (1:2–3, 6, 8, *etc.*). But this is no more Hellenistic than the similar procedure adopted by Paul in Colossians. Peter is simply taking the language of the opposition, disinfecting it, and using it back on them, charged with Christian meaning.

A third mark of lateness is the phrase 'that you may participate in the divine nature' (1:4). This certainly looks startling, but the form of the expression has now been paralleled by the Decree of Strationicea to the honour of Zeus and Hecate.[2] Further, con-

---

[1] *Ibid.*   [2] See A. Deissmann, *Bible Studies*, pp.360 ff.

temporaries such as Philo, Stobaeus and Josephus use similar language,[1] which shows that this sort of talk was current coin in the first century AD, and as such Peter could have used it for his purpose as readily as the modern preacher talks of the quantum theory without in the least necessarily understanding all its implications. But is the idea, of being partaker of the divine nature, too advanced for Peter? It is intrinsically no different from being born from above (Jn. 3:3; Jas. 1:18; 1 Pet 1:23), being the temple of the Holy Spirit (1 Cor. 6:19), being in Christ (Rom. 8:1) or being the dwelling-place of the Trinity (Jn. 14:17–23). In this whole introductory paragraph of his Epistle, the writer is putting his Christian doctrine into Greek dress[2] for the purposes of communication, without in the least committing himself to the pagan associations of the terms. Indeed, in 1:3–4 he makes a frontal assault on Stoic and Platonic presuppositions, who taught, respectively, that by *phusis* (nature) or *nomos* (law) a man became partaker of the divine. No, says our author; it is by grace, by the gospel promises, that this comes about (1:3–4). Furthermore, the aorist *apophugontes* reminds us that we are not moving in the realms of Platonism but Christianity. We are made partakers of the divine nature not *in escaping* from the natural world of time and sense, but *after escaping* the 'world' in the sense of mankind in rebellion against God. Attention to this point would have saved Käsemann from some very careless exegesis of this verse.[3]

2. *The parousia teaching of 2 Peter.* For one thing, the apostles are said to be spoken of as a past generation (3:2). But *are* they?

---

[1] For the details, see my 2 *Peter Reconsidered*, p.23.

[2] That this is quite deliberate is clear from the Stoic *prokopē* which he adapts in 1:5–7. What both Käsemann and Kümmel fail to see is that the Hellenistic flavour of the Letter is matched by the strong strand of apocalyptic Judaism that runs through it. See Bauckham *op.cit.* p.246–251, 265 ff. As he observes, drily, 'whereas scholars have rather often stressed one-sidedly either the Hellenistic or the Jewish character of 2 Peter, it is wiser to recognize both aspects'.

[3] 'It would be hard to find in the whole New Testament a sentence which . . . more clearly marks the relapse of Christianity into Hellenistic dualism' (*Essays on New Testament Themes*, pp.179 f.). Käsemann supposes that 2 Peter's goal is that of the pagans, to escape from the physical (and corruptible) world to gain a spiritual (and divine) nature. 'Apotheosis is his true destiny' (*ibid.*). He fails to recognize that this participation in the divine nature is not the goal but the starting-point of Christian experience; and the world from which the

The text specifically denies this! That an apostle could write in these terms about his fellow apostles is clear from Ephesians 2:20, where apostles and prophets are again linked as the foundation for the Christian church. Käsemann sees here the 'primitive Catholicism' of a later generation, when the apostles have become the organs of the church's being, and the possession of the ecclesiastical authorities.[1] But how natural, and how primitive, for Peter, like Paul, to stress that the apostles are given to the church for the sake of the church (cf. 1 Cor. 3:21ff.), and in that sense are 'your apostles'. See further the note on 3:2.

Then again, the reference to the decease of 'the fathers' (3:4) is thought to imply that the first Christian generation has long passed away. This is very questionable. Normally in New Testament usage 'the fathers' means the Old Testament fathers (Heb. 1:1; Rom. 9:5), and it seems clear from the context (Genesis and the flood) that this is what is meant here. Peter's opponents are claiming that, so far from there being a sudden parousia, nothing has changed since the foundation of the world. If they were saying merely that nothing had happened since the foundation of the church, Peter's reply, namely that there was once an interruption (the flood), would have been irrelevant.

Furthermore, the hope of the second coming has been abandoned (3:4). Surely this implies a late date? We must remember that to the false teachers it was not a hope but a threat; and they were laughing because it had not been fulfilled. Had the hope not been prominent in the church in which they worked, they would not have spoken slightingly of it. It is surprising to find this objection raised to the authenticity of the Epistle by the very scholars who are constantly reminding us what a shock to mid-first-century Christians the delay of the parousia proved to be, how it stimulated the writing of Gospels and how it influenced Lucan and Johannine theology. So far from having to wait for 1 *Clement* in AD 95[2] for the first appearance of surprise at the delay,

---

believer escapes is not the physical universe but the world in the Johannine sense of man at odds with his Creator (cf. 1 Jn. 5:19).

[1]Käsemann, pp.174 f. See, however, the powerful refutation of his position in A. L. Moore, *The Parousia in the New Testament*, 1966, pp.151–156, and in R. J. Bauckham, *op.cit.*, pp.151–4 and his *2 Peter: an account of research*, pp.17–25, and my *2 Peter Reconsidered*, pp.14–23.

[2]1 *Clem.* xxiii. 3 f.

the earliest New Testament letters we possess, 1 and 2 Thessalonians, were written primarily to meet this question.[1] It would inevitably become a problem as soon as Christian leaders began to die off, and thus would be a very natural thing to find in the sixties when Peter must have written, if he was the author. On the contrary it would have been a very surprising thing to find in the second century, when there was, both among Apologists and Fathers, a decay in the hope of a personal return of Christ, and increased emphasis on eschatology in terms of cold rewards and punishments.

This brings us to another point sometimes made. Does not our Epistle share this second-century eschatology? Schelkle, for instance, wonders if it does not concentrate on judgment and reward to the exclusion of the characteristic New Testament hope of a personal return.[2] Quite the reverse. For one thing the primitive eschatological tension between the 'now' and the 'then', between what we have, and what we yet await, is strongly present.[3] For another, the parousia hope is adduced, as in Paul and John, for practical and not for speculative reasons. The three ethical inferences regularly drawn by New Testament writers from their confident expectation of Christ's return, namely watchfulness, holiness, and Christian service, are all here.[4] In all these points the second-century church lost contact with the apostolic message.[5]

---

[1]See 1 Thes. 4:11–18; 5:1–4 (incidentally quoting the thief analogy also cited in 2 Pet. 3:10), 2 Thes. 1 and 2, and 1 Cor. 15:6, 50–58.

[2]Käsemann asks rhetorically, and wrongheadedly, 'What have we to say about an eschatology which, like that of our epistle, is concerned only with the hope of the triumphal entry of believers into the eternal kingdom and with the destruction of the ungodly?' (Käsemann, p.195). One wonders whether he read the latter part of 2 Pet. 3 attentively.

[3]The tension between realized and unrealized eschatology is the very nerve of the New Testament concept of *elpis*, hope. Thus Christians are already partakers of the divine nature, yet they have still to enter the everlasting kingdom (1:4, 11). Elect already, they must make their election sure (1:10). Just because they have escaped the world's corruption, they must, for that very reason, add to their faith(1:4–5). 'What is this if not the typical New Testament tension between the church and the world, between the present and the future, the ideal and the phenomenal, faith and works, in fact between the Christian *simul justus et peccator?*' (2 *Pet. Re.*, p.18).

[4]3:10–12, 14; *cf.* 1 Jn. 2:28; 3:3; 1 Thes. 5:2, 6, 8. See also Peter's hope of 'hastening the day of the Lord' in Acts 3:19–21; *cf.* 2 Pet. 3:12.

[5]Dr A. L. Moore (*The Parousia in the New Testament*, p.152) points out seven respects in which the parousia teaching of 2 Pet. 3 accords precisely with that of 2 Thes. 2:2–13 and Mk.

But does 2 Peter not teach the Stoic doctrine of the destruction of the world by fire? As a matter of fact it does not.[1] What the Stoics taught was not a once-for-all but a periodic conflagration. The idea of a fiery doom is to be found in Plato's *Timaeus* 22D, in Persian sources, in the Qumran literature,[2] in Jewish intertestamental and apocryphal works[3] and not least in the Old Testament.[4] 2 Peter shares the characteristic Jewish tension between believing that the end is imminent, and wrestling with the problem of delay. In an important article P. E. Testa[5] has shown the distinctiveness of the Christian teaching found in 2 Peter. After examining Persian and Stoic views, he makes it clear that the Petrine teaching belongs without question to the Jewish-Christian tradition.[6] Unlike the Persians, Peter stresses the moral purpose of the conflagration, to punish and purify. Unlike the Stoics, he stresses its uniqueness – it is not to be repeated and it issues in a new heaven and a new earth, not, as they believed, in the same old earth and sky in readiness for the next fire or deluge. Unlike the Old Testament, Peter presents a unified apocalyptic picture of a single future event. Testa makes the ingenious suggestion that the impulse for this imagery may have come from baptismal symbolism, where the flood and the final conflagration are linked (*cf.* Mt. 3:11). Be that as it may, the doctrine taught in 2 Peter became widely accepted in Christian circles in the second century,[7] and Bigg may well be right in tracing this conviction ultimately to this Epistle.[8] Were it not for

---

13:5–37. 'Comparison with the earlier material', he writes, 'shows that the Christology is parallel, the ethics similarly orientated, and the place and status of eschatology the same.'

[1]Origen had to answer this accusation, and does so very effectively (*Contra Celsum* iv. 11. 79). See on 3:7.

[2]There is a remarkable parallel in 1 QH iii. 29–35. Also 1 QS ii. 8; 1 QM xiv. 17.

[3]See *Ps. Sol.* xv. 6; *Apoc. Abraham* xxxi; *Enoch* xvii. 1; 2 *Esdras* v. 8; *Sib. Orac.* iv. 172 ff.; iii. 54, 542; *Baruch* xxvii. 10; lxx. 8.

[4]See *eg.*, Is. 66:15 f.; Je. 4:4; Ezk. 21:31; Am. 5:6; Zp. 1:18 (P.E. Testa pays particular attention to Is. 24–27; 34–35; 65–66).

[5]'La distruzione del mondo per il fuoco nell 2 Ep. di Pietro 3:7, 10, 13' in *Rivista Biblica*, 1962, pp.252–281. Earlier, J. Chaine had come to much the same conclusion in his article in the *Revue Biblique* for 1937.

[6]Independently, D. S. Russell agrees (*Method and Message of the Jewish Apocalyptic*, 1964, p.281), and so does R. J. Bauckham, *op.cit.*, pp.296 ff.

[7]Clement, *Strom.* v. 14. 121, Justin, *Apol.* i. 20, *Sib. Orac.* iv. 172 ff., the prophecies of Hystaspes (Clement, *Strom.* vi. 5. 43), Origen, *Contra Celsum* iv. 11, 2 *Clem.* xvi, etc.

[8]Bigg, pp. 214 f.

the authority of an apostolic document it is hard to think that a doctrine barely hinted at in the rest of the New Testament should have gained such widespread acceptance so soon.

On other difficulties concerning the parousia teaching, see the Commentary; in particular on 1:19 and 3:8.[1]

3. *2 Peter's teaching about Paul* (3:15f.). This is often held to tell decisively against Petrine authorship. He would not, so many scholars believe, have called Paul his 'beloved brother'. He would not have alluded to the heretical misuse of Paul's letters, whose publication as a *corpus* must have been long after Peter's death. And he would not have ranged them alongside Scripture.

All three points are questionable. Peter could certainly have called Paul his beloved brother. He espoused his cause at the Council of Jerusalem (Acts 15:7ff.) and gave him the right hand of fellowship (Gal. 2:9). It is a great mistake to see Peter and Paul through Tübingen spectacles, and suppose that they were always rivals, simply because of the disagreement on one occasion at Antioch (Gal. 2:11ff.).[2]

We do not know when Paul's letters were published as a *corpus* – certainly not in his lifetime. But Peter says nothing about a *corpus*, or about publication, for that matter.[3] He simply refers to a recurring characteristic throughout the Pauline letters, which both he and the recipients had read. We need not suppose that they had read all the Paulines. Indeed, if our Epistle was written by a forger, who had the whole of the Pauline *corpus* before him, it is very surprising that he should not have been influenced by it at all. After about AD 90 the subapostolic literature is full of allusions to Paul. It would be strange indeed if a pseudepigrapher, writing to show the unanimity between the two great apostles, should have entirely neglected the Pauline *corpus* to which he drew specific attention.

[1]See also my *2 Peter Reconsidered*, where they are dealt with more fully.

[2]See J. Munck, *Paul and the Salvation of Mankind*, 1959, chapter 3.

[3]There is no real difficulty in supposing Peter to have read most of Paul's letters. They were, according to Acts and Paul's own letters, in close and frequent contact with each other, and had Mark and Silvanus as common secretary-colleagues. Further, both Peter and Paul operated in Asia Minor; it would have been difficult for them not to have known of each other's teachings and movements.

Of course, the greatest difficulty lies in supposing that Peter could have classed Paul's letters with 'the other Scriptures', whatever the precise meaning one gives to 'other' (*i.e.*, whether Paul's letters are included in or distinguished from the others). But is this such a difficulty?[1] The apostles were in no doubt that their written words were as authoritative as their spoken utterances.[2] And they were no less clear that the Holy Spirit of God who had inspired the prophets was at work through them. That is precisely the point of 1 Peter 1:11–12, as it is of 2 Peter 1:18–21. That is why they expected their letters to be read in church (*i.e.* alongside the Old Testament; *cf.* Col. 4:16; Rev. 1:3). The apostle claimed to have the very mind of Christ, to teach in words inspired by the Spirit, to proclaim the word of God, to act as the mouthpiece of God (1 Cor. 2:16; 2:13; 1 Thes. 2:13; 1 Pet. 4:11). The apostle is the plenipotentiary representative of Jesus Christ.[3] That is why he is able to issue commands (3:2; 1 Cor. 7:17), excommunicate (1 Cor. 5:3; 14:38, RSV), and make adherence to his teaching the norm of orthodoxy and the condition of fellowship (2 Thes. 3:14; 1 Tim. 6:3, 5; 2 Jn. 10). When this is borne in mind, is it so remarkable that one apostle should mention another's writings in the same breath as the other Scriptures? Why must we deny the equal applicability of the term 'scripture' to prophetic and apostolic writers when the ultimate authorship of God's Spirit is claimed for both (1 Pet. 1:11–12; 4:11; 2 Pet. 1:18–21)? Peter, certainly, was not disposed to do so. There is nothing in the doctrine of Scripture found in the Second Epistle that could not have been written by the author of the First.

e. Conclusion

That there is a weighty case against the apostolic authorship of 2 Peter it would be idle to deny. Its style, diction, poor attestation,

---

[1] The erudite Lagrange sees no difficulty in this, and draws attention to some of the verses here quoted. See his *Histoire ancienne du Canon du Nouveau Testament*, 1933, pp.9 f.

[2] 2 Cor. 10:11; 1 Cor. 5:3; 2 Thes. 2:15; 3:14.

[3] His authority is, accordingly, that of his Lord. Hence the finality of Rev. 22:18 f., and the anathema of Gal. 1:6–12. This unique position of the apostles was envisaged by Jesus (Jn. 14:26; 15:26; Mt. 10:40; 28:18, 19; Jn. 20:21) and recognized by the subapostolic church (*e.g.*, Ignatius, *Rom.* iv, *Philad.* v, Polycarp, *Ep.* vi). This unique position of the apostles is now

relationship with Jude, as well as its idiosyncrasies of content might incline one to assign it to the second century. F. J. A. Hort, when once asked what his view of 2 Peter was, replied that if he were asked he would say that the balance of argument was against the Epistle – and the moment he had done so he would begin to think that he might be wrong![1] The solid worth of 2 Peter, so manifestly superior to anything the second century had to offer, the striking contrast it affords to the undoubted Petrine pseudepigraphs, the absence of any credible motive for its origin as a pseudepigraph,[2] all make one pause. What is more, the document does not fit what we know of the second century. There is no hint of second-century problems like church leadership, developed Gnosticism, Montanism, or chiliasm. This consideration, coupled with the material common to Jude and 2 Peter, led J. A. T. Robinson to argue (improbably) that Jude wrote 2 Peter as Peter's agent, and then wrote Jude in his own name on hearing that the troubles persisted.[3] It is, no doubt, possible that 2 Peter was produced by a disciple of the apostle, as Reicke, Chaine and Schelkle suggest. It was customary both in Jewish and pagan circles to put out a pseudonymous work and attribute it to a great man in whose honour or style it was composed. Thus in his *Life of Pythagoras* Iamblichus, a neo-Platonist writer of the third century AD, congratulates the school of Pythagoras because they prefix his name to their writings in a desire to honour him as the source of all that is true and original in their thought. A great deal of Jewish pseudepigraphy sprang from the same motive, perhaps taking its cue from Deuteronomy. This accounts for writings like the *Psalms of*

---

increasingly widely recognized. See K. H. Rengstorf, s.v. 'Apostolos' in Kittel's *Wörterbuch*; O. Cullmann, 'The Tradition' in *The Early Church*, 1956; N. Geldenhuys, *Supreme Authority*, 1953 and B. Gerhardsson, *Memory and Manuscript*, 1961.

[1]W. Sanday, *Inspiration*, 1894, p.347.

[2]The *Apocalypse of Peter* professes to add to our knowledge about the future life. The *Gospel of Peter* is written in the interests of a docetic Christology. The *Letter of Peter* is Ebionite, the *Travels of Peter (Periodoi Petrou)* sheer romance. The *Kerygmata Petrou* was a writing designed to claim apostolic precedent for heretical tendencies, and the *Acts of Peter* is a sort of novel for the entertainment of the faithful who were not supposed to go to theatres and other pagan entertainments. 2 Peter has little in common with any of these undoubted forgeries. It has no heretical axe to grind. It tells us next to nothing we did not already know about Peter. It contains no secret tradition claiming Peter for its fountain-head. As a pseudepigraph it has no satisfactory *raison-d'être*.

[3]*Redating the New Testament*, p.192 ff.

Solomon, the *Wisdom of Solomon* and a host of others, orthodox and heterodox. It is suggested that there is nothing immoral in pseudepigraphy of this sort; we ought not to think of it as forgery but rather as creative poetry, saying in the contemporary situation what the great man would have said had he survived. It was not long before this type of writing invaded the Christian church. There are plentiful survivals from the second century AD. Why not from the first?

The only *a priori* argument against such an apparently reasonable hypothesis is the moral one. How is it that writers who urge the highest moral standards in their letters should stoop to deceit of this type? In this case, the author not only claims to be Peter; he constantly implies it (1:1, 14, 16–18; 3:15). It may be that nobody was taken in by those claims, or that if they were they would have seen no harm in what was the accepted practice of the day. It *may* be, but those who hold this view have scarcely succeeded in demonstrating it. It seems rather that pseudepigraphy was not so leniently viewed in Christian circles. Thus Paul inveighed against the practice in the Thessalonian correspondence (2 Thes. 2:2; 3:17). By no stretch of the imagination could he be regarded as condoning what P. N. Harrison claims were 'the very different standards of literary proprietorship which prevailed in those days'.[1] Then in the second century, the author of the *Acts of Paul and Thecla* was unfrocked for this very practice. He protested that he attributed his work to Paul only in order to increase the latter's honour; but to no avail.[2] He explained that he had acted in good faith, and from the highest motives 'from love of Paul', but it made not the slightest difference. He was deposed from his office as presbyter and was disgraced.[3] We have here a valuable insight into the attitude towards pseudepigraphy adopted in high places in the second century. Precisely the same conclusion emerges from the story of Serapion and the *Gospel of Peter*. Serapion, bishop of Antioch about AD 180, heard of the partiality of a small town in

---

[1] *The Problem of the Pastoral Epistles*, 1921, p.12.   [2] Tertullian, *de Baptismo* xvii.

[3] It is true that Tertullian is anxious to attack any who use the example of Thecla to maintain the right of a woman to baptize, but this is not the reason he gives for the disgrace of the author. It was not because he represented a woman baptizing but because he misrepresented himself as Paul that he was removed from office.

his diocese for the *Gospel of Peter*. When he had investigated the matter he forbade its use.[1] He says, 'For our part, brethren, we both receive Peter and the other apostles as Christ, but the writings which falsely bear their names we reject, as men of experience, knowing that such were not handed down to us.' It was not so much its mildly docetic Christology which determined the bishop's attitude, as the fact that it was falsely attributed to Peter, and was not handed down from earlier generations of the church.

It was into a church exercising this sort of discrimination that we are asked to believe 2 Peter was surreptitiously inserted. I find it very hard to believe. It is not as though we were plentifully supplied with examples of orthodox pseudepigrapha which were cheerfully accepted by the second-century church and later generations. After carefully examining the whole problem Guthrie feels obliged to say, 'There is no evidence in Christian literature for the idea of a conventional literary device, by which an author as a matter of literary custom, and with the full approbation of his circle of readers, publishes his own productions in another's name. There was always an ulterior motive.'[2]

It is precisely at this point that we must consider the detailed work done on this Epistle by Richard Bauckham[3] which leads him to maintain that he has discovered the very thing Guthrie thinks never existed – the publication by a disciple of Peter in Rome of this Letter under the literary convention of a last 'Testament'. For he believes that the literary genre to which 2 Peter belongs made it perfectly evident to the first readers that it was a pseudepigraph. Accordingly, no possible question of morality arises. 2 Peter is both a letter and also an example of the type of work we meet in the *Testaments of the Twelve Patriarchs*. That is to say, it sets out the supposed message of the deceased Peter to meet the exigencies of a late-first-century situation where antinomianism was present, heresy was rife and the parousia was mocked. The author's aim was to defend apostolic Christianity in a subapostolic situation, and this he does, not by having recourse to his own authority, but by

---

[1] In Eusebius, *H.E.* vi. 12.   [2] *Vox Evangelica*, 1962, p.56.   [3] *2 Peter and Jude*, 1983.

faithfully mirroring apostolic teaching which he adapts and interprets for his own day. 'Peter's testament' formed the ideal literary vehicle for his plans. Not only did the Testament genre have a long and honoured history in Judaism both within and outside the Old Testament; not only do the two main contents of 2 Peter (ethical admonitions and revelations of the future) precisely correspond to those found in most Testaments; but everyone knew these were pseudepigraphs. It went without saying that the same held good of 2 Peter. Nobody ever imagined it came from Peter himself. The literary convention of the Testament was too well known. Such is the theory.

There are three elements in the Testament genre which persuade Bauckham that 2 Peter belongs to it. Traditionally the testator gives the essence of his teaching, reveals that he is about to die, and prophesies the future. In 1:3–11 'Peter' encapsulates his message; in 1:12–15 he knows he is about to die and wants his last warnings to be heeded; and in 2:1–3; 3:1–4 he predicts the future. The rest of the Letter is, Bauckham believes, structured round these paragraphs. It is designed to defend Peter's teaching against the false teachers who make the following four objections to Peter's core message. Firstly, the preaching of the apostles was a myth (1:16–19). Secondly, Old Testament prophecy was not inspired (1:20–21). Thirdly, divine judgment is idle and ineffective (2:3–10). Fourthly, where is the promise of his coming? (3:5–10). All four objections cut at the parousia hope and allow freedom to sin as you please since judgment can be discounted. The author, accordingly, shows the importance and interdependence of eschatology and ethics (1:3–11), and then defends his position first by denouncing the ethics of the false teachers (2:10–22) and then by demonstrating ethics for true disciples (3:11–16). Within the genre of the Testament, therefore, the subapostolic author can skilfully counter the errorists of his day, and make a powerful defence and reassertion of apostolic Christianity. And everyone would know that this is what he was about.

But might not Peter himself have cast his material into the combined shape of Epistle and Testament? Bauckham thinks not. For one thing the essence of the Testament genre is that it should be pseudepigraphical: 'In Jewish usage the testament

35

was a fictional literary genre.'[1] So the readers would not expect it to be from Peter himself: in any case the evidence for its attribution to the apostle personally is weak, so it is improbable that Peter, wishing to write his own testament, adapted the (normally fictional) genre in order to do so. Moreover, when we come to the predictions of false teachers in chapters 2 and 3 the author alternates between the future and present tense thus making the fictional nature of the genre very explicit: the apostolic 'prophecies' are now being fulfilled. 'Such deliberate breaches of the fiction of Petrine authorship are possible only if the fiction was a transparent one.'[2]

Dr Bauckham has written a massive and learned commentary which will long remain the standard work in English on this Epistle. His view is important and, if correct, removes all moral stigma from the pseudepigraphal publication of 2 Peter. It justifies the place of 2 Peter in the Canon, for it champions orthodox apostolic Christianity in contest with false teaching, and probably emerged from the Petrine circle in Rome somewhere between AD 75 and 100. Like the Gospel of Mark it contained apostolic material penned by a subapostolic man. Therefore from the viewpoint of the ancients there would be no problem in having it in the Canon. From a modern viewpoint its inclusion is appropriate, since the main principle of canonicity is to assert the uniqueness and normativeness of the apostolic message – which is above all what 2 Peter sets out to do.

If he is right in his thesis, therefore, it is not only possible but proper to recognize 2 Peter as a pseudepigraph which is rightly included in the Canon, and he has disproved Guthrie's claim that 'there is no evidence in Christian literature for the idea of a conventional literary device, by which an author as a matter of literary custom, and with the full approbation of his circle of readers, publishes his own production in another's name'.

But *is* he right? This is not the place for a full scale examination of his theory, but a number of questions need to be asked.

In the first place, if it was so evident that 2 Peter was the fictional Testament which Bauckham takes it to be, why is it that this has not been apparent to Christians down the ages until

[1]*Op. cit.* p.134.   [2]*Op. cit.* p. 135

Bauckham wrote his book? This is not an unfair *ad hominem* argument. The position Bauckham advances depends on the assumption that the literary genre of a fictional testament *was apparent to all*.

Secondly, if it was possible for works to be put into the Canon on the ground of early date and orthodox content, it is hard to see why Hermas, the Epistle of Diognetus, The Epistle of Barnabas and the First Epistle of Clement were not included. Yet the very Councils that accepted 2 Peter into the Canon decisively rejected Clement, Barnabas, Diognetus and Hermas. It is not possible to find a closer analogy to what Bauckham puts forward than Origen's position on Hebrews (that the content is Paul's but who actually penned it probably God alone will ever know). The analogy is far from compelling: Hebrews, of course, is not pseudepigraphical at all.[1]

Thirdly, it is far from clear that all 'testaments' must be fictional. The final testaments of David or Moses in the Old Testament need not be fictional. Nor need a later writer, in re-editing them, necessarily adopt the trappings of pseudepigraphy such as the author of 2 Peter is supposed to do here. Josephus 'wrote up' the Song of Moses – but he did so in the style of his own day. In any case, the farewell address of Moses in Deuteronomy is both prophetic and strongly ethical in content. Why should not a genuine Testament from Peter share those same two characteristics?

But, fourthly, one must ask whether Bauckham has not greatly exaggerated the influence of the testamentary genre on our Epistle. What grounds are there for supposing that it is a Testament at all, or that it owes anything substantial to the testamentary tradition? Whatever grounds there may be have certainly escaped the majority of commentators over the centuries. The basis really must be sought in 1:13–15, and is that passage not explicable as it stands, embodying the concern of an apostle who knows he may not have long to live and is passion-

---

[1] Much confusion haunts the subject of pseudepigraphy. Fritz Neugebauer brings some fresh air into the discussion in his paper 'Zur Deutung und Bedeutung des 1 Petrusbriefes' (*NTS*,26, 1980, p.61–86) where he differentiates three categories: anonymity, onymity and pseudonymity. Of course, the Hebrews case is anonymity: 2 Peter, if Bauckham is right, is pseudonimity, and therefore quite dissimilar.

ately concerned for the continuance of a healthy faith among the next generation?[1]

These considerations put substantial question marks against Bauckham's able and well-argued hypothesis.

If, however, it could be conclusively proved that 2 Peter is that otherwise unexampled thing, a perfectly orthodox epistolary pseudepigraph, I, for one, believe that we should have to accept the fact that God did employ the literary genre of pseudepigraphy for the communicating of his revelation. I would accept it as I accept the history and proverb, the myth and poetry, the apocalyptic and wisdom literature, and all the other types of literary form which go to make up Holy Scripture. It is not, therefore, from any obscurantism or *parti pris* that I am advocating the Petrine authorship of this Epistle. If I part company from the majority of critics on this Epistle, and with Zahn, Falconer, Bigg, Wohlenberg and others am inclined to maintain its Petrine authorship, it is because I remain unconvinced by the arguments brought against it, because I have yet to see a convincing pseudepigraph from the early days of Christianity,[2] and because there are few arguments brought against the authenticity of 2 Peter which do not equally militate against the view

---

[1]Reisner, commenting (in *Zukunftserwartung in biblischer Sicht*, 1984, p.132) on the testamentary hypothesis, which, as he perceives, is really based on 1:12–16, is forthright in his dismissal. 'Richtig daran is, dass die Passage deutlich auf die Todesprophetie anspielt, die der Auferstandene nach Joh. 21:18, 19 über Petrus aussprach. Die Annahme, dass 2 Petrus eine Situation direkter und unabwendbarer Lebensbedrohung anspiele, ist dagegen nicht Zwingend. Ταχινή in 2 Petr. 1:14 dürfte 'plötzlichen' und nicht 'baldigen' Tod meinen; Ἔξοδος bedeutet nicht unbedingt den Tod, sondern kann auch einfach die Abreise meinen.' ('(The hypothesis) is correct in that the passage clearly alludes to the prophecy of Peter's death spoken by the risen Christ, according to Jn. 21:18–19. On the other hand, the assumption that 2 Peter alludes to a situation in which (the writer's) life is under direct and inescapable threat, is not convincing. Ταχινή in 2 Pet. 1:14 could well refer to 'sudden' rather than 'imminent' death; Ἔξοδος does not necessarily mean 'death', but may mean simply 'departure'.')

[2]Bigg's comment on this point is worth reproducing. 'The pseudonymous writers of the early church, from the nature of things, were never either intelligent or critical. They did not attempt to qualify themselves for their task by an accurate study of the past; indeed, it would not have been possible for them to do so. There is hardly an instance of a really good pseudo-antique except the Platonic Letters, the work of an otiose scholar, who had thoroughly studied his exemplar, and could reproduce his style and circumstances to a nicety. But what was difficult for an Athenian professor with a library at his command, was quite beyond the capabilities of an uneducated Christian. Such a man does not comprehend even the simplest rules of the forger's art. We may apply to him the words of Persius, *digitum exsere, peccas*' (Bigg, p.233).

that it was the product of a pseudepigrapher.[1] On a more positive note, I am impressed by the similarities between 2 Peter and 1 Peter both in diction and doctrine, and also to some extent with the reported Petrine speeches in Acts,[2] though the value of this argument depends, of course, both on Peter's authorship of the First Epistle and the substantial reliability of Acts. I am impressed by the absence of any suggestion of chiliasm in 3:8[3] when quoting the very verse used by Barnabas, Justin, 2 Clement, Methodius and Irenaeus to support it. I find this almost incredible if 2 Peter did in fact come from a second-century hand. I am equally impressed at the contrast between the parousia teaching of 2 Peter and that of the early second-century *Apocalypse of Peter*.[4] I am impressed by the absence of interest in church organization (one of the main preoccupations of second-century works like the *Didache* and the *Ascension of Isaiah*), by the undeveloped nature of the heresy against which the Epistle is directed, and by the fact that the delay of the parousia is still a burning scandal. For these reasons the Commentary which follows will assume, provisionally, that the author is Simon Peter.

II THE OCCASION AND DATE OF 2 PETER

We are almost completely in the dark about the place of origin of this letter. If it is a genuine letter of Peter, it was probably

[1] E. I. Robson, at the outset of his book *Studies in the Second Epistle of Peter*, 1915, says rightly, 'The arguments of Chase against Petrine authorship are equally arguments against "forgery" or even capable imitation'(p.1).

[2] Thus 'received' (1:1) comes in Acts 1:17 and otherwise only twice in the New Testament. 'Godliness', a common word in 2 Peter, comes in Acts 3:12 and otherwise only in the Pastorals. 'Lawlessness' (2:8) occurs in Acts 2:23 and rarely elsewhere, while the only New Testament passages that speak of 'the wages of wickedness' are 2 Pet. 2:13, 15 and Acts 1:18. The rare 'punish' comes in 2:9 and Acts 4:21, and, of course, 'the day of the Lord' occurs in 3:10 and Acts 2:20. These parallels are merely verbal, and may be of no significance; they may, on the other hand, be echoes of one man's vocabulary.

[3] This verse, Ps. 90:4, became, in the second century, the main proof-text of chiliasm, the doctrine that Christ would reign for a thousand years on earth at the parousia. This belief became almost an article of Christian orthodoxy from the time of the writing of Revelation to Irenaeus. It would have been almost impossible for any second-century writer to use this verse, as 2 Peter does, without commenting on it at all either in favour of or against the chiliast hope. This in itself suggests the antiquity of our Epistle.

[4] This latter displays, in any case, literary dependence on our Epistle, which it would hardly do if 2 Peter, like itself, was second-century production. For the *Apocalypse* to allude

written from Rome shortly before his martyrdom (1:15). This remains the most likely place even if Peter was not the author. Barnett[1] points to the abhorrence of heresy, the eirenic picture of the relations between Peter and Paul, the reference to Peter's approaching death, and the hint of Mark's Gospel (1:15) as all being indicative of a Roman origin, and points out that 1 Peter and Jude, with both of which our Epistle has strong affinities, were also Roman publications in all probability. Certainty, however, is impossible.

The destination of the letter is equally puzzling. The crux here is 3:1. If, as most commentators take it, this is a reference back to 1 Peter, then the recipients of the second letter are obviously meant to be the same people to whom 1 Peter was despatched, the Christians in the provinces of Asia mentioned in 1 Peter 1:1. If, however, 3:1 refers to another (lost) letter and not to 1 Peter at all, then it is more difficult to be sure of the recipients. However the probabilities still favour Asia Minor; the letter was early received here (as it was in Egypt, another possible destination), and Asia Minor was one of the main seed-beds of those gnostic tendencies of which 2 Peter gives us an early example. At all events, the letter was sent to a particular congregation or congregations where the author knew trouble was afoot. It was certainly not a 'catholic' epistle designed for everyone in general and nobody in particular.

Much ink has been spilt on the question of whether the recipients were Jews or Gentiles. For the former[2] can be urged the implied contrast between 'your apostles' (3:2) and the rest, and the affinities between some of the language of 2 Peter and the Qumran writings.[3] But a Gentile, or at all events mixed, community is much more likely. Not only is Paul, the apostle to the Gentiles, a recognized authority, but the author is chary of explicit allusions to Jewish pseudepigrapha which Jude is quite

---

to it in order to suggest verisimilitude, 2 Peter must have enjoyed real prestige as an authentic production of the apostle. See above, p.14, n. 1.

[1] Barnett, p.164.

[2] So Zahn, Spitta. Falconer (*Expositor*, VI, 6, 1902) thinks it was written to Samaritans.

[3] W. F. Albright is impressed by the reminiscences in 2 Peter of the Qumran literature, 'including the true way, light in darkness, the final destruction by fire, *etc.*' (*From Stone Age to Christianity*, 1957, pp.22 f.). So is R. H. Harrison, *Archaeology of the New Testament*, 1964, p.81. So too, most recently Rainer Reisner, (*op. cit.*).

happy to adduce, and certain phrases such as 'a faith as precious as ours' (1:1) and 'that . . . you may . . . escape the corruption in the world caused by evil desires' (1:4) suggest that the readers are Gentiles. It is probable that a mixed community (living in and influenced by a pagan community – Fornberg) is nearest the truth; they are people to whom the author had personally written and ministered (1:16; 3:1) and who had received at least one letter from Paul (3:16). It is impossible to be more precise than this; hence the variety of guesses by commentators about where they lived.

The date, again, is widely contested, from AD 60–160. Whether or not 2 Peter used Jude, whether or not his letter is prior or subsequent to 1 Peter, there are certain pointers which help in determining the date of the Epistle. It cannot have been written until most, if not all, of the Paulines had been penned (3:16); thus it cannot precede the mid-sixties. If Peter wrote it, a date between AD 61 and his death (? 64, 66 or 68) would be indicated. If not, what is the latest reasonable date? Early enough to have been used by the *Apocalypse of Peter* which is dated by the most recent authorities to the first quarter of the second century.[1] It must have been written by that time, in any case, to have imposed itself on Clement of Alexandria as worthy of a commentary. A date around AD 80 commends itself to several scholars, such as Reicke, Albright, Bauckham and Chaine, for a variety of reasons.[2] The views of many critics that it comes from a much later date[3] than this are governed by several misconceptions (that 3:16 implies a fixed collection of Paulines already recognized as canonical, that 3:4 implies the death, long ago, of the first Christian generation, and that 1:14, 17 imply familiarity with the four Gospel canon) and by the

[1]So E. Hennecke, *New Testament Apocrypha*, vol. II, p.664.

[2]Chaine favours such a date because he believes it was written by a close disciple of Peter, Albright because of the similarities with Qumran, and Reicke because he thinks there could hardly have been such a favourable attitude to imperial magistrates in a Christian document written after the persecution of Domitian. Bauckham links its publication with the dying out of the first generation (*cf.* 3:4), and its literary affinities with Hermas, 1 and 2 Clement, all deriving from the Roman church. His dating of Hermas and 2 Clement in the first century AD is surely tendentious. Normal dating places Hermas and 2 Clement in the mid-second century AD, and they thus become early testimonies to 2 Peter's use.

[3]Thus Windisch suggests 120, Mayor 125, von Soden 150, Jülicher 125–175, Harnack 150–175.

desire to 'close the gap' between the publication of 2 Peter and its relatively widespread attestation in the third century.[1] Such a view runs foul of the external evidence that 2 Peter was prior to the *Apocalypse of Peter*. Furthermore, it fails to account for a number of other features which make a second-century date very hard indeed to visualize. But it is perhaps the undeveloped nature of the heresy attacked which is the strongest evidence of a first-century origin in the lifetime of St Peter, and to this we now turn.

III. THE FALSE TEACHING IN 2 PETER AND JUDE

It will be convenient to treat the false teaching attacked by 2 Peter and Jude together, because, despite the differences between them, it is clear that they have a great deal in common and are almost certainly manifestations of the same problem.[2]

There is wide agreement among commentators that the heresy envisaged is in both cases a primitive form of what in the second century became Gnosticism. The main characteristics that emerge are as follows. The lives and teaching of these men denied the Lordship of Jesus (2 Pet. 2:1; Jude 4). They defiled the Agape (love-feast), were immoral themselves and infected others with their lascivious ways, through minimizing the place of law in the Christian life and emphasizing freedom (2 Pet. 2:10, 12ff., 18ff.; Jude 4, 12). In their teaching, which was very voluble, they were plausible and crafty, fond of rhetoric, out for gain, and obsequious to those from whom they hoped to gain some advantage (2 Pet. 2:3, 12, 14–15, 18; Jude 16). Both writers represent them as arrogant and cynical, not only to the Lord, but to church leaders and angelic powers as well (2 Pet. 2:1, 10–11; Jude 8). They appear to have posed as either visionaries or prophets, in support of their claims (2 Pet. 2:1; Jude 8). They are self-willed and set up divisions, confident of their own

---

[1] On this point B. B. Warfield has some pertinent things to say in his *Syllabus on the Special Introduction to the Catholic Epistles*, pp.116 ff. He reminds us that Herodotus is quoted only once in the century following its composition, and Thucydides not at all until the second century after it was written.

[2] Fornberg, Neyrey and Bauckham unconvincingly seek to differentiate them.

superiority (2 Pet. 2:2, 10, 18; Jude 19). The errorists against whom 2 Peter writes scoff at the parousia (chapter 3), but there is no trace of this in Jude, although his antagonists, too, are mockers in a general sense (v.18). Peter's opponents twist the Old Testament prophets and Pauline writings to their own ends (1:18–2:1; 3:15–16),[1] while Jude's antagonists twist the (Pauline) doctrine of free grace into an excuse for licence (v. 4). There are other indications in Jude that the recipients had a basically Pauline understanding of the gospel. The same distinction between spiritual and carnal Christians that Paul makes in 1 Corinthians 2 appears in Jude 19. The false teachers described themselves as *pneumatikoi*, the 'spiritual ones', though in fact they did not even possess the Spirit at all! Though 2 Peter does not use precisely the same language, much the same impression is given by the repeated use the author makes of the *gnōsis* and *epignōsis* roots. He is repudiating the claims of the heretics to a superior knowledge by showing them what true Christian knowledge comprises. Jude writes in haste to rectify the situation where this sort of heresy has arisen; Peter writes, partly at least, in order to have a preventive effect, for many of his verbs are in the future tense (though this may be a rhetorical device to show that what has happened is in accordance with prophecy; see 2 Pet. 2:1ff.; *cf.* Jude 4). The other difference in the treatment of the false teachers is that Peter avoids the explicit use of apocryphal material to enforce his points, while Jude has no such scruples.

Here, in an undeveloped form, are most of the main characteristics which went to make up later Gnosticism – emphasis on knowledge, which emancipated them from the claims of morality; arrogance towards 'unenlightened' church leaders; interest in angelology; divisiveness; lasciviousness. The later Gnostics perverted the grace of God into licence, confident that the true 'pneumatic' could not be affected by what the flesh does. They thought they had no duty to civil or ecclesiastical authorities – had they not been delivered from the old aeon and its powers? They were, moreover, antagonistic to eschatology,

---

[1]This dishonest handling of Scripture was a characteristic failing of later Gnostics, and is attacked by Irenaeus (*A.H.* i. 3.6, 8.1, 9.1).

for, as Käsemann observed,[1] the Gnostic had the fullness of the divine nature already. Salvation is present to the Gnostic, and transcends time; to the Hebrew mind, of course, which took time seriously, salvation could never be complete until the last day. That is why the Gnostic had no use for apocalyptic and the future element in salvation. It was at this point, no doubt, that they thought they had an ally in Paul, for he, too, stresses the present tense in salvation – though without neglecting the future.

It must be emphasized, however,[2] that there is no trace in the opponents either of Jude or Peter of that cosmological dualism which lies at the heart of Gnosticism. There is no trace of a demiurge or of antipathy to bodily resurrection. There is no evidence that their libertinism was based on dualism, nor that their eschatological scepticism resulted from a Gnostic concentration realized rather than future eschatology. It is plain, therefore, that to call the false teachers Gnostic is an anachronistic misnomer. The most we can do is to realize that many of their characteristics reappear in second-century Gnosticism.

But we do not need to wait for the second century to find these characteristics. Indeed, as Kümmel rightly points out, the heresy here depicted 'does not fit any specific Gnostic system of the second century'.[3] Immediate parallels spring to mind within the first century. In Corinth, as early as the fifties, a movement had gained a foothold which advocated an 'enlightened' sexual programme based on promises of liberty (1 Cor. 6:12–13). The Lord who had bought his servants was, in practice, denied (6:18–20). Laying emphasis on the emancipating effects of knowledge, these people justified participation in heathen cults (1 Cor. 8; cf. 2 Pet. 2:10), abused the love-feasts (1 Cor. 11:21), despised angelic powers (1 Cor. 11:10) and fostered separatist tendencies (1 Cor. 3; 11:18f.). Their claim to élitism in the Spirit and in visions was also to be found at Corinth (1 Cor. 12:1–13; 14:37–39; 2 Cor. 12:1–3). Most significant of all, they encouraged disbelief in the future element of the kingdom of God, the

---

[1]Käsemann, p.171.
[2]See especially Fornberg, *An Early Church in a Pluralist Society* and 'The Form and Background of the polemic in 2 Peter' by J. H. Neyrey (JBL, 1980, pp.407–431).
[3]*Introduction to the New Testament*, p.300.

parousia and resurrection (1 Cor. 15); and this, naturally, led to licence (15:32). A similar sort of heresy is found in the Asian churches, advocated by the Nicolaitans (Rev. 2 and 3). While much about these sectaries is obscure, it is at least plain that sexual immorality, emphasis on *gnōsis*, participation in idolatrous feasts, and separatism were among their main characteristics, possibly coupled with political cooperation with Rome (for which Bo Reicke[1] argues strongly, if at times bizarrely, in the case of 2 Peter and Jude). The occurrence of the name Balaam in 2 Peter 2:15; Jude 11 and Revelation 2:14 perhaps suggests some connection with the Nicolaitans. In short, there is no antinomian movement known to us from the second century[2] which more closely tallies with that of 2 Peter and Jude than the Nicolaitans of Revelation[3] and the proto-gnostic libertines of Corinth. Similar tendencies were to be found at Colossae in the sixties (with speculative thinking, immorality, and concern with angels) and in the Johannine churches in the eighties or nineties (insubordination, separatism, immorality, emphasis on knowledge, and lack of love). The heresy we meet in 2 Peter and Jude is entirely credible within the first century, and the mid-first century at that.

[1]Bo Reicke assumes that 2 Peter, Jude, and James, together with 1 Clement all belong to the type of background suggested by Suetonius, *Domitian* x, where we read of various attempts among the aristocracy to unseat this most unpopular and cruel emperor. Reicke tortures the evidence of these Epistles to fit them into this political mould; though ingenious, it hardly carries conviction.

[2]Were 2 Peter and Jude of a late date, we might expect a reference to the distinctive tenets of the false teachers; as it is we find nothing of the sort, not even the suggestion of 'genealogies' and 'aeons' and the Demiurge, which were stock-in-trade of various Gnostic sects. There is no hint either of the various schools in which Gnosticism became defined in the second century, Carpocratianism, Severianism, Valentinianism, and so forth. Indeed the primitive nature of the heresy here stands out in even bolder relief since the discovery of Valentinus' *Gospel of Truth*, the *Gospel of Thomas* and the *Gospel of Philip* which display genuine developed Gnosticism.

[3]This is the conclusion of the most recent treatment of the problem by Dr Rainer Reisner, 'Der zweite Petrus-Brief und die Eschatologie' in *Zukunftserwartung in biblischer Sicht*, hrsg. von Gerhard Marier, Wuppertal, 1984, p.124 ff. He is attracted by possible links with Qumran (he lists six such), which would be very apt if 2 Peter and Mark's Gospel were in fact sent to Qumran. But his explanation of how the strict ascetics of Qumran turned into the libertines presupposed by 2 Pet. is unconvincing. He is strong, however, in stressing the Jewish elements in this heresy; not only the many allusions to apocryphal Jewish traditions, but 'the way' phrases (2:1, 15, 21) which are very Jewish. Probably Peter, like Paul, has to face a syncretistic, libertine opposition bent on combining certain elements of Christianity with life in a pagan culture.

To put the matter positively, what does the letter actually say? Reisner (*op.cit.*) addresses himself to this question, and shows succinctly that the contents of the Epistle can be summarized under five heads, all of which are in line with early Christianity, and not nearly so applicable to a late date.

First, the author seeks to bind them to the apostolic tradition (1:19ff.), for it is the apostles, not the false teachers, who stand in true succession both to the Old Testament prophets and to the Lord Jesus who revealed himself in glory on the Mount. As in 1 Cor. 12:10, 29 the prophetic charisma remains alive.

Secondly, he stresses that there is no credibility in claims to spirituality which are not backed by a holy life (1:5, 9). It is noticeable that he interprets the Old Testament paraenetically (*i.e.* as ethical exhortation) not speculatively as was so common in Jewish mysticism: ethics are more important than knowledge (Mt. 7:15–27; 1 Cor. 13:2).

Thirdly, he urges respect for the supernatural powers. There is no arrogant *securitas* in Peter as there is in the false teachers: he knows that it is all too possible to fall from grace by presumption (2:9, 15, 18). Balaam, Lot and Noah all underline the point that the pious can be tempted and can fall.

Fourthly, he teaches that the world will have an end and will be replaced by God's new creation. How different from Plato and the Stoics! Who today dares to pray for the end of the world? But the first apostles did (1 Cor. 7:31; Rev. 6:10).

Finally, the author has wise words to say both on the delay and on the acceleration of the parousia. God is not the slave of some programmed eschatological plan which we have to decode. We are forbidden to speculate (Mt. 22:43; 2 Pet. 3:10). As in the prayer 'your kingdom come' Peter suggests that we can accelerate the return of Christ. Delay is no cause for embarrassment, rather for relief, for it still affords time for repentance. Jesus had said the same (Lk. 13:6–9).

Thus not only is the nature of the false teaching entirely compatible with a mid-first-century date, but so is Peter's way of handling it in the Letter. The author has shown himself a true disciple of his Lord.

IV. THE UNITY OF 2 PETER

From time to time suggestions have been made that 2 Peter is made up of two or more sources. Some years ago, for example, M. McNamara[1] suggested that chapter 1 circulated independently, and that is the letter referred to in 3:1. Thus chapter 3 is one of the 'reminders' promised by the short letter which constitutes our chapter 1. He thinks chapter 2 also circulated as an independent tract against false teachers. This is quite an attractive hypothesis, and gives an excellent rapport between chapters 1 and 3 while recognizing the individuality of chapter 2 as a document in its own right with strong affinities to Jude. The snag is the continuity of style throughout the Epistle which makes it certain that the whole work proceeds from the same man. McNamara recognizes the force of this, and regards his three letters as all coming from the same hand. This is possible but far from necessary, and has no atom of external support.

E. I. Robson[2] invented a more complicated theory to account for the apparent genuineness and apparent spuriousness of different parts of the Epistle. He could neither reckon it as entirely Petrine, nor yet accept the view that it was a pseudepigraph. He maintained, accordingly, that there are four genuine Petrine parts of the letter (1:5–11, Teaching; 1:12–18, Autobiography; 1:20–2:19, Prophecy; 3:3–13, Apocalyptic), and that the whole thing has been written up by a redactor.

A somewhat similar view was expressed by M. E. Boismard in his review[3] of my 2 *Peter Reconsidered*. He acknowledged the force of the case for Petrine authorship but indicated a hypothesis I had not considered, namely that a redactor combined an authentic Epistle of Peter (chapters 1 and 3) with the Epistle of Jude. Thus, he suggested, the affinities and the differences between 1 and 2 Peter might be explained. However, the unity of style is against this. Furthermore, 2 Peter does not use Jude only in chapter 2. Thirdly, one may wonder whether the 'Asiatic' style in which 2 Peter was written[4] was carried through to the second century. And finally, the difficulties of chapters 1

---

[1]*Scripture*, XII, 1960, pp.13–19.   [2]*Studies in the Second Epistle of Peter.*
[3]*Revue Biblique*, lxi, 2, 1963, p.304.
[4]*Cf.* p.19.

and 3 still remain, and on this view are Petrine. Why not forget the unevidenced and improbable redactor, and assign the whole thing to Peter, if one is prepared to go so far as to recognize genuine Petrine elements in the Epistle?

V. THE AUTHORSHIP OF JUDE

The external attestation to this small letter is early and good. It finds a place in the second-century Muratorian Canon; Tertullian recognized it as an authoritative Christian document,[1] so did Clement of Alexandria,[2] who wrote a commentary on it.[3] Origen hints that there were doubts in his day ('if anyone should add the Epistle of Jude', *Comm. in Matth.* 17:30), but clearly did not share them,[4] for he quotes Jude as authoritative with enthusiasm: 'And Jude wrote an Epistle, tiny in the extreme, but yet full of powerful words and heavenly grace' (*ibid.* 10:17). In addition, Athenagoras, Polycarp and Barnabas[5] seem to have cited the Epistle early in the second century, so it could hardly have been composed later than the end of the first. Eusebius classes it among the disputed books, and it was not admitted into the early Syrian Canon, the *Peshitta*. The reason is not hard to discover. Jude quoted apocryphal writings, and although in some circles in the West this tended to add stature to the apocryphal works in question,[6] in the East this link with apocryphal material was sufficient to cause Jude's rejection.[7] Jerome says as much. He explains the cause of the doubts about Jude as 'because he appealed to the apocryphal book of Enoch as an authority it is rejected by some'.[8] As late as the end of the fourth century Didymus of Alexandria had to defend Jude against those who attacked it because of its use of apocryphal

---

[1] *De cult. fem.* i.3. So authoritative, in fact, that it led him to accept *1 Enoch*!

[2] *Paed.* iii.8. 44, *Strom.* iii. 2. 11.

[3] Summarized in the *Adumbrations*.

[4] Kümmel astonishingly says 'Origen did not regard it as part of the canon' (*Introduction to the New Testament*, p.301). He must have overlooked Origen's *Comm. in Rom.* 3:6 where he calls Jude *scriptura divina*.

[5] See Bigg, pp.307 f. for the details.   [6] So Tertullian, *De cult. fem.* i.3.

[7] See Introduction, section viii.

[8] *De vir. ill.* iv.

material.[1] It is clear that this was the only reason for the hesitation felt in some quarters about Jude. By AD 200 it was accepted in the main areas of the ancient church, in Alexandria (Clement and Origen), in Rome (Muratorian Canon), and in Africa (Tertullian). Only in Syria were there objections, and even there these could hardly have been in unison, because Jude was accepted into the Philoxenian and Harklean recensions of the New Testament.

Clement of Alexandria in the *Adumbrations* says that this letter was written by Jude, the brother of James the Lord's brother. So does Epiphanius, but he calls him an apostle as well, as do many of the Fathers (Origen, Athanasius, Jerome, Augustine). That the Lord's brethren were loosely known to others as apostles appears from Galatians 1:19. But Jude was no apostle. He styles himself 'a servant of Jesus Christ and brother of James'. There can be no doubt who is meant. Kümmel summarizes the matter well when he writes 'As "brother of James" he is characterized clearly enough. There was only one eminent, well known James, the brother of the Lord (Jas. 1:1; Gal. 1:19; 2:9; 1 Cor. 15:7). Then Jude is one of the brothers of Jesus, the third named in Mark 6:3, the fourth in Matthew 13:55. Otherwise we know nothing about this Jude.'[2] The author could hardly be Judas, the son (or brother) of James (Lk. 6:16), one of the twelve, because the author of this letter expressly dissociates himself from the apostles (v. 17). Nor is Streeter's[3] suggestion likely, that it was written by the third bishop of Jerusalem who, according to the fourth-century *Apostolic Constitutions* (but not according to Eusebius[4]) was Judas. But even if this was the case, did he have a brother called James, and, furthermore, a brother of such distinction that one had only to mention his name in order to identify him? Surely this is special pleading. The letter claims to be by Jude, the brother of James and therefore of the Lord. Can this claim stand?

Many scholars accept it, noting the deeply Jewish colouring of the letter, especially the love for Jewish apocalypses and the

---

[1]For the text, see Migne, *Patrologia Graeca* xxxix. 1811 ff.
[2]Kümmel, *Introduction to the New Testament*, p.300.
[3]*The Primitive Church*, 1929, pp.178–180.
[4]Who calls him Justus, along with several later lists.

Aramaic sentence structure with its triple arrangements coupled with the good Greek that one might expect from a native of bilingual Galilee. Mayor has made an interesting study of the affinities in thought and expression between the Epistles of Jude and James and this, so far as it goes, supports the attribution.[1]

But why, if Jude is the brother of the Lord, does he not say so? The answer, as old as Clement of Alexandria, is his humility. The church called James and Jude brothers of the Lord (1 Cor. 9:5), but they preferred to think of themselves as his servants, remembering, no doubt, that in the time of their actual intercourse with him as brethren, they did not believe in him (Jn. 7:5). But both letters combine unquestioned authority with personal humility, which is precisely what one would expect from a converted member of the family circle of Jesus.[2]

But could Jude have lived long enough to write this letter? It manifestly comes from the close of the apostolic age. The apostolic faith is crystallized (v. 3), the apostolic words are remembered (v. 17), and the apostolic warnings have been fufilled (v. 18). This could hardly be the case much before about AD 70, though there is no need to assume with Luther that the writer 'speaks of the Apostles as a disciple long afterwards'.[3] Could Jude have survived till the last quarter of the first century? If Jude was a younger brother of Jesus (as his placing in the lists in the Gospels suggests) there would be no difficulty about this dating, were it not for a story recorded by Hegesippus.[4] He tells us that the grandsons of 'Jude the brother of the Lord after the flesh' were brought before the Emperor Domitian (AD 81–96) as potential revolutionaries (belonging, of course, as they did to the line of David), but were released when their horny hands attested that they were small farmers with no political aspiration, and their kingdom was seen to be a heavenly one! Hegesippus informs us that they became bishops in the church, and survived to the time of Trajan (AD 98–117). Surely, it is argued, if Jude had grandsons who were mature men in Domi-

---

[1]Mayor, pp. cxlviii ff.

[2]For a discussion of the relationship of Jude and James to Jesus see R. V. G. Tasker's commentary on *James* in this series, pp.22–25, and J. B. Lightfoot's Excursus 'The Brethren of the Lord' in his *Epistle to the Galatians*, 1869, pp.247–282.

[3]*Preface to Jude.*   [4]Eusebius, *H.E.* iii. 20. 1 ff.

tian's time, he must have died long before, and too early to have written this Epistle. J. B. Mayor makes short work of this view:[1] 'Jude, as we have seen, was apparently the youngest of the Brethren of the Lord, probably born not later than 10 AD, if we accept the date of 6 BC for the Nativity. Taking into account the early age at which marriage generally took place in Judaea, we may suppose that he had sons before 35AD and grandsons by 60 AD. These may have been brought before Domitian in any year of his reign. Jude himself would thus have been 71 in the first year of Domitian. If his letter was written in 80 AD, he would have been 70 years of age, and his grandsons about 20.'

The other objections against Jude's authorship of the Epistle are trifling. The fairly good quality of his Greek should surprise only those who are unaware of the extent of Hellenization in first-century Palestine, particularly Galilee.[2] The fact that the quotation of *Enoch* in verse 15 corresponds fairly closely to the Greek translation of that work need not tell against Jude's authorship; after all he would hear the Septuagint read each sabbath in the synagogue. In any case, it is not improbable that the substance of Jude and 2 Peter 2 comes from a common source, a catechetical tract against false teaching; in which case it may well have been an unknown catechist, not Jude, who made this citation of the Greek of *Enoch*. We have already examined the view that the nature of the false teaching denounced in Jude is indicative of a late date.

There is, then, a good deal to support and little to militate against the traditional view that Jude wrote this letter. If we reject this, we are reduced either to the improbable conjecture that an unknown Jude whose brother was an important (but unknown!) James wrote the letter, or else to pseudepigraphy. And the failure to specify just who this Jude was is most unlikely on either supposition. In the case of pseudepigraphy, it is very hard to see why so obscure a person as Jude should have been chosen for the attribution. It was normal to choose some well-known person on whom to 'father' pseudepigraphic writ-

[1]Mayor, p. cxlviii.
[2]See E. R. Goodenough, *Jewish Symbols in the Graeco Roman Period,* 1953, and N. Turner, 'The Language of Jesus and his Disciples' in *Grammatical Insights into the New Testament,* 1965, who argues that Jesus and his family habitually spoke a type of Septuagintal Greek.

ings. A pseudepigraph attached to the name of someone of whom nothing else is known is almost inconceivable.

Barclay's conclusion is fair. He writes, 'When we read Jude it is obviously Jewish; its references are such that only a Jew could understand them, and its allusions are such that only a Jew could catch them. It is simple and rugged; it is vivid and pictorial. It is clearly the work of a simple thinker rather than a theologian. It fits Jude the brother of the Lord. It is attached to his name, and there could be no reason for so attaching it unless he did in fact write it.'[1]

VI. THE CHARACTER OF THE LETTER

The Epistle of Jude has received a very poor press. Not only has it lived in the shadow of 2 Peter, but it seems to be little but a string of denunciations, and many regard it as an 'early Catholic' reaction to incipient Gnosticism. Both of these assumptions are highly questionable.

Firstly, the denunciations. True, they predominate from verses 5–19. But the most important and distinctive parts of Jude come in verses 1–4 and 20–25. It is here, not in the denunciations, that the burden of his message is concentrated. In any case, the polemical section is far from mere denunciation. As Earle Ellis has shown,[2] it is in fact a carefully composed 'pesher' (or 'commentary') exegesis, in which Jude argues that the libertinism of his opponents marks them out as the sinners of the last days who were prophesied by the Old Testament, by some intertestamental works, and by the words of the apostles. Moreover, Jude is not addressing his opponents in this letter. It is not a case of 'argument weak: shout louder'. He is writing to warn his orthodox, if wobbly, Christian readers of the dangers of succumbing to the blandishments of the false teachers, and when he comes on to his positive teaching at the end of the letter he gives wise advice on how to help those who are carried away into error, and shows a deep pastoral concern for them (vv. 22–23).

[1]Barclay, pp.202 f.   [2]*Prophecy and Hermeneutic in Early Christianity*, p.220 ff.

Secondly, the 'early Catholicism'. This somewhat pejorative epithet arose in Germany to denote the reaction of the second-century church to the twin threats of Gnosticism and Montanism. It denoted a hardening of the arteries, a fossilization of the faith into set forms, an emphasis on church leaders, a fading of the parousia hope and a distancing from the apostolic age. Many commentators have seen Jude as a representative of 'early Catholic' literature, and have dated it, accordingly, in the first part of the second century. 'The faith' has become straitjacketed (v. 3), the apostles belong to a bygone era (v. 17), and the opponents, since patristic days, have been seen as Gnostics. Nevertheless such a conclusion is too bland. It assumes what it seeks to prove. For there is nothing in the letter itself to point to any of the distinguishing marks of Gnosticism proper. Such identification is read into the letter rather than out of it. You did not need to be a Gnostic to have visions, be fascinated by the apocrypha, live a sensuous life and defile the love feasts! Even if it were possible to demonstrate that marks of what later became Gnosticism are prevalent in Jude's false teachers, that would be a most unsafe criterion for dating. Many of the seeds of later Gnosticism were clearly there in the first century, as the Letters of John and indeed the Corinthian Epistles make plain. Furthermore, the author does not refer to the apostles as belonging to a bygone era; he simply states that he himself did not belong to their number, and he urges his readers to pay attention to their predictions that false teachers would arise, for this has in fact taken place (hence his letter). The fact that Jude refers to what the apostles *said* rather than *wrote* suggests we still are moving within the oral period, when apostolic teaching was passed on largely by word of mouth.

Nor does the reference to 'the faith that was once for all entrusted to the saints' (v. 3) require a late date. 'The faith' is used in this objective way as early as Galatians 1:23 and Philippians 1:27. There is no need to take 'the faith' here as meaning anything more than 'the gospel'. Paul makes it plain that the idea of Christian orthodoxy was well established by the fifties of the first century (*e.g.* Rom. 6:17; Gal. 1:8ff.; 1 Thes. 2:13; 2 Thes. 2:15; 3:6, 14). To suppose Jude means more than this may well be gratuitous. Indeed, the 'early Catholic' interpretation of 'the faith' here is particularly inept, for Jude is not discussing fixed formulations of the faith at all, but the moral content of Christianity which is so greatly at variance with the behaviour of the false teachers. Ethics, not doctrine, is his concern in verses 3 and 4, as he takes pains to make clear in the text!

Of church officials, a bulwark of 'early Catholicism', there is no sign in Jude. It is not the responsibility of bishops and presbyters to uphold the faith, but of *all* his recipients. Church officials are not invoked to quell false teaching. Rather, he urges the whole Christian community to engage in charismatic prayer, pastoral argument and determined evangelism (vv. 20–23). And they are to do it in lively expectation of the parousia (vv. 1, 14, 21, 24) – it is far from a fading hope! Manifestly, therefore, Jude is not, as is so often maintained, a product of 'early Catholicism'.

No, this letter comes from the heart of Jewish Christianity. It is nourished by the beliefs and assumptions of apocalyptic Judaism. All the evidence points in this way – the rugged Jewishness of the Epistle, the use of those apocalyptic books *1 Enoch* and the *Testament of Moses*, the midrash pesher exegesis (*i.e.* homiletic exposition with, particularly in the Qumran Community, an application of the biblical prophecies to the 'end times') of verses 5–19, the stress on ethics rather than doctrinal formulation, and the Jewish affinities of the language Jude uses.

Jude is no defensive Catholic tract from the second century, but a passionate defence of Jewish Christian faith and life to believers living in the midst of a pluralistic and permissive pagan society. And therein lies one of its great values for Christians the world over in our own day.

VII. THE OCCASION AND DATE OF JUDE

Why did Jude write this letter? And when did he do so?

He wrote in a hurry because of the outbreak of dangerous antinomianism in churches with which he was concerned. It was brought by travelling teachers (v. 4) who 'change the grace of our God into a licence for immorality'. And that remains the burden of his charge against the false teachers. It has been customary to regard them as Gnostics. Wedermann is the most persuasive advocate of this view, but it has been the traditional way to interpret Jude since at least the days of Clement of Alexandria, who thought Jude wrote prophetically against the Carpocratians. Some have seen in the hints afforded by Jude's denunciations the following characteristics in his opponents: a docetic Christology (v. 4), the Gnostic division of mankind into pneumatics and psychics (v. 19), and angelology and dreams (vv. 6–9). But on the one hand we have seen that Jude cannot be placed in the second century, and on the other these very covert allusions would be a singularly ineffective way of countering a major Gnostic heresy. Gnosticism was a second-century, Christian heresy, based on a cosmological dualism of which there is no trace here. We can be confident that Jude's opponents were not Gnostics. We have already seen something of their main characteristics. The errorists were a self-indulgent group of people, antagonistic to the element of law in the Christian life, keen on freedom, rather insubordinate to human and celestial authorities alike, who were arrogant and schismatic and claimed prophetic revelations as authority for their teaching. They did not cut themselves off from the orthodox, but sought to infiltrate them and draw them away: thus they were 'sunken reefs in your love feasts.'

Such were their main characteristics: they found their way (along with much else) into second-century Gnosticism. But there are insufficient criteria supplied us in the letter to arrive at a precise identification of who they were. Bauckham sees them as charismatics who had 'gone over the top', Ellis as Judaizers, Reicke as political agitators, while others find their affinities with Edessa or Qumran. We do not know precisely who they were. What we do know is that they were a dangerous libertine element which had come into the churches with which Jude was concerned, and he was clear that if they remained unchecked they could do untold damage. Their advocacy of liberty was so specious, their way of life so tempting, their pretensions to spirituality so impressive, their initiative and independence so attractive. They were a great danger. That is why Jude wrote.

And when? There is really very little to go on, which accounts for the wide variety of scholarly guesses on the market. Some have seen verse 5b as an allusion to the fall of Jerusalem in AD 70, and accordingly have made that a *terminus a quo* for Jude. Others have seen in verse 17 evidence that the age of the apostles is past. Neither consideration carries any weight. The most important clue we have lies in the relation of Jude to 2 Peter. If Jude used 2 Peter, this fixes an early date for that writing, and makes probable a date shortly afterwards for Jude. If, as most scholars think, 2 Peter used Jude, this again makes for a date for Jude well within the first century in order to fit the external attestation of 2 Peter. If both drew independently on a common source, this again argues for an earlier rather than a later date, when such apostolic 'fly sheets' might have perished. If, as Bigg improbably thought, Jude was an older half-brother of Jesus, he is unlikely to have lived after about AD 65, and consequently a date shortly before that would be necessary if he wrote it. But if, as is much more likely, Jude was a younger half-brother of Jesus (the youngest son, may be, of Joseph and Mary), then he may well have lived until the eighties and could have written his letter any time in the preceding 10 or 15 years.

We have, unfortunately, no means of knowing to whom Jude addressed himself. His was not a general letter, but written to people he knew in a particular situation (vv. 3–5, 17–18, 20). He is clearly a Jew himself, but that does not mean his readers are. However, the probabilities, slight as they are, point in that direction. He assumes their knowledge of Jewish intertestamental and apocryphal literature. He talks of 'our common salvation', which would fit either Jewish or Gentile readers. If Jude the brother of James was indeed the author, it is probable that, like his brother, he would have made himself particularly responsible for the Jewish Christian mission. On the other hand the language of Jude suggests familiarity with Pauline teaching, and it may well be that Wand, Harrison and Guthrie are right in seeing somewhere like Antioch as a probable destination. It is within the Palestine area, to which James, and therefore possibly Jude, confined himself; it comprised Jewish and Gentile Christians; moreover various of the apostles ministered there, which would make good sense of verse 17. Certainty is, of course, impossible; there is inadequate evidence on which to base a considered judgment.

VIII. JUDE'S USE OF APOCRYPHAL BOOKS

There can be no doubt that Jude knew and used at least two apocryphal writings, the *Assumption of Moses* and the *Book of Enoch*, and probably others as well, such as the *Testament of Naphtali* in verse 6, and the *Testament of Asher* in verse 8.

Jude quotes *Enoch* freely. It is a long apocryphal book probably composed at different periods from the first century BC to the first century AD. Jude cites *Enoch* i. 9 in verse 15, almost verbatim. In verse 14 he calls Enoch 'the seventh from Adam', a description which occurs in *Enoch* lx. 8, and there is a good deal in *Enoch* which is drawn on in Jude's description of the fallen angels in verses 6 and 13 (see Commentary).

Jude's indebtedness to the *Assumption of Moses* (v. 9) is no less certain. Indeed it is openly asserted by Origen,[1] Clement[2] and Didymus,[3] who knew the book, which now exists only in fragments: it was probably written at the very beginning of the first century AD. Both the *Assumption* and *Enoch* were highly esteemed in the early church, but we have no means of knowing whether Jude regarded these books as canonical. He quotes them as relevant to the situation for which he writes, and well known both to him and to his readers. It is surprising that the New Testament writers allude so rarely to the vast mass of extra-canonical material which was circulating in the first century. Paul alludes to the rabbinic midrash on the Rock in 1 Corinthians 10:4; the author of Hebrews frequently echoes the works of Philo; in 2 Timothy 3:8 we are told that Jannes and Jambres were the magicians who defied Moses before Pharaoh (a piece of Jewish *haggadah* based on Ex. 7:11 and found in various extra-canonical writings). Similarly the instrumentality of angels in giving the law (Gal. 3:19; Heb. 2:2), and the statements in Acts 7:22, James 5:17 and Hebrews 11:37 all allude to apocryphal material.

This should not surprise us. 'We have no right to assume that inspiration raises a writer to the intellectual position of a critical

---

[1] *De princ.* iii. 2. 1.   [2] *Adumbr. in Ep. Judae.*   [3] *In Ep. Judae Enarratio.*

historian', wrote Plummer.[1] 'St Jude probably believed the story about the dispute between Michael and Satan. But even if he knew it to be a myth, he might readily use it as an illustrative argument, seeing that it was so familiar to his readers.' Paul does not mind using a heathen poet in this way (Acts 17:28; 1 Cor. 15:32–33; Tit. 1:12). Chaine makes the good point that to believe in revelation does not imply a *tabula rasa* mind to all else. An inspired man might well use the contemporary ideas which were not contrary to revelation.[2]

A curious thing happened over Jude's use of this apocryphal material. At first some of these writings were accepted because they bore the stamp of Jude's approval. Thus Clement of Alexandria writes 'with these words he corroborates the prophet' (i.e. Enoch),[3] and again 'here he confirms the *Assumption of Moses'*, and both Tertullian[4] and Barnabas[5] regarded these books as Scripture. But later on the climate changed, and it became apparent how much danger lay in the unrestricted use of apocryphal material. The Apocrypha and its 'blasphemous fables' were attacked by Augustine[6] and Chrysostom.[7] Not only was the authority of Jude insufficient to save the apocryphal writings; Jude himself came under suspicion, and we find, as we saw in section v above, Didymus of Alexandria having to plead that Jude's citation of apocryphal books be not held against him.

IX. JUDE AND 2 PETER: WHERE LIES THE PRIORITY?

Verses 4–16 of Jude have extensive parallels, both in language and subject-matter, with chapter 2 of 2 Peter. The affinities are so close, as anyone can see who reads the two passages through in the Greek or even in an English translation, that there must be some literary relationship between the two writings. Did 2 Peter use Jude, or vice versa, or were both drawing on a common source?

This problem is one of the most enigmatic in New Testament studies. Older commentators recognized this. For example we

[1]Plummer, p.424.   [2]Chaine, p.279.   [3]*Adumbr. in Ep. Judae.*
[4]*Idol.* xv, *Apol.* xxii.
[5]*Ep.* iv. 3, xvi. 5.   [6]*City of God* xv. 23. 4.   [7]*Hom. in Gen.* vi. 1.

find a man like Plummer[1] confessing his own uncertainty of the way in which the relationship lay, and a man like Döllinger changing his mind.[2] More recent writers, such as Wand, Kümmel and Moffatt, have tended to be more confident that they know the answer, but perhaps less painstaking in their examination of the evidence.

What are the main facts in the discussion?

1. There are only three verses in the beginning and seven verses at the end of Jude which do not have extensive parallels in 2 Peter (Jude 1–3, 19–25), though verbal agreement is rare.

2. Jude undeniably arranged his work in triplets which are broken up in 2 Peter; whether or not this is a mark of originality or dependence can be argued both ways.

3. Jude, unlike 2 Peter, explicitly quotes the Apocrypha. This again can be used both ways.

4. 2 Peter's language about the false teachers is often, though not always, couched in the future tense, unlike Jude, who speaks of the heretics as being already present (see below).

5. Linguistically Jude's Greek is less difficult and contrived than that of 2 Peter. Once again opposite conclusions can be drawn from this fact.

6. The mockers in Jude do not appear to mock at the delay of the parousia, as they do in 2 Peter. This again is inconclusive as evidence of date.

Such are the facts. Then we descend to probabilities. Those who favour the priority of Peter lay stress on the unity of style in 2 Peter which makes it unlikely that he made wholesale borrowings from another author; the future tense in the predictions of false teachers in 2 Peter compared with the present in Jude;[3] the improbability that the leading apostle would borrow from an obscure man like Jude; the possibility that Jude 17–18 refer to the prophecy in 2 Peter 3:2–3; and the citation and supposed misunderstanding of some passages in 2 Peter by Jude.[4] Further,

---

[1]Plummer, p.394.   [2]See Plummer's fascinating note, p.400.

[3]2:1–3; 3:3, 17; cf. Jude 4, 8, 10, etc.

[4]Among the more impressive examples are the following: (i) In the parallel passages 2 Pet. 2:4; Jude 6, Jude's words desmois aidiois are most probably a paraphrase of the early variant seirais (chains) for seirois (pits) in Peter. (ii) Jude's omission of Peter's 'before the Lord' (2 Pet. 2:11; Jude 9) and insertion of 'charging the devil with blasphemy' from the Assumption of Moses obscures Peter's good point that the false teachers rail against church leaders (or

the fact that Jude cites the Apocrypha is thought to make it likely that he would make extracts from 2 Peter, and the fact that, as he tells us, he wrote hurriedly in an emergency makes it likely that he would have made use of any suitable material which was to hand, *i.e.*, on this view, 2 Peter.

These arguments are not all of equal value. The unity of style in 2 Peter could be maintained even if he did draw from Jude, for the dependence is by no means mechanical or crude; whatever is taken (by whichever author) is made thoroughly his own. The future tense in Peter's language about the false teachers is not consistently maintained (the present is found in 2:10, 12ff., 20). There is no reason why an apostle should not use material drawn up by a brother of the Lord; indeed, to judge from 1 Peter's indebtedness to traditional and liturgical material, Peter was very ready to borrow from others. While Jude 17–18 could well refer back to 2 Peter 3:2f. it need not do so, and the fact that 'the apostles' and not the particular apostle, Peter, are cited as authority for this prophecy militates against the supposed allusion.

Those who favour the priority of Jude stress the freshness and vitality of the letter compared with the more restrained style of 2 Peter and the probability that the longer letter, 2 Peter, drew from the shorter, rather than vice versa; for then there would only be some ten verses of Jude's own – hardly adequate reason for its publication and preservation. The former point is arguable; judgments on freshness and ruggedness of style tend to be very subjective. But the second point is strongly in favour of Jude's priority.

Advocates of this view see Jude's citing of apocryphal books as spontaneous, which the cautious pseudepigraph, 2 Peter, thought it wiser to drop, while at the same time making pious alterations such as leaving out the fall of the angels, and including the preservation of Noah and Lot. The generalized and watered-down statement in 2 Peter 2:11 becomes intelligible, it

---

angels) in the Lord's presence, and substitutes the charge that they bring accusations of blasphemy, which is much less appropriate. (iii) Jude's mention of the errorists as falling into 'this condemnation' (4), when he has made no mention of any, is best explained that he writes fresh from the reading of 2 Peter, with 2 Pet. 2:3 in mind, 'whose condemnation does not slumber'.

is argued, only when we have read the concrete example cited in Jude 9, and 2 Peter 2:17 is seen as a confused allusion to Jude's clear and powerful verse 12. Mayor[1] lays stress on the divergence in doctrinal emphasis and expression as a mark of Jude's priority, but it is precarious to argue from difference to priority. Many writers also bolster up the priority of Jude by pointing to allegedly late features in 2 Peter. But in each case the arguments are of very varying value. Jude's citation of apocryphal books may merely be the sharpening up of Peter's allusions with material which he knows will be meaningful for his readers. 2 Peter 2:17 is by no means a muddled version of Jude 12 but a thoroughly coherent, though different, metaphor (see Commentary). And the allegedly late features in 2 Peter are capable, as we have seen (section Id above), of a very different explanation.

I believe E. I. Robson was right when he wrote, 'The very fact that arguments either way appear to their maintainers to be of equal cogency, seems to show that on traditional lines we shall never reach a conclusion.'[2] He considered that behind 2 Peter and Jude there stood a document or documents denouncing false teaching. Bo Reicke inclines to the same view. He is impressed not only by the similarities between the two Epistles but by their differences in language, ideas, and order. 'Jude would seem to be mainly of secondary origin, since it summarizes in an elegant style points which 2 Peter expands with greater effort and more detail. Such smoothness of style is frequently characteristic of editors who condense and revise what has been laboriously drawn up by others. If this is the proper explanation here, then Jude was an arrangement of material already in existence'.[3] He concludes that both Jude and 2 Peter depend on a common tradition which may have been oral, 'a sermon pattern formulated to resist the seducers of the church'. M. E. Boismard, who had been studying this problem for some years, has come to the same conclusion,[4] which is

[1]Mayor, pp.xvi ff.
[2]Robson, p.52. Spicq (op. cit. p.197) and Michaels (op. cit. p.355) agree.
[3]Reicke, p.190.
[4]In a letter to me he writes, 'J'étais arrivé à la conclusion que les deux épîtres utilisaient un document commun, de ton eschatologique.'

given high probability in the New Testament Introductions by Harrison[1] and Guthrie.[2] In a footnote the latter has worked out some fascinating statistics which should give pause to those who assume without further argument the dependence of one of these writings upon the other. 'Out of the parallel passages comprising 2 Peter 1:2, 12; 2:1–4, 6, 10–12, 15–18; 3:2–3 and Jude 2, 4–13, 17–18, the former contain 297 words and the latter 256 words, but they share only 78 in common. This means that if 2 Peter is the borrower he has changed 70 per cent of Jude's language and added more of his own. Whereas if Jude borrowed from 2 Peter, the percentage of alteration is slightly higher, combined with a reduction in quantity. Clearly there can be no question of direct copying or of editorial adaptation. It is also significant that out of twelve parallel sections, Jude's text is verbally longer than 2 Peter's on five occasions, showing that neither author can be considered more concise than the other.'

If both authors drew independently on some standardized form of catechesis denouncing false teaching of an antinomian type, the similarities and differences between the two presentations will be easy to understand, since neither writes in slavish dependence on his outline.[3] It would appear, from the parallels before us, that such a common source began with the indication of the false teachers, their subtle infiltration, their denial of the Lord, and the doom awaiting them as had long ago been foretold in the sacred writings. This was spelt out in some detail, and followed by further description of the false teachers in language drawn from the Old Testament, the world of nature and the words of Jesus, the whole thing concluding either with the doom of the errorists or some teaching to the 'beloved' readers on positive Christian living.

It is highly probable that a document like this did exist in the early church.[4] It would soon have proved very necessary. It is

---

[1]E. F. Harrison, *Introduction to the New Testament*, 1966, pp.396 f.

[2]D. Guthrie, *New Testament Introduction*, 1970, pp.925 f.

[3]Indeed only one clause (in Jude 13; 2 Pet. 2:17) is almost identical in both letters.

[4]Both 1 *Clement* (xxiii) and 2 *Clement* (xi) quote as 'scripture' and 'the prophetic word' respectively just such a document as this (see Commentary on 2 Pet. 3:4). In both there is a reiterating of the truth of the parousia, despite its delay. In both there is the emphasis on righteousness and single-mindedness which we find in 2 Peter and Jude. Both refer to the

becoming increasingly widely recognized that several such tracts circulated during the early period. The existence of a document containing sayings of Jesus has long been suspected (it is generally referred to as Q), so has the independent circulation of Mark 13 as a basis for eschatological teaching in the early church. If we are to follow the suggestions of Carrington[1] and Selwyn,[2] there were catechetical tracts (pre- and post-baptismal) and a tract on how to deal with persecution. Rendel Harris,[3] supported to some extent by Dodd,[4] suspected the existence of a list of *testimonia* and W. L. Knox's theory of Gospel origins requires several such fly-sheets.[5] It is by no means unlikely that there was another decrying false teaching. This appears to me to be the simplest explanation of the perplexing literary phenomena linking 2 Peter with Jude. If it be objected that it is bad scholarship to postulate the existence of lost sources when alternative explanations are possible, it must be remembered that dependence on a common source is widely admitted in Synoptic criticism of the sayings material common to Luke and Matthew. Either Matthew used Luke, or Luke used Matthew, or both drew from a common source. If 'Q' be not regarded as an otiose hypothesis in the Synoptic problem, why should a lost common source be ruled out in this instance?

The other consideration which has prevented the majority of scholars from adopting the hypothesis of a lost source is this. It leaves very little for Jude to have said on his own account. Merely the first three verses, and verses 19–25.[6] But is this an

---

mockery at parousia teaching which is found in 2 Pet. 3:4 and to the analogy of the fruit tree which is found in Jude 12.

[1]*The Primitive Christian Catechism*, 1940.   [2]*The First Epistle of St. Peter*, 1946, Essay 2.

[3]*Testimonies*, 1916.

[4]*According to the Scriptures*, 1952, pp.28 ff.; his position has been challenged in M. D. Hooker's *Jesus and the Servant*, 1959, pp.21 ff. in favour of Harris's position. See also E. E. Ellis, *Paul's Use of the Old Testament*, 1957, pp.98–107.

[5]*Sources of the Synoptic Gospels*, II, 1957.

[6]'This argument loses a good deal of its force in the light of the view, argued in the Commentary on Jude, that the *most* important part of Jude, which fulfills the author's main purpose in writing, is the appeal (vv. 20–23). These verses are precisely those (together with the opening vv. 1–3 and the closing doxology) which Jude would have added to the hypothetical source. This is an intelligible procedure, and the possibility of a common source cannot be ruled out.' (Bauckham, p.142). The only reason he gives for rejecting the hypothesis is that it is more complicated than that of direct dependence. Would that one could solve the Synoptic problem in so cavalier a fashion! Surprisingly, he accepts the

insuperable difficulty? After all, he expressly tells us that he had been planning to write on another subject when news came to him of the outbreak of this heresy, and he snatched up his pen in haste to deal with it. Is there any reason why, under these pressing circumstances, he should not have dashed off the main themes of the apostolic counter to false teaching, adding, in his haste, little of his own apart from advice to the faithful on continuance? The rest could wait, like the proposed letter which he had perforce to lay aside, until a more convenient season.

---

existence of a much less clearly defined common source linking 2 Peter 3:4–13; *1 Clem.* xxxiii. 3–4; *2 Clem.* xi. 2–4. He regards it as a Jewish apocalyptic source, and is inclined to identify it with the *Book of Eldad and Modad*.

2 PETER:
ANALYSIS

CHAPTER ONE

    a. Introduction and greeting (1:1–2).
    b. The Christian's privileges (1:3–4).
    c. The ladder of faith (1:5–7).
    d. Barren and fruitful Christians (1:8–9).
    e. A worthy goal (1:10–11).
    f. Truth will bear repetition (1:12–15).
    g. The truth is attested by apostolic eyewitnesses (1:16–18).
    h. The truth is attested by prophetic scriptures (1:19–21).

CHAPTER TWO

    a. Beware of false teachers (2:1–3).
    b. Three examples of judgment and deliverance (2:4–10a).
    c. The insolence of the false teachers (2:10b–11).
    d. Their arrogance, lust and greed (2:12–16).
    e. The emptiness of the false teachers (2:17–22).

CHAPTER THREE

    a. The purpose of the letter reiterated (3:1–2).
    b. The taunts of those who scoff at the second coming (3:3–4).
    c. Peter argues from history (3:5–7).
    d. Peter argues from Scripture (3:8).
    e. Peter argues from the character of God (3:9).

f. Peter argues from the promise of Christ (3:10).
g. The ethical implications of the second coming (3:11–14).
h. Peter quotes Paul for support (3:15–16).
i. Conclusion (3:17–18).[1]

[1]Bauckham's outline of the structure of 2 Peter is so ingenious that it is worth citing:
1:1–2 Address and Salutation.
1:3–11 Theme: a summary of Peter's message.
1:12–15 Occasion: Peter's Testament.
1:16–18 Reply to Objection 1: a) apostolic eyewitness.
1:19 Reply to Objection 1: b) the value of Old Testament prophecy.
1:20–21 Reply to Objection 2: the inspiration of Old Testament prophecy.
2:1–3a Peter's prediction of false teachers.
2:3b–10a Reply to Objection 3: the certainty of judgment.
2:10b–22 Denunciation of the false teachers.
3:1–4 Peter's prediction of scoffers (including Objection 4 – v. 4).
3:5–7 Reply to Objection 4: a) the sovereignty of God's word.
3:8–10 Reply to Objection 4: b) the forbearance of the Lord.
3:11–16 Exhortation.
3:17–18 Conclusion.
The validity of this analysis does not depend on the testamentary hypothesis which Bauckham adopts. It shows superbly the inner coherence of the structure of this letter.

2 PETER: COMMENTARY

CHAPTER ONE

A. INTRODUCTION AND GREETING (1:1–2)

1. *Simon Peter.* At the outset of a letter which will have to involve a good deal of rebuke, the author first identifies himself and then presents his credentials.

The combination of the two names appears to be a primitive trait; it is found in Matthew 16:16; Luke 5:8, and often in John (*e.g.* 21:15–17, where Jesus three times addresses his penitent disciple by his patronym, because the name Peter, 'man of rock', was so inappropriate at that juncture to one who had denied his Master). Some have seen in this combination of the two names an attempt to appeal both to Jewish and to Gentile readers, but it is hard to see any signs of different groups of recipients in the letter itself. Others think, with more probability, that the double name, if significant at all, is meant to draw the reader's attention from the Jewish fisherman to the Christian apostle, from the old life to the new, from Simon, the name given him at his entry into the Old Covenant, to Peter, his distinctively Christian name.

The form 'Symeon', attested by Sinaiticus and Alexandrinus, is to be preferred to the normal spelling, *Simon*, attested by Vaticanus and Papyrus 72. It is the old Hebrew form, which is found elsewhere only in the Apostolic Decree (Acts 15:14) framed by James, the leader of the Jerusalem church. This Hebraism impresses some critics as a hallmark of authenticity (Bigg, Mayor, Zahn, James). Barnett, however, thinks it betrays 'the pseudonymity of the letter. The author clearly wishes to be identified with the author of 1 Peter'. He fails to explain why the pseudepigrapher clumsily chose a form of introduction different from that in 1 Peter, and why this supposedly deliberate archaism of Symeon never recurs in the pseudo-Petrine literature of the second century. J. A. T. Robinson is impressed by the Hebraism, and uses it to support his view that the Epistle was actually penned by Jude, the Lord's brother. It would be natural, if so, that he should refer to 'Symeon' in precisely the same way as did his brother James in the Apostolic Decree (Acts 15:14).

The writer's credentials are twofold. He is both *a servant (i.e.* 'bondslave') *and apostle of Jesus Christ.* Personal humility, so noticeable in 1 Peter, is combined with a sense of the authoritativeness of his apostolic position, and with good reason (see Mt. 10:40; Jn. 20:21–23). 'Apostle' stresses his solidarity with Christ, 'servant' with his readers. The latter term prepares the way for his statement that they have obtained *a faith as precious as ours.* There is no distinction between believers. All alike are sinners who owe their presence in the heavenly city to the amnesty of the King. *Isotimos* can mean 'of equal value'. Here it probably means 'of equal standing' (Abbott-Smith 'equally privileged'). There is a political nuance to the word: there are no second class citizens in God's kingdom. The *faith* in question appears to be, *pace* Boobyer, not the faith as a body of doctrine, which would scarcely make sense in the context, but the faith or trust which brings a man salvation as he grasps the proffered hand of God. Faith is the God-given capacity to trust him, available alike to Jew and Gentile, to apostle and twentieth-century Christian. This equality of opportunity and status is all due to *the righteousness of our God* which refuses to make distinctions between the various recipients of his mercy and love. Peter's use of *righteousness (dikaiosunē)* has none of the forensic overtones which we find in Paul. As in 1 Peter (2:24; 3:12, 14, 18; 4:18), so in this Epistle (2:5, 7–8, 21; 3:13) the word has the ethical associations which we find given to it in the Old Testament; here it means the fairness, the justice of God.

The phrase *our God and Saviour Jesus Christ* raises the question whether Peter is distinguishing God and Christ, or is in fact calling Jesus God. From the grammatical aspect, the two nouns are bound together in Greek by a single article, which strongly suggests that a single Person is meant. As Bigg points out, 'it is hardly open for anyone to translate in 1 Peter 1:3 *ho theos kai patēr* by "the God and Father", and yet here decline to translate *ho theos kai sōtēr* by "the God and Saviour".' Furthermore, in the other four cases where Peter writes of *our Lord and Saviour* (1:11; 2:20; 3:2, 18), it always clearly refers to Jesus. When Peter wishes to distinguish the two Persons (1:2) his construction is quite different: *the knowledge of God and of Jesus our Lord*. Probably, therefore, the author *is* calling Jesus God here. It is objected that nowhere in the Epistles is Jesus unambiguously called God. This may mean no more than that the New Testament writers were careful to guard against ditheism for, quite apart from some probable instances of the attribution 'God' to Jesus (Jn. 1:1; 20:28; Rom. 9:5; 2 Thes. 1:12; Tit. 2:13; Phil. 2:6; Heb. 1:8; 1 Jn. 5:20), the early Christians were utterly convinced that Jesus embodied God. To claim with Paul that 'in Christ all the fulness of the Deity lives in bodily form' (Col. 2:9) is even more emphatic than simply calling Jesus God.

The word *Saviour*[1] is used here because Peter is building his plea for Christian development and his attack on Christian licence upon the fact that his readers have found salvation. It is the conviction of the whole Bible that every believer belongs to a God who saves. Saviour is one of the great names of God in the Old Testament. Peter is in fact boldly taking the Old Testament name for Yahweh and applying it to Jesus, just as he did in his sermon on the day of Pentecost (Acts 2:21).

2. Peter's prayer for his readers is identical with that in 1 Peter 1:2. *Grace* and *peace* were Paul's constant prayer for his Christian friends (Rom. 1:7; 1 Cor. 1:3; 2 Cor. 1:2, *etc.*), based, no doubt, upon the characteristic Greek and Hebrew greetings respectively. This is no barren formula to Peter, however, for he makes both the experience of God's peace and the reception of his grace (or help) to be dependent upon the deep *knowledge of*

[1] See my *The Meaning of Salvation*, 1965, pp.195 f. 'Saviour' is found sixteen times in the New Testament applied to Jesus, five of them in 2 Peter. There is, as Bauckham shows, no difficulty in Jesus being hailed as 'God and Saviour' in the first century AD.

God and of Jesus. In so doing, he is at one with both John and Paul. John 17:3 states emphatically that eternal life consists in knowing God and Jesus Christ whom he has sent; while Paul, who had for many years enjoyed this knowledge of God in Christ, still cherished the longing to know his Master better (Phil. 3:8, 10). For Christ's gifts, such as grace and peace, cannot be enjoyed in independence of himself.

No doubt the insertion of *knowledge* here (it is not used in the greeting in 1 Peter) has a polemical thrust. It occurs three other times in 2 Peter (1:3, 8; 2:20). Elsewhere, apart from a single reference in Hebrews (10:26), it appears only in the later Epistles of Paul where it comes fifteen times. Peter was writing to people who claimed a real knowledge of God and of Christ, but continued in immoral behaviour. *Knowledge* may have been a catchphrase of theirs which Peter takes up and fills with authentic Christian content. True knowledge of God and Christ produces grace and peace in the life; what is more, it produces holiness (v. 3). The whole New Testament unites in denouncing a profession of faith which makes no difference to behaviour.

The exact significance of the compound noun, *epignōsis* (as compared with the simple *gnōsis*), is disputed. Thus J. Armitage Robinson in his commentary on Ephesians[1] thought the difference between them to be that between abstract (*gnōsis*) and particular (*epignōsis*) knowledge. J. B. Lightfoot, however, defined *epignōsis* as a 'larger and more thorough knowledge' than *gnōsis*.[2] In 2 Peter, at all events, Lightfoot's understanding is more apposite than Robinson's; for in each of the occurrences it is *epignōsis* of Jesus Christ that Peter is talking about. It is 'the decisive knowledge of God which is implied in conversion to the Christian religion' (Bultmann). A deeper knowledge of the Person of Jesus is the surest safeguard against false doctrine.

Of God and of Jesus our Lord. Many MSS read simply 'in knowledge of our Lord', possibly correctly. The shorter reading is generally preferable; it fits the singular *his* of verse 3; and elsewhere in this Epistle it is Jesus alone who is the object of *knowledge* (*epignōsis*). P [72] omits the *and*, thus indicating one

---

[1] *St. Paul's Epistle to the Ephesians*, 1903, pp.248 ff.
[2] *St. Paul's Epistles to the Colossians and Philemon*, 1879, comment on 1:9.

divine Person, Jesus and Lord. It is noteworthy that right at the outset of this letter Peter should strike the note of that knowledge of God and of Jesus Christ as Lord which is brought about in conversion, and issues in a life not of libertinism and error, but of growing conformity to the mind and life of Christ.

B. THE CHRISTIAN'S PRIVILEGES (1:3–4)

The punctuation of these verses is a puzzle. Either, we may put a comma after verse 2, in which case verses 3 and 4 explain the greeting: grace and peace are multiplied in knowing him because God has given us all we need. Or we may put a full stop after verse 2. There is then no main verb in the sentence. Unless, therefore, the *that* (4) represents an old use of the imperative 'see that you become', we should regard the sentence as an anacoluthon; Peter began his sentence but never ended it grammatically. If so, NIV is correct in simply omitting the '*that*'.

3. The apostle is making their divine call the ground for his appeal for holy living. Christ has taken the initiative in calling them to himself (*cf.* Eph. 2:8). It is not entirely certain whether Jesus or the Father is conceived of as issuing the call and offering the divine power. There is a similar ambiguity in 1 John 2:28f. But Jesus is the last person mentioned, and so the *glory and goodness* are more appropriate to him than the Father. In either case, the point is that the One who calls, enables. He does not give us all we might like, but all that we need for *life and godliness* (*cf.* 1 Thes. 4:7f.). These gifts are enshrined in Jesus Christ himself, and in getting to know him we enjoy the power to live a holy life. But what is it that attracts a man to Jesus? His own unique (*idiā*) 'glory and excellence' (RSV). Jesus Christ calls men by his moral excellence (*aretē*[1]) and the total impact of his Person

---

[1] *aretē* is a rare New Testament word. It comes three times here (verses 3 and 5), Phil. 4:8 and 1 Pet. 2:9. 'Goodness' is a pagan quality; Christianity calls a man to holiness. That is why the word is largely neglected in the New Testament. Here, however, the language is polemical, the allusion to the Old Testament is probable, and the meaning is Hebrew, not Greek – goodness in action, concrete deeds of excellence. There is much the same thought in 1 Pet. 2:9. Christians are to show forth the *aretas* of their Redeemer. In both cases the excellence in question is manifested in saving actions; it is no mere static quality.

(*doxa*[1]). Perhaps Peter is looking back to the life of Jesus which made such an impression on him that he once cried, 'Go away from me, Lord; I am a sinful man!' (Lk. 5:8), and that one of the major themes in his First Epistle was the imitation of Christ. No doubt he is thinking, too, of the glory of Jesus which shattered him at the transfiguration, to which he refers in verse 17. But it was not only the transfiguration which revealed the impact of Jesus' Person. It was his whole life. That is why John was able to say 'we have seen his glory, the glory of the one and only [Son], who came from the Father' (Jn. 1:14). It is not without significance that these two words, *aretē* and *doxa*, belong to God in the Old Testament (Is. 42:8, 12, LXX); Peter claims them for Jesus, through whom the divine excellence and glory have been supremely manifested.

The text is once again uncertain. Some MSS read 'through . . . his glory and goodness' (*dia*, 'through', would be an easy mistake for *idiā*, 'by his own'). They are wrong, for *idios* is a characteristic word of 2 Peter; it is used seven times in the Epistle. The datives are instrumental, *by* not 'to' (RSV).

4. There seem to be verbal allusions to 1 Peter in the words 'call', 'glory' and 'excellence' (*goodness*, NIV). Unusually, it does not seem to be God the Father who calls us in this instance, but Jesus himself, as in the Gospels. His person attracts men: his power enables them to respond. And, as 2 *Clement* v.5 put it later, 'the promise of Christ is great and marvellous.' He is echoing Peter's words here: *he has given us his very great and precious promises*. How has Christ done this? *Through these, i.e.* his own glory and goodness. The divine virtue and transcendent goodness manifested in Jesus both constitute and validate the call to come and *participate in the divine nature*. We are promised a share in his moral excellence during this life, and of his glory hereafter. For, taken together, the triple agency of the promises, the power and the person of the Lord Jesus regenerate a man and make him a sharer in God's own nature, so that the family likeness begins to be seen in him.

But there must be the proper response to all this. We have

---

[1]*doxa* is a favourite word of Peter's, coming ten times in 1 Peter and five in 2 Peter.

already seen the place of faith (1:1). Now he speaks of its correlative, fleeing the world. By *the world* Peter means society alienated from God by rebellion (2:20; *cf.* 1 Jn. 2:15–17; 5:19). We *participate in the divine nature* only after we have *escaped* or turned our backs on (note the decisiveness of the aorist participle) that attitude (*cf.* Jas. 1:21). On the problems associated with this phrase and *participating in the divine nature* see Introduction, pp. 25f. The ancient world was haunted by the conception of *phthora, corruption*. The transitoriness of life, the pointlessness of it all, oppressed many of the best thinkers in antiquity (as it does today). Peter tells them that there is a way of escape – through Jesus Christ.

What contrasts these verses contain! *Corruption* and *life and godliness; evil desires* and *knowledge of him who called us.* Like Paul, Peter begins with the theological indicative. They are in God's family; they have left the world; they possess precious promises; they know Christ. That is the basis for his ethical imperative, which comes so strongly in the succeeding verses. They must become in practice what they already are in God's sight.

These two verses abound in rare and daring words. Peter is very subtly using language uncommon in the New Testament but full of meaning in the pagan world, as we know from Jewish literature and the Carian inscription.[1] The false teachers laid emphasis on knowledge; so Peter stresses that the object of knowledge in the Christian life is the Lord who calls men. They thought that knowledge dispensed with the need for morality, so Peter emphasizes two words common in pagan circles for ethical endeavour, *eusebeia* (*godliness*) and *aretē* (*goodness*). They appear to have thought that holiness of living was impossible (see 2:19–20), so Peter speaks to them of the *divine power*, a Hebrew periphrasis for God. Rival pagan schoolmen asserted that you escaped from the toils of *corruption* (*phthora*) by becoming *participants in the divine nature* either by means of *nomos* ('lawkeeping') or *phusis* ('nature'). Peter takes up their language, and replies that it is by sheer grace. Did the false teachers, Gnosticwise, suggest that their adherents became more godlike as they escaped the trammels of the material world? Far from it,

---

[1] See Introduction, p. 19, and Bauckham, *op. cit.*, p. 181.

says Peter. Participation in the divine nature is the starting-point, not the goal, of Christian living. He writes to those who have *escaped* from the seductive allegiance to society at odds with God.

Peter is assuredly sailing very close to the wind in using pagan language in this polemical way; it is not surprising that his letter has been treated with great misgiving in many quarters as a result. The most daring phrase of all is, of course, *participate in the divine nature*, which has a deliberately Hellenistic ring about it, for this polemical reason.[1] But in substance it is saying much the same as John 1:12. Peter does not mean that man is absorbed into the deity; that would at the same time dissolve personal identity and render impossible any personal encounter between the individual and God. But as in 1 Peter, he speaks of a real union with Christ. If we are partakers of Christ's sufferings (1 Pet. 4:13), and partakers of the glory that shall be revealed (1 Pet. 5:1), it is because we are partakers of Christ. What Peter is saying here, though couched in this unusual form, is just the same in content as Paul's claim in Romans 8:9; Galatians 2:20; John's, in 1 John 5:1; and his own, in 1 Peter 1:23. It paves the way for Ignatius, a few years later, to say that Christians 'partake in God.' To repent, believe and be baptized into Christ is, so the whole New Testament asserts, to enter into a totally new relationship with God, in which he becomes our Father and we members of his family. It is in this sense that Peter rightly claims that believers are *already* participants in the divine nature.

It would be naïve, therefore, to suppose, as many have done, that this verse proves Peter's surrender to pagan ideas of divinization current in late Platonism and the mystery religions. In contrast to Hellenistic ideas, Peter maintains that corruption and mortality are not due to matter, but to sin. You do not escape them by cult initiation now and the immortality of the soul after death, but by God implanting a new nature, Christ's own, within you, which will produce holiness of life now, and will flower into the fullness of knowing him after this life is over. Bauckham, whose detailed Commentary is incomparably the

[1]Otherwise, Käsemann, p.182; Wand, pp.150 ff.

best in English, sees that Peter is not surrendering to Hellenism here, but wrongly regards 'the Christian eschatological goal of escaping mortality and attaining immortality' as the essence of Christ's promises, rather than the new birth of which Peter speaks in both his letters.

This verse has also been a classic proof-text for the Greek patristic and Eastern Orthodox doctrine of the deification of man. This needs to be treated with great circumspection. In its context, the verse does nothing to support such a doctrine: it is very plain from this letter that Peter, like Paul, believed in the two natures, the new and the old at work within the Christian, and we shall never be totally freed from the endemic tendency to evil until we receive a rich welcome into his everlasting kingdom (1:11). Doctrinally it is important to balance any teaching on the 'deification' of man with equally strong teaching on his continued fallenness this side of the grave.

C. THE LADDER OF FAITH (1:5–7)

5. *For this very reason*: because of our new birth and the precious promises and the divine power offered us in Christ we cannot sit back and rest content with 'faith' (*cf.* Jas. 2:20). The grace of God demands, as it enables, *effort* in man. We are to bring *into* this relationship *alongside* what God has done (such is the force of the prepositions in *pareisenenkantes*) every ounce of determination we can muster. To illustrate the way in which the Christian faith must be worked out in behaviour, Peter, like Paul before him,[1] and many after him,[2] selected a list of virtues which should be found in a healthy Christian life. The practice of making lists of virtues was already well established among the Stoics, who called it a *prokopē*, 'moral advance'. Bo Reicke, commenting on this adaptation of Stoic material, says rightly, 'he did not wish to Hellenize the church, but only employed such expressions because they would be familiar to his readers.' The

---

[1]Gal. 5:22–23; 1 Tim. 6:11; Rom. 5:3 f.
[2]Barnabas, *Ep.* ii. 2, 3; Hermas, *Vis.* iii. 8. 1–7; Clem. Rom., *Ep.* lxii.

great difference between Stoic and Christian ethics is that the latter are not the unaided product of human effort, but the fruit of our being partakers of the divine nature. Nevertheless, human effort is indispensable, even though it is inadequate. There is enough truth to hurt, in Moffatt's quotation of a cynic's description of Christian experience as 'an initial spasm followed by a chronic inertia'. If this danger is to be avoided, the Christian must always be adding to his faith.

The word *epichorēgō*, *add*, is a fascinating one. It is a vivid metaphor drawn from the Athenian drama festivals, in which a rich individual, called the *chorēgos*, since he paid the expenses of the chorus, joined with the poet and the state in putting on the plays. This could be an expensive business, and yet *chorēgi* vied with one another in the generosity of their equipment and training of the choruses. Thus the word came to mean generous and costly co-operation. The Christian must engage in this sort of co-operation with God in the production of a Christian life which is a credit to him.

Peter begins his list with *faith*. This initial acceptance of the love of God, this response to his gracious willingness to receive us, is the foundation stone on which the virtues which follow are built. Compare the primary position Paul also gives to it in Romans 5:1–5.[1]

Goodness, the first quality Peter mentions as springing from true Christian faith, is a rare word in biblical Greek, but very common in non-Christian literature. It means 'excellence', and was used to denote the proper fulfilment of anything. The excellence of a knife is to cut, of a horse to run. But what is the excellence of a man? This was a question much and inconclusively discussed in antiquity. Peter hints strongly at the answer. For he has already used this word in verse 3, when speaking of the impact of Christ's character on a man which leads him to commitment. Here he claims that the same quality of life is to be worked out in the character of the believer. The Christian must

[1]The same holds good in the subapostolic literature as well. Barnabas puts faith first, with reverence and endurance, long-suffering and self-control as its allies; while Hermas not only puts faith first, but specifically says 'through her the chosen of God are saved'. Faith is here represented as a woman, who has several daughters (*i.e.* other virtues), and the culmination of them all, as here, is love.

work out the salvation which God works in him.[1] In a word, his life must reflect something of the attractive character of Christ. For he was the man *par excellence*, the proper man. True human excellence, then, is the manliness which is Christlikeness. That likeness cannot be acquired except through personal and continuous encounter with him by faith. This is where the false teachers had gone wrong. They talked a good deal about faith, but exhibited in their lives none of that practical goodness which is indispensable to genuine Christian discipleship.

Christianity, however, is not merely a matter of personal faith and practical goodness; the intellectual element in our personalities has an important place. *Knowledge* is therefore mentioned next. (See also on v. 2). It is not certain whether *gnōsis*, the word used here, is significantly different in meaning from *epignōsis* employed there. If there is a difference, the nuance of *gnōsis* would be 'sagacity', 'practical wisdom'. This is its customary meaning in Greek ethical language. Bengel has caught its meaning when he describes it as the wisdom 'which distinguishes the good from the bad, and shows the way of flight from the bad' (*cf.* Heb. 5:14). This knowledge is gained in the practical exercise of goodness, which, in turn, leads to a fuller knowledge of Christ (v. 8; *cf.* Jn. 7:17). *Knowledge* was, of course, one of the favourite words of the false teachers, but Peter was not, on that account, afraid to use it. He was confident that the God who had revealed himself in Jesus was the God of truth. Knowledge, therefore, could never harm the Christian. Peter would have no truck with that so-called faith which shrinks from investigation lest the resultant knowledge should prove destructive. Trust has nothing to do with obscurantism. The cure for false knowledge is not less knowledge, but more.

6. Third in the list comes *self-control*, (*enkrateia*). This is to be exercised not only in food and drink, but in every aspect of life. The word is not common in the New Testament (though it comes in Paul's list of virtues in Gal. 5:23) but, like *goodness* above, it was highly prized in Greek moral philosophy. It meant controlling the passions insead of being controlled by them.

[1] Phil. 2:12.

Aristotle[1] saw through the shallowness of Socrates' dictum that no-one willingly rejects the best course once he sees it.[2] He knew full well that men do willingly and wilfully sin, and he has a lot to say about *akrasia*, being mastered by one's lusts. But he had no answer to the problem of human wickedness. That answer is to be found in the Christian way of life. For Christian self-control is submission to the control of the indwelling Christ; and by this means mature virtue (what Aristotle wistfully called 'divine virtue which is beyond man'[3]) does become a possibility for men. Once again Peter uses a word which must have cut the false teachers like a whiplash. They claimed that knowledge released them from the need for self-control (2:10ff.; 3:3). Peter emphasized that true knowledge leads on to self-control. Any system which divorces religion from ethics is fundamental heresy.

From the habit of self-control springs *perseverance*, the temper of mind which is unmoved by difficulty and distress, and which can withstand the two Satanic agencies of opposition from the world without and enticement from the flesh within. The mature Christian does not give up. His Christianity is like the steady shining of a star rather than the ephemeral brilliance (and speedy eclipse) of a meteor. There are few more reliable tests of faith than this; true faith endures (*cf.* Rom. 5:1–3; Mk. 13:13).

This patience is no stoic quality of accepting all that comes as from the dictates of blind fate. It springs from faith in the promises of God, knowledge of Christ, experience of his divine power (vv. 3–4). And so it produces in the Christian a deepened awareness of a Father's wise and loving hand controlling all that happens. Like Jesus himself, who for the joy set before him endured the cross (Heb. 12:2), we are enabled to see our apparent misfortunes in the calm light of eternity. Mayor points to an interesting passage in Aristotle where self-control and endurance are contrasted. 'Self-control', says Aristotle, 'is concerned with pleasures . . . and endurance with sorrows; for the man who can endure and put up with hardships, he is the real example of endurance.'[4]

[1]*Nic. Eth*. vii. 3.   [2]Plato, *Protag*. 352 C.   [3]*Nic. Eth*. vii. 3.
[4]*Magn. Moral*. ii. 6. 34.

To this steadfastness of character *godliness*, or rather 'reverence', must be added. The word *eusebeia* is rare in the New Testament, probably because it was the primary word for 'religion' in popular pagan usage. The 'religious man' of antiquity, both in Greek and Latin usage (where the equivalent word was *pietas*), was careful and correct in performing his duties both to gods and men. Perhaps Peter uses it here in deliberate contrast to the false teachers, who were far from proper in their behaviour both to God and their fellow men. Peter is at pains to emphasize that true knowledge of God (which they mistakenly boasted they possessed) manifests itself in reverence towards him and respect towards men. There is no hint of religiosity here. *Eusebeia* is a very practical awareness of God in every aspect of life. (See also on verse 3.[1])

7. But *godliness* cannot exist without *brotherly kindness*. 'If any one says, "I love God," yet hates his brother, he is a liar' (1 Jn. 4:20). Love for Christian brethren is a distinguishing mark of true discipleship, and represents yet another area where the false teachers were so distressingly deficient. Those who have become partakers of the divine nature, or, as he puts it in 1 Peter, those who have been born again (1:23), must show their royal birth in royalty of behaviour towards other children of the King, whatever their differences in culture, class and churchmanship. But this gift has to be worked at. Love for the brethren entails bearing one another's burdens, and so fulfilling the law of Christ; it means guarding that Spirit-given unity from destruction by gossip, prejudice, narrowness, and the refusal to accept a brother Christian for what he is in Christ. The very importance and the difficulty of achieving this *philadelphia* is the reason for the considerable stress on it in the pages of the New Testament (Rom. 12:10; 1 Thes. 4:9; Heb. 13:1; 1 Pet. 1:22; 1 Jn. 5:1).

---

[1]Barclay appropriately cites Xenophon's (highly imaginative!) description of Socrates at this juncture, to illustrate the noblest conception of *eusebeia* to be found in the pagan world. 'He was so pious and devoutly religious that he would take no step apart from the will of heaven; so just and upright that he never did even a trifling injury to any living soul; so self-controlled, so temperate, that he never at any time chose the sweeter instead of the better; so sensible, so wise, and so prudent that in distinguishing the better from the worse

The crown of Christian 'advance' (to return to the martial metaphor of the stoic *prokopē* on which this list of qualities seems to be modelled) is *love*. 'The greatest of these is love' (1 Cor. 13:13). This word *agapē* is one which Christians to all intents and purposes coined, to denote the attitude which God has shown himself to have to us, and requires from us towards himself. In friendship (*philia*) the partners seek mutual solace; in sexual love (*erōs*) mutual satisfaction. In both cases these feelings are aroused because of what the loved one is. With *agapē* it is the reverse. God's *agapē* is evoked not by what we are, but by what he is. It has its origin in the agent, not in the object. It is not that we are lovable, but that he is love. This *agapē* might be defined as a deliberate desire for the highest good of the one loved, which shows itself in sacrificial action for that person's good. That is what God did for us (Jn. 3:16). That is what he wants us to do (1 Jn. 3:16). That is what he is prepared to achieve in us (Rom. 5:5). Thus the Spirit of the God who is love is freely given to us, in order to reproduce in us that same quality. For men will never believe that God is love unless they see it in the lives of his professed followers.

Such is the fruit of the tree of faith. To be a partaker of the divine nature, so far from granting a dispensation from the claims of ethics, both confirms them and makes possible their achievement. 'Each step', said Bengel, 'gives birth to and facilitates the next. Each subsequent quality balances and brings to perfection the one preceding.'

Far from being a mere repetition of pagan ideals, Peter's list is qualitatively different. For it begins with faith and ends in love, and these are the indispensable root and fruit of Christian ethical behaviour. It may share a good deal in the goals and aspirations of secular moralists (God has not left himself without witness even in the hearts of those who do not know him) but it will transform them by trust in the Jesus who has called us by his own glory and goodness, and will embody them in that selfless *agapē* love which flows only from those who have come to participate in his divine nature.

---

he never erred' (*Memorabilia* i. 5. 8–11). It is something of this type of character which Peter means to delineate by the comprehensive word, *eusebeia*.

D. BARREN AND FRUITFUL CHRISTIANS (1:8–9)

8. The true knowledge of Christ, as opposed to the false, does produce these moral and spiritual qualities in the believer. They are implicit, already, within the new nature imparted to him (*cf.* Eph. 1:4). If already *you possess these qualities* (*huparchonta*), you must allow them to manifest themselves *in increasing measure* (*pleonazonta*). There is no excuse for resting content with present attainment. Lack of spiritual growth is a sign of spiritual death. Nor is there any room for indolence and the slackening of effort (*argous*); otherwise the Christian becomes *unproductive*, like the wheat choked by weeds (the cares, riches and pleasures of life) which produces no fruit (*akarpous*).[1]

The *knowledge* (*epignōsis*) of Jesus Christ is a significant phrase, and is perhaps directed against the false teachers boasting of their knowledge already complete. Peter reminds his readers that the full knowledge of Christ belongs to the future, when we shall see him face to face. He makes the same point, though not in an argumentative context like this, in 1 Peter 1:8. Meanwhile he sees the knowledge of Christ as spanning the whole arch of Christian experience. It begins with the knowledge of him who calls us (1:3); it continues in the knowledge of God and of Jesus (1:2); and it will end in the full knowledge of him who has made possible (and actual) the ladder of virtues in the lives of the redeemed. Paul, too, saw that the knowledge, not *about* but *of* Jesus Christ, was both the root and the goal of Christian experience (Phil. 3:10).

9. But the man who does not manifest these qualities is *blind*. *Tuphlos* is often used in Greek in this metaphorical sense, and the New Testament offers numerous examples. Such a man lacks insight (*cf.* Jn. 9:39–41). He fails to realize there is a war on, the war with evil (Rev. 3:14ff.). He remains still largely under the effective control of 'the god of this world' whose choice stratagem is to blind the mind (2 Cor. 4:4). The NIV, unjustifiably, reverses the order of adjectives here, by the rendering

---

[1] *Cf.* Mt. 13:22. The phrase *ouk argos oude akarpos*, 'neither slack nor fruitless', is quoted in the *Letter from the Gallic Churches* (AD 177) as recorded in Eusebius, *H.E.* v. 1. 45.

nearsighted and blind. Peter wrote *blind and nearsighted.* Why this strange order? The rare word *muōpazō* (only here in the New Testament) usually means 'short-sighted'. If a man is blind, how can he be short-sighted? If Peter had this meaning in mind, he may mean that such a man is blind to heavenly things, and engrossed in the earthly; he cannot see what is afar off, but only what is near. This makes excellent sense in view of the immorality and earthinesss of the false teachers. But probably Peter was thinking of the other meaning of *muōpazō,* namely 'to blink', 'to shut the eyes'. If so, the participle is causal. Thus the meaning is that such a man is blind because he blinks or wilfully closes his eyes to the light. Spiritual blindness descends upon the eyes which deliberately look away from the graces of character to which the Christian is called when he comes to know Christ. The whole phrase is a trochaic tetrameter; possibly Peter culled it from some poem or ditty current at the time, as Paul sometimes did (Tit. 1:12). This may account for the rather curious form of expression.

The next phrase *has forgotten* supports this interpretation of *muōpazōn. Lēthēn labōn* can only mean that the man has deliberately forgotten, put out of his mind, the fact that he has been *cleansed from his past sins.* Peter may have in mind here the public confession and vows taken by converts at their baptism (*cf.* Acts 2:38; 22:16). Their *past sins* would then be those committed before they became Christians, the cleansing of which would be an essential corollary of being made a partaker of the divine nature. The man who makes no effort (v. 5) to grow in grace is going back on his baptismal contract. This could be the start of apostasy.

E. A WORTHY GOAL (1:10–11)

10. *Therefore, my brothers,* may refer to what immediately precedes. The meaning would then be 'since there is a danger of the coming on of spiritual blindness, be still more on your guard' (Mayor). More probably, however, it refers to the whole of the preceding paragraph (vv. 3–9). Because of God's wonderful gifts, because the use of those gifts leads to an increased knowledge of Christ, therefore they must the rather exert themselves. Peter repeats the call for zeal he had uttered in verse 5, and the aorist imperative, *spoudasate*, stresses the urgency of his plea that they should determine to live for God. He enforces his appeal by calling them *my brothers*, as often in his speeches in Acts.[1]

Make your calling and election sure is an appeal that goes to the heart of the paradox of election and free will. The New Testament characteristically makes room for both without attempting to resolve the apparent antinomy. So here; election comes from God alone – but man's behaviour is the proof or disproof of it. Though 'good works' (gratuitously read here by some MSS) are possible only through the appropriation of God's gracious aid, they are absolutely necessary, and fairly and squarely our responsibility. Hence the use of the middle voice, *poieisthai*, 'make sure for yourself'. Christian calling and Christian living go together. It seems that the false teachers boasted of their divine calling and election, while making that an 'excuse for every kind of licence, as though they had permission to sin with impunity because they are predestined to righteousness' (Calvin).

Chronologically speaking, of course, *election* precedes *calling* (*cf.* Rom. 8:30). There is nothing arbitrary or unfair about it. Christ is the Elect One. Election is in Christ. Outside him is ruin. God calls men to commit themselves to Jesus Christ, and, once they have done so, that call must be implemented by holy living. Whether or not it is possible for one so chosen and called to apostasize, Peter does not consider here (see, however, on 2:1, 19–22). At all events it is true enough, as Strachan put it, that 'not all who hear the Divine voice (*klēsis*) progress in Christian conduct, which is the token of election (*eklogē*)'.

If you confirm your calling with a life agreeable to it, Peter concludes, two results will follow. In the first place, *you will never fall*. Of course, in many ways we all stumble (Jas. 3:2). But what Peter means is that the Christian will be spared a disastrous coming to grief (NEB; *cf.* Rom. 11:11). The metaphor is

---

[1] *Cf.* 1 Pet. 2:11 and 2 Pet. 3:1, 8, 14, 17 where, at a critical point in his challenge, he addresses his readers as 'dear friends'.

drawn from the surefootedness of a horse. A life of steady progress should characterize the Christian. His radiant life should be the silent proof of God's election.

11. Furthermore, you will reach your heavenly destination, *and you will receive a rich welcome into the eternal kingdom* . . . . The second result of loving obedience is put before us as the goal of a long journey. Words are piled upon one another to excite the weary pilgrim's heart at the splendour of that destination. *Epichorēgēthēsetai* is used again in verse 5 (q.v.). If we generously put ourselves out in obedience to God and give him what we have, he will generously put himself out for us, so to speak, and lavishly equip us for life in the everlasting kingdom. *Richly* (*plousiōs*) is thrown in to underline the point. And the metaphor of entry into the kingdom may well go back to one of the honours paid to a victor in the Olympic Games. His home city, in her joy and pride in his success, would welcome him back not through the usual gate, but through a part of the wall specially broken down to afford him entrance. *Eternal Kingdom* (*aiōnion basileian*) is a phrase which, curiously enough, hardly recurs in the New Testament or Apostolic Fathers,[1] despite the frequency of both 'kingdom' and 'eternal'. A close parallel is afforded by the 'eternal dominion' (*aiōnios archē*) of the Stratonicean inscription[2] and the phrase here may well be an implicit rejection of the claims to 'eternal rule' made by imperial Rome.[3]

Despite the amount of emphasis Peter has been laying on the need for growth, perseverance and effort in the Christian life, the concluding verses of this section (vv. 10–11) make it abundantly plain that 'final salvation is not man's achievement but the gift of God's lavish generosity' (Bauckham).

Peter has three things to say about this kingdom. First, it is eternal. That is to say, it belongs to what Jewish thought had named the 'Age to Come'. Particularly during times of difficulty and persecution in the last few centuries BC, men of faith had increasingly become disillusioned with 'this Age', and longed for the time when God would break in and vindicate himself

---

[1] With the sole exceptions of *The Apocalypse of Peter* and Aristides' *Apology* (AD 129) which cite this verse, and thus become very early witnesses to the antiquity of this Epistle.
[2] See Introduction, pp.19, 25.   [3] *urbs aeterna, etc.*

and his people in the coming age. The New Testament conviction is consistently this; that in the Person of Jesus Christ the
'Age to Come' has invaded 'this Age'. The last things have been
inaugurated, though, of course, they await completion. It is of
this consummation in the eternal[1] kingdom that Peter speaks.

Secondly, in striking contrast to Hellenistic ideas of divinization, our entry into this kingdom is still seen as future. Like
Abraham, the Christian traveller is called in faith and obedience
to rest content with nothing ephemeral, but to press on towards
that city which has foundations, whose builder and maker is
God (Heb. 11:10). By saying that we are already partakers of the
divine nature (v. 4), and that we have nevertheless still to enter
the everlasting kingdom, Peter retains in his own characteristic
way the New Testament tension between what we have and
what we still lack, between realized and future eschatology.

Thirdly, this kingdom is characterized as belonging to *our Lord
and Saviour Jesus Christ*.[2] This is the qualitative definition of the
kingdom. It is his kingdom (Mt. 16:28; Jn. 18:36; Ps. 2:6). It is
entered by relationship to him.[3] The noblest description of
heaven is in personal categories like this. It will embody utterly
harmonious relationships between the Saviour and the saved. It
seems probable that once again Peter has the scoffers in mind
(*cf.* 3:3) as he makes these three points about the heavenly
kingdom.

Thus the apostle concludes his first paragraph, a stirring
appeal to his wavering followers not to allow intellectual
appreciation of Christianity to become a substitute for moral
application. Is his 'activist' emphasis on heaven for the obedient
in verses 10–11 a contradiction of his 'receptionist' teaching on
the divine nature in verse 4? No. Heaven is not a reward *pro
meritis* but *de congruo*. It accords with the nature of a good and

---

[1] *aiōnios* is quite widely applied in the New Testament. We read of eternal fire (Mt. 18:8),
life and punishment (Mt. 25:46), glory (2 Cor. 4:17), home (2 Cor. 5:1), destruction (2 Thes.
1:9), consolation (2 Thes. 2:16), power and glory (1 Tim. 6:16), salvation (Heb. 5:9), judgment (Heb. 6:2), redemption (Heb. 9:12), the Holy Spirit (Heb. 9:14), inheritance (Heb.
9:15), covenant (Heb. 13:20), glory (1 Pet. 5:10), and gospel (Rev. 14:6).
[2] 'The exact correspondence of words here, "our Lord and Saviour Jesus Christ" with
those in verse 1, "God and our Saviour Jesus Christ" is a strong argument in favour of the
translation "our God and Saviour Jesus Christ" in that verse' (Caffin).
[3] *Cf.* Mk. 10:21 'come follow me' and 10:24 'enter the kingdom' and 10:26 'be saved' or
10:17 'inherit eternal life'.

generous God towards those who trust and obey him. This passage agrees with several[1] in the Gospels and Epistles in suggesting that while heaven is entirely a gift of grace, it admits of degrees of felicity, and that these are dependent upon how faithfully we have built a structure of character and service upon the foundation of Christ.[2] Bengel likens the unholy Christian in the judgment to a sailor who just manages to make shore after shipwreck, or to a man who barely escapes with his life from a burning house, while all his possessions are lost. In contrast, the Christian who has allowed his Lord to influence his conduct will have abundant entrance into the heavenly city, and be welcomed like a triumphant athlete victorious in the Games. This whole paragraph of exhortation is thus set between two poles: what we already are in Christ and what we are to become. The truly Christian reader, unlike the scoffers, will look back to the privileges conferred on him, of partaking in the divine nature, and will seek to live worthily of it. He will also look forward to the day of assessment, and strive to live in the light of it.

F. TRUTH WILL BEAR REPETITION (1:12–15)

12. It is the importance of this issue, nothing less than their eternal destiny, which leads Peter to write like this to his readers. They knew it all, of course; the twin themes of faith and works, grace and effort, were not new to them or to any of the early Christians. But they needed to be reminded *of these things*, particularly in their present situation when the grace of God was being used as a cloak for licence (2:19; *cf.* Rom. 6:1) and the knowledge of God as a substitute for obedience (*cf.* 1 Jn. 2:4). Such is the (sometimes wilful) forgetfulness of the human heart that one of the prime functions of a Christian minister must be to keep the basic facts of Christian truth and conduct always before the minds of his congregation. Reminders have this additional value. They are intended to stir up the recipients into action for themselves. Thus Peter's determination to remind them is balanced by his hope that they

[1] *E.g.* Lk. 15:11–32; 12:47 f.   [2] 1 Cor. 3:10–15.

will be able to remind others of them (see v. 15).

In this verse Peter speaks of his intention to continue this work of reminding, whether we read *ouk amelēsō, I will not be negligent* (AV) or, with RSV, *mellēsō*, 'I intend', which is more probable, but very difficult. Even in koinē Greek the future tense of *mellō* followed by the present infinitive is strange. It could mean 'I am always going to be reminding you' (which would exclude a reference to the present Letter as the reminder) or 'I will take care to' (which could embrace the present Letter, but is much more awkward Greek). Bauckham has to decide for the latter option because he believes that, after the model of the *Testaments of the Twelve Patriarchs*, 2 Peter is written by a disciple of the apostle after his death, to act as a farewell sermon and testament. See, however, on verse 15. Bauckham's case is precarious. Had he been right we would have expected not two future reminders (vv. 12, 15) but two present tenses, alluding to 2 Peter itself. Moreover his comparison of 2 Peter with *The Testaments* is unconvincing, and 1:12–15 seems to refer not to this Letter alone, but to some additional reminder. See on 1:15 and the Introduction.

It is at first sight somewhat surprising that Peter should address his readers as *established in the truth you now have*. From what he has already said, and what he is yet to say about them, it is very evident that their lives left a lot to be desired – and yet they were established Christians. Surely this is a solemn warning that it is all too easy for those who have been Christians for some time to lapse into serious sin or doctrinal error. There is no safeguard against this except living in direct touch with the Lord and Saviour.

There is an illuminating parallel to Peter's concern for the stability of his readers in the face of heresy: the *Epistula Apostolorum* was written 'that you may be established and not waver, not be shaken nor turn away from the word of the gospel that you have heard'.

It is interesting that Peter, like Jude, can see the Christian tradition given through the apostles (1:16f.) as a unity and as the truth (*cf.* Jude 4), in contrast to the divisive tendencies, unhistorical myths, and unworthy behaviour of the false teachers. And there may be something poignant in his use of the word *established* to describe his hesitant and wavering readers. For that is the word which Jesus used of him on one memorable occasion when, although so fickle, he was sure that *he* was established in the truth and could not possibly apostasize (see Lk. 22:32). It seems to have become a favourite word of this turbulent man who now really was established. He uses it in his final prayer at the end of 1 Peter (5:10), and a similar word occurs in a significant context in 2 Peter 3:17.

13. Peter[1] can hardly overemphasize the importance of reminders. Here he has just reminded his readers of the call of God, the need for growth in grace, and the heavenly home which awaits them. In 1 Peter 2:11 he reminds them of their Christian warfare, a theme to which he returns in 2 Peter 3:1ff. It would seem that he could never forget his Lord's commission, 'When you have turned back, strengthen your brothers' (Lk. 22:32). He determines to continue with it to the end of his days.

He is well aware that this may not be very long. If this letter was written in the early sixties of the first century, when under Nero Christians were becoming increasingly unpopular in Rome, it would not be necessary for an eminent Christian leader to have prophetic insight in order to anticipate a sudden and violent death. *As long as I live in the tent of this body. Skēnōma*, literally 'tent', was a common Greek word for the body. Like all the early Christians, Peter was very conscious of the transitoriness of life. The men of faith, in God's Israel, had always been tent-dwellers (Heb. 11:9).[2] Like Paul (2 Cor. 5:1), Peter uses the metaphor of striking tent for death. It has often been thought that this sort of language betrays infection by Greek dualism, with its perishable body and immortal soul. But both writers are much more likely to have been influenced by the pilgrim theme which is so prominent in the Old Testament, to which Epictetus's words might well be applied, 'While he alloweth thee to enjoy it (*i.e.* thy property), use it as a thing that does not belong to thee, as a traveller uses a hostel.'[3]

---

[1]Like Paul (Phil. 3:1; 2 Tim. 2:14; Tit. 3:1).

[2]Indeed, according to Stephen's speech, the rot set in when 'Solomon built the house' (Acts 7:47).

[3]Cited by Selwyn, *The First Epistle of St. Peter*, 1946, p.169.

14. Peter writes this reminder to them, conscious not only of the intrinsic transitoriness of life, but also of the occasion recorded in John 21:18–19 where Jesus foretold a drastic ending to his life by crucifixion. This allusion makes it very probable that we should translate *tachinē* by 'suddenly' rather than *soon* (the former meaning fits 2:1 better, as well). Bauckham rejects this translation as illegitimate, but neither Hermas (who uses *tachinos* several times in this sense) nor the Arndt-Gingrich Greek Lexicon support his view. However, the rendering *soon* is just possible, and would equally fit the prophecy that he would suffer a violent death when he grew old. As he would be over sixty when he wrote this, he would anticipate its fulfilment soon.

It is interesting that the roots of both *skēnōma* (*tent*) and *exodos* (*departure* v. 15) should occur in the Lucan account of the transfiguration, to which Peter goes on to refer. If 2 Peter is a pseudepigraph, its author must have been sophisticated in the extreme to produce so delicate a touch.

We have much to learn (in our generation, when death has replaced sex as the forbidden subject) from Peter's attitude to death. He had for years been living with death; he knew that his lot would be to die in a horrible and painful way. And yet he can speak of it in this wonderful way, apparently without fear or regret. It means entry into the everlasting kingdom. It means the exit from this world (v. 15) to some other place prepared for us by God. It means the laying aside of the tent we have been inhabiting. 'There is no reason why we should take its removal so badly. There is an implied contrast between the failing tabernacle and the eternal dwelling place, which Paul explains in 2 Cor. 5:1' (Calvin).

15. It is in view of Jesus' words that Peter is so anxious to carry out his work of establishing Christians by means of continual reminders. And so he says that he *will make every effort* (the future, *spoudasō* is better attested than the present, *spoudazō*) to ensure that after his death they will have, any time they care to turn to it, a permanent written reminder of his teaching. What is he referring to? Clearly not to this Epistle (*pace* Bauckham and Kelly). But his words fit Mark's Gospel admirably.

Here is a work which from the earliest times was closely associated with Peter. Papias, early in the second century, wrote: 'This
also the presbyter used to say – Mark, having been Peter's
translator, wrote accurately, not however in order, as much as
he remembered of the things said or done by the Lord . . . . For
he was concerned for one thing only, not to omit any of the
things he had heard, or to falsify anything in them.'[1] This, then,
was good tradition early in the second century: it was traditional
before Papias, who was himself born about AD 70. And it is
backed up by all the second-century writers who refer to Mark,
notably Clement[2] and Irenaeus.[3] The latter is particularly
interesting. He says, 'After their (*i.e.* Peter and Paul's) death
(*exodon*) Mark, the disciple and interpreter of Peter, himself
handed down to us in writing the substance of Peter's preaching.'[4] It is significant that Irenaeus uses the same word for death
as Peter does here. *Exodos* is a rather rare word for death, used
by itself (though common enough in conjunction with *biou*). It
was so used by Luke of Christ's death foreshadowed at the
transfiguration (Lk. 9:31). It is used here in the same context.
And it is used in this passage of Irenaeus. It seems probable that
Irenaeus knew this passage in 2 Peter, and took the implicit
promise to refer to Mark's Gospel.

In recent years a fascinating discovery from Cave 7 at Qumran
has emerged which may support Irenaeus' assumption that
2 Peter 1:15 refers to the Gospel of Mark. A fragment from that
Cave, 7Q5, is perhaps part of the Gospel of Mark embodying
verses 52–53 of Mark 6.[5] Another fragment from the same Cave,
7Q10, may be a part of 2 Peter 1:15. The identification,
advocated by José O'Callaghan, is far from certain as only six
letters are extant. However what seems certain is that if this tiny
fragment comes from the Greek Bible at all, there is no passage
other than 2 Peter 1:15 from which it could come. See further the
Introduction.[6] Qumran was fascinated by extraneous religious

---

[1]Recorded in Eusebius, *H.E.* iii. 39. 15, v. 8. 3.
[2]Recorded in Eusebius, *H.E.* vi. 14. 5–7.
[3]*A.H.* iii. 10. 6.   [4]*A.H.* iii. 1. 1; *cf.* Eusebius, *H.E.* v. 8.
[5]See however C. J. Hemer in *ZNTW*, 1974, pp.155–157 who is unconvinced by the
identification.   [6]P.16.

works, and it is perhaps not impossible that 2 Peter was sent as a covering letter for the Gospel of Mark to this community by the Dead Sea shortly before the cave was closed in AD 68.

Needless to say, if the identification of these two fragments at Qumran can be established, the implications for the date of Mark's Gospel, and the authenticity and date of 2 Peter would be decisive. At present it remains no more than a fascinating possibility.

However that may be, and despite the patristic conviction that this verse alludes to Mark's Gospel, the reference in this verse is sufficiently vague to have picqued the curiosity and encouraged the inventiveness of later writers. Bigg conjectures with great probability that 'the composition of the later pseudonymous literature was suggested by these words. If so, the fact goes to prove that 2 Peter was well known and regarded as authentic in very early times. It seems hardly likely that such extensive liberties would have been taken with the name of Peter unless there were a phrase, in a writing generally recognized as his, which gave plausibility to the forgery'.

G. THE TRUTH IS ATTESTED BY APOSTOLIC EYEWITNESSES (1:16–18)

16. Here Peter is clearly defending himself against some accusation of the false teachers. But what? All hangs on the word *muthois*. It could mean *stories* and this word accompanied by the same verb 'to follow' occurs in Josephus in this sense.[1] It could also mean 'allegories' (Bigg thinks the false teachers regarded the Gospel miracles in this sense rather than sober fact), or 'fictitious prophecies' (Mayor), or 'old wives' tales' as in the Pastorals (Tit. 1:14; 2 Tim. 4:4). When the whole phrase, including *sesophismenois* (*cleverly invented*), is taken into consideration the meaning 'fables' seems the most probable. Peter is arguing that when he talks (as he has done in the preceding verses) of the present power of the risen Lord to equip the Christian for holy living, and of the glorious future which awaits the faithful Christian, he is not guilty either of embellishment or of specul-

---

[1] Josephus, *Antiq.*, *proem.* 3.

ation. They are respectively the present and the future manifestations of the historical Jesus, to whose reality he could bear
personal testimony.

It is impossible to decide from this reference the precise
character of the false teachers. They were not Gnostics in anything like a developed sense, however, or they would never
have attacked 'myths'; they had too many themselves! It seems
that, like Hymenaeus and Philetus,[1] they explained away the
future element in salvation in terms of the past.[2] Thus they
could very well have said that the resurrection is past already,
when the believer died and rose with Christ at his baptism (Col.
2:12; Rom. 6:3–5), and that the future coming of Christ was
realized in the coming of the Spirit. This seems the most natural
way of taking the words, accords well with what is said of the
false teachers in chapter 3, and explains Peter's use of the
transfiguration incident to refute them. Men who explained
away the resurrection and scoffed at the parousia could best be
refuted by reference to the incarnate life of Jesus.[3]

The Synoptic Gospels all see the transfiguration as a foretaste
not so much of the resurrection as of the parousia of Jesus.[4] In
all three Gospels it follows immediately on the promise of Jesus
that some of his hearers would not taste death until the kingdom came with power. Whatever the meaning of this myster-
ious promise, it is clear that there was a strong link in the minds
of the evangelists between the transfiguration and the parousia.
In subapostolic days the transfiguration seems to have attracted
very little comment. At all events, references to it are rare.[5] But
one of them is in the *Apocalypse of Peter*, an early second-century
work which is acquainted with our Epistle.[6] There the trans-
figured bodies which appeared to the praying disciples are
presented as the foretaste of 'your righteous brethren whose
form ye did desire to see'.[7] It is clear that the unknown author of
the *Apocalypse* understood 2 Peter in this sense, and in fact

[1] 2 Tim. 2:17–18. [2] See further, Introduction, pp.43 ff.
[3] See further, Introduction, p.21 f.
[4] See G. H. Boobyer, *St. Mark and the Transfiguration Story*, 1940.
[5] See A. M. Ramsey, *The Glory of God and the Transfiguration of Christ*, 1949, chapter 13.
[6] See Introduction, pp.14.
[7] See Hennecke, *New Testament Apocrypha*, vol. II. pp.680 f.

quotes him, as we shall see on verse 18.

The power and coming may be taken as above, but there are several other possibilities. The phrase may be a hendiadys, 'the mighty coming', as in Matthew 24:30 ('coming . . . with power and great glory'). It could possibly be a reference to Jesus' claim to power in Matthew 28:18 and his demonstration of it in the miracles: Peter had been an eyewitness of both. It might refer to the power and glory given Jesus at his ascension, of which the transfiguration might be thought a foretaste. It is perverse, with Chase, to make *parousia* mean the first coming of Christ. It refers, as in 3:4, 12 and normally in the New Testament, to his future coming, his regal advent. The papyri show that the word was often used of the official state visit of a king.

Peter emphasizes the first-hand nature of the apostolic teaching his readers had received. 'We' – the apostolic 'we' – *were eyewitnesses*, he says. The word used for this, *epoptēs*, is an unusual[1] and interesting one. It was commonly used to denote one initiated into the Mystery Religions. Peter's point in using this word here is probably polemical. He may be suggesting that the false teachers were outside the circle of the initiates to which the author and his readers belong. In so doing Peter effectively reverses their exclusive boasts to superiority over ordinary Christians on the grounds of being initiated into the higher *gnōsis* to which their humbler brethren could never aspire. But he may simply be asserting his eyewitness status, and this is the most common meaning of epoptēs. There is frequently a stress on apostolic eyewitnesses whenever the historic Christian faith is being defended against false teaching (*e.g.* 1 Cor. 15:3–8; 1 Jn. 1:1–3; 4:14).

Megaleiotēs, majesty, is a very rare New Testament word: in both its other occurrences it means the majesty of the Divine.[2] So here it expresses the divine majesty as revealed in the transfiguration of Jesus.

17. The Greek construction breaks down at the end of verse 17 and the subject changes. This complicates the understanding

[1] It occurs only here in the New Testament. But the corresponding verb, *epopteuō*, is to be found only in 1 Pet. 2:12; 3:2. Is this yet another indirect indication of common authorship?
[2] Lk. 9:43; Acts 19:27.

of verse 19a. From the *power* and *coming* of Jesus at the transfiguration Peter turns to the *honour* and *glory* displayed there: 'honour in the voice which spoke to him; glory in the light which shone from him' (Alford). There may possibly be an allusion to Daniel 7:14, one of the most important Old Testament texts for the understanding of Jesus as the glorious Son of man, and one which had enormous influence in the early church. We should read 'by' *the Majestic Glory*, not *from*. This rare phrase, a typically Hebraic periphrasis for God, comparable with the 'divine power' and 'divine nature' of 1:3–4, is found in Clement of Rome,[1] who may have drawn it from our Epistle, though *megaloprepēs* is a word he is fond of. The 'bright cloud' which overshadowed Jesus at the transfiguration is another way of expressing the same reality – none other than God himself (*cf.* Ex. 16:10; Nu. 14:10; Ezk. 1:4).

Notice how Jesus is said to *receive* honour and glory from God the Father. What a contrast to the supposed Hellenistic *theios anēr* (divine man). It shows how far off the mark Ernst Käsemann was in supposing that 2 Peter saw the transfiguration as an epiphany of Jesus' hidden divinity. In line with primitive Christian understanding, Jesus is given divine glory because he is appointed to the task of carrying out God's salvation and judgment.

It is instructive to compare Peter's account of the *voice* with the Synoptic record in the Gospels, which it may well antedate if Peter is indeed the author. If he is not, it is hard to see why a later author did not quote direct from one of the Gospels rather than insert the independent touches we find here. If a psuedepigrapher was at work with the Synoptics before him, why does he not tell us something about the behaviour of the disciples on the mount? Why does he make no mention of Moses and Elijah? Most surprising of all, why does he omit the significant 'listen to him', common to all three accounts, which would have fitted the context here so well? The voice from heaven, too, occurs in a different form from any of the Synoptics (though the word order here is uncertain[2]). Peter gives the unique construction, *eis hon*

---

[1] *ix. 2.*
[2] Thus B and P 72 read 'My son, my beloved is this', P 'This is my son, the beloved, this is', and the majority of MSS 'This is my son the beloved' (under the influence of the Matthaean version).

eudokēsa;[1] *with him I am well pleased*, which is, of course, a rough translation of Isaiah 42:1. It suggests the good pleasure of the Father alighting and remaining on Jesus. Again, Peter's version 'my Son, my Beloved' (NEB) is remarkable and independent. It means that whereas in other versions *beloved* qualifies *Son*, the repetition of the preposition in 2 Peter shows 'my Beloved' must constitute a second title. It may derive either from Genesis 22:2, 12, 16 and mean that, like Isaac, Jesus is God's only son. Or it may spring from Isaiah 42:1 (like the 'with him I am well pleased') and mean to identify Jesus with God's suffering and vindicated Servant. Now 'the Beloved' was a very early Messianic title, not just an epithet to describe 'Son' (itself a Messianic title in Judaism, because of Psalm 2:7, as 4Q Flor. 1.18–21 makes certain). J. Armitage Robinson has shown this in an important note,[2] in the course of which he argued that the right reading in Mark 9:7 should be not 'the beloved' with most MSS, but 'my Beloved' with the Old Syriac. This he regarded as a very primitive touch. If so, it is equally primitive in 2 Peter, where the 'my' is actually in the best Greek text, and does not hang on a later Syriac translation.

18. Two features which bear on the question of authorship are to be found in this verse. In the first place, the writer stresses that he was *with* Jesus when the voice from heaven came. It is widely held that this claim denotes the imitator at work. The author tries too hard to identify himself with Peter. Some of the difficulties in such a view are mentioned in the comment on verse 17 and in the Introduction.[3] Furthermore, although some forms of pseudepigraphy were common in the ancient world, where copyright did not exist, Dr Guthrie has argued convincingly that the writing of *letters* in someone else's name was not

[1]The nearest parallel is Mt. 12:18, where the best text reads simply *hon eudokēsen hē psuchē mou*. Matthew alone among the Synoptists gives 'in whom I am well pleased' at the transfiguration, but reads *en hō eudokēsa*.

[2]*St Paul's Epistle to the Ephesians*, 1903, pp. 229–233, 'The Beloved as a Messianic Title'. See also Bauckham's most careful note on this verse, and his conclusion that '2 Peter's phrase *ho agapētos mou*, my Beloved, has a good claim to be closer to the Semitic basis than the Synoptic versions, and must be regarded as at least as original as they are.' He shows conclusively that 'in his account of the Transfiguration the author of 2 Peter was not dependent on the Synoptic Gospels'.

[3]See pp.31 ff.

an accepted practice,[1] certainly not in the name of a recently deceased person. Further, the assumption that every phrase which alludes to some incident in the life of Peter betrays the work of an imitator is a very unfair method of criticism, and merits Bigg's sarcastic comment, 'If a writer declared his identity in the address only of an epistle, as in 1 Peter, the address is treated as a forged addition. If he hints in an unmistakeable way who he is, as in the case of the Gospel of John, his words are regarded as so suspicious, even indecent, that he must be a forger. But if he does both, as in the case of 2 Peter, the case against him is treated as irrefutable.'[2]

Secondly, *the sacred mountain* is thought to presuppose a time when the transfiguration had been 'taken up and sanctified in the religious consciousness of the church' (Strachan). But this is to import into the text a quite unbiblical understanding of *sacred*, or holy. In the Bible it means 'belonging to God', and the mount is holy just as the prophets (1:21) and apostles (3:2) are holy, because it was visited by God. How could Peter help thinking of that mount as holy when it was there that the divine glory of Jesus was disclosed to him? This is why the mount where Moses met God was called holy (Ex. 3:5), and the epithet was applied to the other Old Testament locations where God revealed himself, supremely to Mount Zion.[3] Interestingly enough, the mountain never was 'taken up into the religious consciousness of the church'! There was, in later times, not even unanimity about which mountain it was, Tabor or Hermon. The *Apocalypse of Peter* quotes this phrase,[4] as Jesus is made to say 'Let us go into the holy mountain'.

This whole passage has a great interest in showing the impact made by the transfiguration upon those who were present. Peter uses the incident here to emphasize his authoritative knowledge of the historical Jesus (and thereby to rebut the false teachers' talk of 'myths'), to stress the solidarity between the Old Testament and the apostolic message (against false teachers who were twisting both), and to draw from the incarnate life of

---

[1]*New Testament Introduction*, 3rd ed. 1970, pp.671 ff., Appendix C, 'Epistolary Pseudepigraphy'.
[2]Bigg, p.232.   [3]Ex. 15:13; Jos. 5:15; Pss. 2:6; 3:4; Is. 52:1, *etc*.
[4]See Hennecke, *New Testament Apocrypha*, vol. II, p.680.

Jesus a positive pledge of the future coming in glory which the false teachers laughed at.[1]

H. THE TRUTH IS ATTESTED BY PROPHETIC SCRIPTURES (1:19–21)[2]

19. From personal eyewitness testimony Peter now turns to 'the prophetic word'. As in all other occurrences of the term, Peter means the Old Testament, and he adduces it in support for his teaching in verses 3–11. The verse can be understood in two quite different ways. The crucial word is *bebaioteron, more certain*. Does it mean that the Scriptures confirm the apostolic witness (AV, NEB mg.)? Or does it mean that the apostolic witness fulfils, and thus authenticates, Scripture (RV, RSV, NEB, NIV)?

Most commentators follow the second alternative and take it that the voice at the transfiguration makes even more certain the Old Testament prophecies about the coming of the Lord. Thus 'the transfiguration bears witness to the permanent validity of the Old Testament. . . . It is a distortion of the truth to say (like Marcion and many moderns) that the transfiguration shows the supersession of the Old Testament by the Gospel, for "the fulfilment of the Old Testament" means not its abolition but its vindication as a perpetual witness to the supremacy of Christ.'[3] This view, though excellent doctrine, is exposed to two criticisms. It is extremely difficult to squeeze this meaning 'we have the prophetic word made more sure' out of *echomen bebaioteron*, lit. 'we have more sure'. If Peter had meant to say this, why did he not use the normal construction and write *echomen bebaiō-thenta*? And it is even more difficult to squeeze such a sentiment

---

[1] The view of Bultmann and others that the transfiguration itself was a post-resurrection appearance, read back by the disciples into the incarnate life of Jesus, has been demolished by Boobyer and Stein.

[2] Theophilus of Antioch, who wrote about AD 170, three times alludes to these verses, 19–21. In *ad Autol.* ii. 13 he speaks of 'his word shining like a light in a small house'. In ii. 9 he writes, 'the men of God, carriers of the Spirit, have become prophets, and have been taught by God because God's own Spirit has been breathed into them.' Finally, in ii. 33 he writes, 'we are taught by the Holy Spirit who spoke through the holy prophets'. Not only do these allusions show how Theophilus had steeped himself in 2 Peter, and therefore support the antiquity of the Epistle; they also show how shrewdly he had understood the meaning of this difficult passage.

[3] A. M. Ramsey, *The Glory of God and the Transfiguration of Christ*, p.126.

out of a first-century Jew, let alone a Christian apostle. The Jews always preferred prophecy to the voice from heaven. Indeed they regarded the latter, the *bath qōl*, 'daughter of the voice', as an inferior substitute for revelation, since the days of prophecy had ceased.[1] And as for the apostles, it is hard to overemphasize their regard for the Old Testament. One of their most powerful arguments for the truth of Christianity was the argument from prophecy (see the speeches in Acts, Rom. 15; 1 Pet. 2, or the whole of Heb. or Rev.). In the word of God written, they sought absolute assurance, like their Master, for whom 'it is written' sufficed to clinch an argument. Peter's meaning seems to be that given in the first alternative above. He is saying 'If you don't believe me, go to the Scriptures'. 'The question', says Calvin, 'is not whether the prophets are more trustworthy than the gospel.' It is simply that 'since the Jews were in no doubt that everything that the prophets taught came from God, it is no wonder that Peter says that their word is more sure'.

The metaphor of Scripture as *a light* or torch, illuminating a murky room, is both well known and apt (*cf.* Ps. 119:105; 4 Esdras xii. 42), though *auchmēros*, 'murky' (NEB), does not recur in biblical Greek. It does, however, come in the *Apocalypse of Peter* as a description of hell. The thought is that the light shows up the dirt, and makes possible its removal. We are to walk by the torchlight of Scripture *until the day dawns and the morning star rises in your hearts.* What does this mean? There are several possibilities.

It is possible that Peter stands as a precursor of the Alexandrian school as an advocate of a truly Christian *gnōsis.* Thus the newly converted still walk in a murky light, and are to progress in study of the Scriptures until they arrive at the light of day, where mature knowledge of Christ (or illumination by the indwelling Spirit) has imparted to them Christian truth in its fullness. Plumptre, who adopts something like this view, points out that so understood it gives a close parallel with the 'wonderful light' of 1 Peter 2:9 and the 'rising sun from heaven' of Luke 1:78.

However, both the dawning of the day and the rising of the

[1]See C. K. Barrett, *The Holy Spirit and the Gospel Tradition*, 1947, pp.39 f.

morning star refer most naturally to the parousia. On the dawn-ing of the day of the second coming see Romans 13:12. On the *phōsphoros*, 'the morning star', it is interesting to note that it is applied in Greek literature not only to the morning star (*i.e.* Venus) but also to royal and divine persons. We possess part of a first-century AD Orphic hymn beseeching the *phōsphoros* to bring his light to bear.[1] In Christian writings, the Messiah is seen in the star symbolism of Numbers 24:17 (as in the Mes-sianic Anthology found in the Dead Sea Scrolls), and the rising Sun of righteousness of Malachi 4:2. In the Benedictus, Christ is 'the day star from on high' or 'the morning sun from heaven' (Lk. 1:78, AV, NEB); the primitive hymn enshrined in Ephesians 5:14 says that Christ will shine on you, and in Revelation 2:28; 22:16 he is called the 'morning star'.

This all suggests a third interpretation: 'Take heed to the prophetic scriptures until the full light of the parousia dawn.' This would make good sense, and would fit in well with the emphasis on the second coming in chapter 3. The objection to it is that the parousia does not rise *in your hearts*. Does this mean, as Käsemann thinks, that the author's Petrine mask slips, and shows that for all his orthodox talk about the parousia in chapter 3 he belongs to a generation which has spiritualized away that final culmination of world history into pure subjectivity? Not necessarily. Just possibly the phrase 'in your hearts' could belong at the beginning of the next clause (there were, after all, practically no punctuation marks in ancient MSS). If we put a colon after 'rise' instead of after 'hearts', the meaning would be 'knowing this first and foremost in your hearts. . .'. Alterna-tively, the rising of the morning star in Christian hearts at the dawning of the day may mean the glow of anticipation in Chris-tian hearts when 'the signs of the approaching Day are manifest to Christians. The fulfilment of their hope is at the door: the Lord is at hand' (von Soden). But probably we should think not so much of *anticipation* as of *transformation*. Our inner trans-formation, deepened continually by the Spirit as we study the Scriptures (2 Cor. 3:18), will be completed on the great day when we shall see him as he is, and be made like him (1 Jn. 3:2).

[1] Moulton and Milligan, *Vocabulary of the New Testament*, 1949, p.680, s.v. *phōsphoros*.

Bauckham makes two important points here. He believes that it is not the parousia as a total event which is in Peter's mind here, but rather the full revelation which it will bring in contrast to the partial knowledge we have in the Old Testament Scriptures and the apostolic tradition about Jesus. 'Naturally it will be in their hearts that Christian believers will perceive this revelation.' He points out that Paul, too, uses both subjective and objective terms to denote the coming age (1 Cor. 13:8–12).

His second point about this parousia reference is that it assumes the readers may be alive at the parousia – hardly the case if Käsemann is right in thinking that the author has abandoned primitive Christian expectation of the return of Christ!

Whatever the precise details, the main emphasis is manifest: we are on pilgrimage throughout our lives in this dark world. God has graciously provided us with a lamp, the Scriptures. If we pay attention to them for reproof, warning, guidance and encouragement we shall walk safely. If we neglect them, we shall be engulfed by darkness. The whole course of our lives ought to be governed by the Word of God.

20–21. *Above all, you must understand that no prophecy of Scripture came about by the prophet's own interpretation. For prophecy never had its origin in the will of man, but men spoke from God as they were carried along by the Holy Spirit.*

This passage has been interpreted in many ways. The main problem concerns the meaning of *epiluseōs*, a noun which does not occur again in the New Testament, though the verb comes in Mark 4:34 and Acts 19:39: in both instances it means to unravel a problem. The two main ways of taking it are, first, no prophecy arises from the prophet's own interpretation – *i.e.* it is given by God; and second, no prophecy is to be understood by private interpretation – *i.e.* but as the church interprets it. In the first case it is the prophet's understanding of his prophecy which is at issue, in the second it is our interpretation of the prophet's words.

The second view prevails today among most commentators. In its favour is the fact that the false teachers certainly did misinterpret Scripture (2:1; 3:16). If this were the meaning it would be important. Scripture is neither given (v. 21) nor interpreted by man (v. 20); the Spirit does both tasks. Again, if this were the meaning, it would provide a good introduction to chapter 2, which is, in fact, where the NEB puts it (but it so doing it starts its new paragraph in the middle of a Greek sentence!). Peter would then be claiming that only the Spirit-filled church could properly interpret the Spirit-inspired Scriptures.[1] The false teachers read the Bible amiss; they have not got the clue to its proper understanding, which the orthodox have, through the light of the indwelling Holy Spirit.

However there are difficulties about this view. Grammatically, this clause goes with what precedes, not what follows. The same is true of the sense. In the preceding paragraph, Peter is not talking about *interpretation* but *authentication*. His theme is the origin and reliability of the Christian teaching about grace, holiness and heaven. The same God whom the apostles heard speak in the transfiguration spoke also through the prophets. The argument in verses 20–21 is a consistent and indeed necessary conclusion to the preceding paragraph. Thus, we can rely on the apostolic account of the transfiguration because God spoke. And we can rely on Scripture because behind its human authors God spoke. The prophets did not make up what they wrote. They did not arbitrarily unravel it. 'They did not blab their inventions of their own accord or according to their own judgments' (Calvin).[2] In the Old Testament, this was the characteristic of the false prophets, who 'speak visions from their own minds, not from the mouth of the Lord' (Je. 23:16, *cf.* Ezk. 13:3). But true prophecy came from God and, men as they were, the prophets were *carried along* by the Holy Spirit.[3]

[1] As a curiosity of exegesis, Käsemann's view might be mentioned. He sees verses 19–21 as a careful bolstering up of the Catholic ministerial position against the *gnōsis* of the Enthusiasts. Primitive Christian prophecy has disappeared – it was too dangerous to be allowed by the hierarchy, represented by 2 Peter. So 'prophecy is now confined to the Old Testament'. But even this does not help. Enthusiastic exegesis replaces prophecy! The church, accordingly, has to exercise control over the interpretation of Scripture. The community must obey what the teaching ministry says to it (Käsemann, p.190). Of all this, needless to say, there is no hint in the passage itself.

[2] von Soden may be right in suspecting a reference here to the false teachers. The true prophets, unlike the false teachers, did not rely on their own ideas. The voice of God was brought to them, as to the apostles at the transfiguration (1:17, 21).

[3] *epilusis*, then, almost comes to mean 'inspiration', as J. P. Jacobszoon of Leyden translated it as early as 1599. No prophetic Scripture comes from self-inspired ecstasy, but from God. So J. Loow in *Nederlands Theologische Tijdschrift*, 3, 1965, pp.202–212.

Peter, then, is talking about the divine origin of Scripture, not about its proper interpretation. If interpretation were his subject in this verse, then verse 21 would be utterly irrelevant to his argument. What is more, a very forced meaning would have to be given to *ginetai*, viz. 'comes under the scope of' (Mayor). And Mayor was too good and honest a scholar not to be troubled about this. In point of fact, as Bauckham shows, the use of *epiluō* in the LXX and the Fathers strongly supports the conclusion that it is the prophet's own interpretation of God's revelation which is under consideration here.

It should now be apparent that Peter has been replying to two charges by the false teachers. To their contention that the apostles were purveying myths about Jesus, his power and coming, Peter says 'Not so: we were with him at the transfiguration. We were eyewitnesses.' He then adduces the Old Testament as a witness which is even more unimpeachable than the apostles themselves, and should be common coin both to the sectaries and the orthodox. But they respond by rejecting the authority of the Old Testament, denying its divine origin, and saying that the prophets simply produced their own ideas. So Peter strongly reasserts the conviction, common to Jews, Jesus and Christians alike, that the Old Testament has indeed a divine origin, and when the prophets spoke the prophecies recorded in Scripture they were men in touch with God who acted as his spokesmen.

It is interesting that in this, perhaps the fullest and most explicit biblical reference to the inspiration of its authors, no interest should be displayed in the psychology of inspiration. The author is not concerned with what they felt like, or how much they understood, but simply with the fact that they were the bearers of God's message. The relative parts played by the human and the divine authors are not mentioned, but only the fact of their co-operation. He uses a fascinating maritime metaphor in verse 21 (*cf.* Acts 27:15, 17, where the same word, *pheromenē*, is used of a ship carried along by the wind). The prophets raised their sails, so to speak (they were obedient and receptive), and the Holy Spirit filled them and carried their craft along in the direction he wished. Men spoke: God spoke. Any proper doctrine of Scripture will not neglect either part of this truth. Certainly those who are convinced of God's ultimate authorship of Scripture will take every pains to discover the background, life situation, limitations, education and so forth of the human agent who co-operated with God in its production. For revelation was not a matter of passive reception: it meant active co-operation. The fact of God's inspiration did not mean a supersession of the normal mental functionings of the human author. The Holy Spirit did not use instruments;[1] he used *men*. God's way is ever one of truth through personality, as was perfectly demonstrated at the incarnation. Moreover, he did not use *any* men, but *holy men*, those who were dedicated and pledged to his service. And even with such men, he did no violence to their personalities, but co-operated with them while revealing himself through them. 'He says they were *moved*, not because they were out of their minds (as the heathen imagine *enthousiasmos* in their prophets), but because they dared nothing by themselves but only in obedience to the guidance of the Spirit, who held sway over their lips as in his own temple' (Calvin).

CHAPTER TWO

A. BEWARE OF FALSE TEACHERS (2:1–3)

This chapter is closely linked with the preceding verses. Indeed, it has been observed that 1:16–2:3 has a chiastic order:
  A. apostles (1:16–18)

---

[1]There is nothing here remotely analogous to the Montanist claim, that they were like a lyre struck by the plectrum of the Holy Spirit. Montanism arose in the middle of the second century. Had this Epistle been written after that, the author would have said a good deal more than verse 21 if he were a Montanist. If not, he would have taken pains to distinguish his position from theirs. The personal concept of inspiration here is in striking contrast to the mechanical views which soon began to prevail.

Peter's words are in equally strong contrast to the mechanical understanding of inspiration to be found in Philo, his Jewish contemporary. Philo sees it as a compulsive divine possession which turned man into a *theophoros*, a 'God-bearer' (*Mut. Nom.* i, p.609, *de Somn.* p.689). Peter sees it as a personal and ethical co-operation between God and holy men. There is no suggestion that the sacred authors are beside themselves like the analogy from Bacchic frenzies cited by Philo; they are carried along in the path of God's will by their own glad and willing consent.

    B. Old Testament prophets (1:19–21)
    B. Old Testament false prophets (2:1a)
    A. false teachers (2:1b–3)
This careful construction makes possible both comparisons and contrasts between the apostles and the false teachers. Moreover, it enables Peter to move from defence against the charges of the opposition into attack. This dominates almost the whole of chapter 2.

1. On the extensive parallels between much of this chapter and the Epistle of Jude, see the Introduction. Peter's thought still lingers in the Old Testament prophecies. In Israel *there were also false prophets among the people* as well as true; and now history was repeating itself. His readers had *false teachers* in their midst. In describing them in this chapter he oscillates between the present and the future tense, as does Paul in a similar context in 1 Timothy 4:1ff. No doubt this is because he sees them as fulfilling the prophecies both of the Old Testament and of Jesus (Dt. 13:2–6; Mt. 24:24, *etc.*). There is a similar play between the future and present in 2 Thessalonians 2:3 and 7, and 2 Timothy 3:1ff and 5. There always have been and there always will be false teachers among the people of God.[1]

That this is the correct interpretation of the change of tense, and not, as some maintain, the failure of some second-century writer to be consistent in his archaism (*i.e.* he keeps slipping into the present tense) is suggested by a passage in Justin Martyr (d. AD 165) who quotes this passage. He says to the Jew Trypho: 'And just as there were false prophets contemporaneous with your holy prophets, so now there are many false teachers amongst us, of whom our Lord forewarned us to beware. Many have taught godless, blasphemous and unholy doctrines, for-

---

[1] It is worth examining this oscillation between present and future more closely because much is made of it by those who see the Epistle as pseudepigraphic. In 2:1; 3:3 the arrival of the false teachers is spoken of as future: in 2:11 f., 17 f., 20; 3:5 it is already present. A similar phenomenon is noticeable in 2 Timothy, where false teaching and living are spoken of in the present tense in 1:15; 2:18, 25 and 3:5 (which refers in the present tense to false teachers who were regarded as future at the beginning of the sentence in 3:1!) and in the future tense in 2:16–17; 3:2 ff., 13; 4:3–4. The combination of future and present is intended to stress the correspondence between prophecy and event. In both cases in 2 Peter where the future is used it is in immediate juxtaposition to references to the prophets (1:19–2: 3; 3:3–4). False teachers are at work in the church, just as the Old Testament prophets foretold.

ging them in his name; have taught, too, and still are teaching, those things which proceed from the unclean spirit of the devil.'[1]

False prophets may mean that they falsely claimed to be prophets, or that they prophesied false things; probably both. The men were as untrustworthy as the message. But as Peter calls them 'false teachers' not 'false prophets' it may be that they made no pretensions to prophecy. Nevertheless three prominent characteristics of false prophets in the Old Testament could apply to them. Unlike true prophets they did not speak with divine authority, their message was one of spurious peace, and they were condemned to be punished by God. Mayor made an interesting collection of the characteristics of the false prophets which were strikingly present in the situation to which Peter addresses himself. Their teaching was flattery; their ambitions were financial; their lives were dissolute; their conscience was dulled, and their aim was deception (see Is. 28:7; Je. 23:14; Ezk. 13:3; Zc. 13:4). *People* translates *laos*, a word used for the people of God in the LXX as well as in the New Testament. According to the speeches attributed to him in Acts, and to the teaching of 1 Peter as well, Peter claims that the Christians have been incorporated into the true Israel of God; there is no split between the Old Covenant and the New.

These *false teachers* (notice the quick change from *pseudoprophētai* to *pseudodidaskaloi*, suggesting that perhaps the false teachers did not, after all, put forward many pretensions to being prophets) are the type of men whom (*hoitines*) you will always find *secretly* or 'surreptitiously' bringing in heretical views. The verb *introduce* (*pareisagō*) has two overtones; it means to 'bring in alongside' (sc. true teaching) and also to 'introduce secretly' (*cf.* Gal. 2:4).

Destructive heresies (lit. 'of destruction' – another Hebraism) means opinions destructive of true faith. The word *hairesis* (lit. 'choice') was applied to a party or sect (*cf.* Acts 5:17; 15:5) or to the views held by such a sect. In the Pauline writings, divisiveness (Gal. 5:20; 1 Cor. 11:18f.) and arrogant independence

---

[1]*Dial.* lxxxii. Again, 'in the interval before His second coming, there would, He warned them, be heresies and false prophets arising in His name' (*Dial.* li).

(Tit. 3:10) are the significant heretical emphases, but as early as Ignatius (*c.* AD 110) the word is used in our sense of 'false doctrine'.[1] Indeed Peter may be alluding to a non-canonical prediction of Jesus, 'there will be divisions and heresies' (Justin, *Dial* 35.3, 51.2).

The effect of their teaching was that they were *even (kai) denying the sovereign Lord who bought them.* This fascinating phrase shows us something of what the cross meant to our author, for *bought* emphasizes both the seriousness of man's plight and the costliness of Christ's rescue (*cf.* Mk. 10:45; 1 Tim. 2:6; Rev. 5:9). The word *agorazō* is used of the redemption of Israel out of Egypt (*cf.* 2 Sa. 7:23). In the cross, as in the Exodus, we see God's personal intervention for his people, not only to deliver them from a fate of bondage and death, but also to redeem them 'as a people for himself', as 2 Samuel 7:23 continues. God redeems man in order that his changed way of life should be a credit to his Saviour; that, as 1 Peter 4:2 puts it, 'he does not live the rest of his earthly life for evil human desires, but rather for the will of God'.[2]

Now these false teachers understood, no doubt, the liberation afforded by the cross of Christ; liberty was one of their war-cries (2:19). But they did not recognize the obligation of holy living imposed by the Crucified. By their lives they denied the Lord who bought them. Christianity is, indeed, a religion of liberty; but it also demands loving bondservice to Jesus the Redeemer. Paul, Jude, James and other leading New Testament figures delighted to call themselves his *douloi*, 'bondservants'. Not so these men. It is interesting that a similar libertine movement in Corinth elicited a similar response, in similar words, from Paul (1 Cor. 6:19–20; 7:23).

Our author is at one with the rest of the New Testament (see Rom. 6 and Heb. 10) in asserting plainly that a man *cannot* run with both fox and hounds. The man who attempts to serve God and self is on the high road to *swift destruction*, for either death or the parousia will cut him off in mid-course. (For a similar use of

---

[1]'Abstain from the noxious weeds of heresy' (*Trallians* vi).

[2]It is interesting that Clement of Alexandria should conflate these two Petrine passages (and 1 Pet. 1:19) in his statement 'The Lord (whom he also calls "Master", *despotēs*, as here) redeems (*agorazei*) us with precious blood' (*Eccl. Proph.* xx).

tachinē, 'sudden', used of Peter's own death, see 1:14.)

Neyrey is probably right in seeing the *destruction* as ironical. These men who taught freedom from destruction (2:19), scoffed at the parousia and gave themselves to immorality would be judged for that immoral way of life at the very parousia which they denied.

2. The denial of *the sovereign Lord who bought them* is primarily ethical, not intellectual. It has two effects. First, it spreads to infect other people, which is why Peter (in ch. 2) is so vehement in his condemnations. Second, it brings discredit on the Christian cause. The theme of God's name being blasphemed by the heathen because of the unsatisfactory life of his people is a commonplace in the Bible (see Rom. 2:24, and Is. 52:5, which has influenced both the general idea and the particular form of expression here[1]; the future tense is due to this allusion). Peter, not without cause, had already shown himself very sensitive on this score in 1 Peter 3:16; 4:14f. The garbled accounts of Christian excesses to be found in pagan writers like Tacitus, Suetonius and Celsus show how necessary it was for the Christians to live blameless lives (Acts 19:9; Rom. 2:24; Tit. 2:5; Jas. 2:7). It still is, if the Lordship of Christ is to be meaningful.

Aselgeiai (*shameful ways*) is a strong word for reckless and hardened immorality, the very antithesis of *the way of truth* (or 'the true way', NEB, if the genitive *tēs alētheias* is a Hebraism). There is only one *way of truth*, Jesus Christ himself (Jn. 14:6); that is why denial of him is the same thing as departure from the truth. For in him the ethical and cognitive aspects of truth (emphasized respectively by Hebrew and Greek thought) cohere. The phrase *the way of truth* springs from Psalm 119:30, and occurs in early second-century literature, not only in the *Apology* of Aristides[2] but also in the *Apocalypse of Peter*.[3] Both appear to be allusions to this passage, for the phrase is nowhere else to be found in the New Testament. It is casual allusions like

---

[1] On the wide use of this theme in the second century see B. Lindars, *New Testament Apologetic*, 1961, pp.22 f.

[2] 'The way of truth which leads those travelling upon it into the heavenly kingdom' (xvi). So also 1 *Clem.* xxxv, Hermas, *Vis.* iii. 7. 1.

[3] 'Those who blaspheme the way of truth' (vii).

this that strengthen the case for an early date for this Epistle, since the *Apology* and the *Apocalypse* both date from *c*. AD 130. Calvin's comment on this verse is apt: 'There is nothing that disturbs godly minds so much as defection. . . To prevent this destroying our faith, Peter interposes with the timely prediction that this very thing will happen.'

3. If verse 2 speaks of the immorality of the false teachers, verse 3 is concerned with their greed and their doom. It is instructive to contrast it with 1 Thessalonians 2:5, where Paul denies that he is a teacher of this type, like the wandering sophists of the Graeco-Roman world, whose main concern was not truth, but success in argument. This accounts for the reference to *stories they have made up*, or phoney arguments, which were designed not for helping the hearers but for fleecing them (hence the mention of *greed*). Peter is turning the false teachers' charge of 'cleverly invented stories' back on themselves. 'It is not the apostles' message, but the false teachers', that is based on sheer invention' (Bauckham). The verb *emporeuomai*, has a commercial background, to *exploit* or 'make money out of'. Like the false teachers of 1 Timothy 6:5, these men thought Christianity could be a source of financial gain to themselves.

The terms in which Peter depicts the doom of the heretics, in this and the following verse, appear to Käsemann to be stiff and stereotyped. 'The enemy', he claims, 'is disposed of in a very primitive fashion; first by accusing him of moral depravity, then by showering him with well chosen proverbs (as in v. 22), and, thirdly, by painting the punishment of the heretics in lurid terms.' Doubtless such stringent condemnations as Peter's appear to twentieth-century readers as old-fashioned and inappropriate, because we have largely lost any sense of the diabolical danger of false teaching, and have become as dulled to the distinction between truth and falsehood in ideas as we have to the distinction between right and wrong in behaviour. But it is impossible to be alive, as Peter was, to the ethical and intellectual importance of 'the way of truth' (*i.e.* Jesus himself) without being incensed when that way is flouted, particularly in the church. Peter reiterates that the *condemnation*, pronounced against false teachers long ago in the Old Testament, is impending (lit. 'from of old has not been idle'). For the thought, see on Jude 4 (*cf.* 1 Pet. 4:17). He concludes by saying that their *destruction* (the third time in three verses that *apōleia* has been used) *has not been sleeping*. NEB renders well, 'perdition waits for them with unsleeping eyes.' The only other New Testament occurrence of this vivid word is applied to the sleepy maidens in Matthew 25:5. No doubt he is rebutting the false claim that God's judgment is nodding off to sleep (*cf.* 1 Ki. 18:27).

B. THREE EXAMPLES OF JUDGMENT AND DELIVERANCE (2:4–10a)

Peter now proceeds to give examples of the impartial judgment of God, and the certainty that it will come even though it linger (*cf.*3:8–10). He speaks first of the fallen angels (v. 4), then of the flood (v. 5) and then of the cities of the plain (v. 6ff.). He gets carried away by his illustrations, and the shape of his sentence suffers. We would expect, 'If God did not spare A, B, C, in the past, he will not spare the false teachers now.' But he is more anxious to encourage than to condemn (though he will do plenty of that before he is through!), to concentrate on the mercy rather than the wrath of God; so he concludes the sentence in verse 9 by putting the salvation of the righteous in the foreground of his canvas, and by relegating the accompanying condemnation of the wicked to the background.

Peter's examples differ slightly from those in the parallel account in Jude 5–7. Peter concentrates on the pride and rebellion of the angels, the apathy and disobedience of the men of Noah's day, and the sheer sensuality of the men of Sodom, presumably because these were all characteristic of the false teachers he was opposing.

4. He begins with the fallen angels of Genesis 6, but does not specify their sin. In Genesis 6:1–4; Jude 6 and Revelation 12:7 it is made clear that rebellion was the prime cause of their fall, though lust is also mentioned. Peter may have been influenced by the embellishment of the Genesis account in the apocryphal *1 Enoch*. Jude certainly was, for he quotes 1*Enoch*, as does the second-century *Gospel of Peter*. But if Peter alludes to this apocryphal book at all, he does so with the utmost discretion (as he does in 1 Pet. 3:19; 4:6 where again he *may* be familiar with apocryphal material, but it is impossible to prove it).[1]

The details of Peter's picture are not quite clear. NIV renders it *putting them into gloomy dungeons*, since most of the best MSS read *seirois* or *sirois*, meaning 'underground pits' (whence the English 'silo'). Others give the rare word *seirais*, meaning 'chains' (so AV), which would be closer to Jude's 'everlasting fetters' and the imagery of *Enoch* x. 4; liv. 4–5 and *Baruch* lvi. 12f. which reads, 'And some of them descended and mingled with women. And those who did so were tormented in chains.' The *Apocalypse of Peter* also represents them in chains. However, both textual and intrinsic probability on balance favour *seirois*.

Sent them to hell is a single word in the Greek, occurring only here in the Bible, and meaning to 'consign to Tartarus'. Tartarus, in Greek mythology, was the place of punishment for the departed spirits of the very wicked, particularly rebellious gods like Tantalus. Just as Paul could quote an apt verse of the pagan poet Aratus (Acts 17:28), so could Peter make use of this Homeric imagery. Josephus does the same, and talks of heathen gods chained in Tartarus.[2] The evil angels are in the place of torment now, although they must await the final judgment. Peter's eschatology is characteristic of the whole New Testament, which sees God's future judgment as finalizing the choices men are making all their lives. There is a close parallel in Revelation 20:10, where the devil, though bound now, is destined for final judgment hereafter.

5. Peter's second instance, the flood, seems to have been a favourite of his: we find it not only recurring in chapter 3 but in 1 Peter 3:20. Here, against the background of judgment on a rebellious and wicked world (*asebōn*, *ungodly*, suggests that they had no time whatever for God), we find God's salvation depicted. Peter insists that it was available for all, but was effective only for few. The fewness of the saved and the certainty of judgment had immediate relevance for his first readers. We

---

[1] It is probable that Peter is alluding to passages in *Enoch* on the punishment of the angels, such as x. 4–6, xviii. 11–xxi. 10.

[2] *c. Apion*. ii. 33.

should probably understand the Greek to mean that God kept Noah safe *because* he was *a preacher* (lit. 'herald') *of righteousness* (note the Old Testament sense of this word, as in 1:1 and in 1 Peter, in striking contrast to the forensic Pauline usage). *Noah . . . and seven others* (literally 'Noah the eighth person'). This is a common classical idiom. It means he was rescued with seven others, *i.e.* his wife, his three sons and their wives, as in 1 Peter 3:20.

The Old Testament does not say that Noah was a preacher of righteousness; nor, incidentally, does 1 *Enoch*. But it was well known in Jewish tradition, and if he was indeed a 'righteous man, blameless' who 'walked with God' (Gn. 6:9) then he *must* have been a herald of righteousness. His very life would have been so different from the wicked men around him, that it would speak volumes; and how could any good man keep quiet when he saw others going to ruin? Any man of God is at least as concerned for the rescue of others as he is in preserving his own relationship with God. And, certainly, the non-canonical writings of the first century are quite clear that Noah was that sort of man; he is called a preacher of righteousness or the equivalent in 1 *Clement* vii. 6, ix. 4, *Sibylline Oracles* i. 128 and Josephus, *Antiquities* i. 3. 1.

The point of the whole Noah illustration is well brought out by Barnett. Peter's readers must, he says, 'choose between apostolic orthodoxy and contemporary heresy. The consequences of their choice will follow as certainly as those illustrated in the fate of Noah and the ancient world'.

6. Peter's third example of divine judgment follows in chronological sequence, unlike Jude's; and Peter, again unlike Jude, merely alludes to the matter without elaboration. There is an artistic appropriateness in the way destruction by fire succeeds destruction by water, and this prepares for a similar effect in 3:7.

The words in this verse are very striking. The word *tephrōsas*, *burning to ashes* or 'covering with ashes', is unique in the Bible, but is used by Dio Cassius (lxvi) in his account of the eruption of Vesuvius in AD 79 when Pompeii and Herculaneum were buried in lava. Many MSS read *katastrophē katekrinen*, *condemned them to*

111

extinction (RSV). NIV is probably correct in omitting 'to extinction', though the textual evidence is evenly balanced. The phrase came in from the LXX account of the destruction of Sodom (Gn. 19:29). This total destruction was allowed by God in order to bring home to succeeding generations that unrighteousness will end in ruin. False teaching and false behaviour ultimately always produce suffering and disaster, be it in Lot's day, in Peter's, or in our own. This is Jude's point when he says that the punishment of these cities has an eternal quality (Jude 7). There are curious parallels between our contemporary scene and Sodom, for that city was as famed for its affluence and softness as for its immorality – and, of course, like any men come of age, they thought they had outgrown the idea of God. They found out their mistake too late.

7–8. But God's way is always to receive the godfearing man who trusts him and hates evil. He delivered Lot, whose rescue was a classic instance of the salvation God offers. The Genesis account does not even claim, with our present verse, that Lot was a *righteous man, who was distressed by the filthy lives of lawless men*. He appears simply as a man of the world (Gn. 13:10–14; 19:16) who had strayed a long way from the God of his fathers. Though hospitable (19:1f.), he was weak (19:6), morally depraved (19:8) and drunken (19:33, 35). His heart was so deeply embedded in Sodom that he had to be positively dragged out (19:16). Time and again it is emphasized that his rescue was entirely due to the unmerited favour of God, which he shows to men because of what he is, not because of what they are (*e.g.* 19:16, 19).

Why then is he called *righteous* here? The answer may partly lie in extra-canonical tradition; thus he is called 'the just one' in *Wisdom* x. 6; xix. 17. It may partly be a matter of comparison with the men of Sodom, in which case NEB's 'a good man' (a decent fellow) may be near the mark. But also, of course, Lot did accept divine intervention on his behalf, as did Elizabeth and Zacharias, who are also called *dikaioi* ('upright') in Luke 1:5–6. Jewish tradition saw Abraham's prayer for the righteous in Sodom as particularly applying to Lot, which says much for the power of intercessory prayer (*Pirqe R.El.* 25, *Gen. Rab.* 49:13). If we are right in reading the article, *ho dikaios*, when the epithet is applied to him again in verse 8, the meaning will be that he vexed his righteous soul with what he saw and heard. If, however, the article should be deleted, with one of the best MSS, the meaning will be 'upright in what he looked at and listened to' (so the Vulgate, *aspectu et auditu justus*). In any case, Peter continues, the licentious behaviour of the lawless society in which he lived *tormented* him, lit. 'knocked him up'. NEB catches the meaning with its translation 'tortured'. It is customary for Christians today, living in a secularized society, no longer to be shocked by sinful things which they see and hear. They will, for example, without protest sit through a television programme presenting material which a generation ago they would never have contemplated watching at a theatre or cinema. But when a man's conscience becomes dulled to sin, and apathetic about moral standards, he is no longer willing to look to the Lord for deliverance.

9. This verse concludes the sentence begun in verse 4. *If this is so, then the Lord knows how to rescue godly men from trials,* or 'the test'. Some MSS have the plural, 'tests', and this would mean temptations in general, particularly the pride, sensuality and disobedience referred to in the previous verses. But the singular 'test' is better attested, and will then bear a meaning somewhat analogous to the 'bring us not to the test' of the Lord's Prayer, the final test of apostasy from God. It was from this test that Noah and Lot emerged victorious; they stood alone among mockers and unbelievers. The New Testament sees the second coming as the final test, the great *peirasmos*. The faithful will be delivered out of that hour of trial which will come upon all the earth (Rev. 3:10), when the returning Lord will test (*peirazō*) the quality of every Christian's service (1 Cor. 3:13). Meanwhile, no temptation from within or test from without is too great to be endured, for God not only regulates it, but gives his people the strength to face it (1 Cor. 10:13). Note that God delivers a man 'out of' (*ek*) not 'away from' (*apo*) trials. Christianity is no insurance policy against the trials of life. God allows them to befall the Christian; he meets us in them and delivers us out of them. Furthermore, the examples of Noah and Lot are instructive for showing *how* God delivers the godfearing (*eusebeis* as opposed to the *asebeis*, the ungodly) from tests. Neither had an immediate deliverance. Noah had to help himself by building an ark in obedience to God's instructions – despite the mirth of his neighbours: Lot had to endure long years of self-recrimination for his foolish decision to go and live in Sodom. Yet, at the time of his choosing, God delivered them both. God may allow us to face long years of waiting before he intervenes; he may use us to help ourselves out of the difficulty. But he well knows how to deliver the godly; he can be relied on.

The faithful to whom Peter wrote may well have wondered, 'Why does God allow us to be plagued with such venomous heresy in our midst?' and again, 'When will God vindicate his name by judging the wicked?' Peter has given his answer to the first of these questions, and now briefly addresses himself to the second, which he will deal with in more detail later. Here he contents himself with asserting that the God who knows how to deliver, long though he may seem to delay, knows equally how to punish. This is clear from the Sodom and the flood illustrations which he has just employed. But Peter's mind goes back to the fallen angels first and foremost, as the phrase *to hold the unrighteous for the day of judgment, while continuing their punishment* indicates; it is almost identical with the language used of the fate of the angels in verse 4. If we are to construe the Greek exactly, it seems to imply that they are now being punished, and are being kept for final judgment later. How can this be? Bigg may be right in taking it to indicate the present torment of deceased sinners, but Calvin probably judges the sense of the passage correctly when he takes *kolazomenous, to be punished*, as proleptic (they are being kept *now* for a judgment that is *future*).

10a. Peter concludes this topic for the time being by assuring his readers that the false teachers are still in God's hand. They have not escaped his control despite their overt immorality. The phrase *opisō sarkos . . . poreuomenous, those who follow the corrupt desire of the sinful nature* (better, 'especially those who in polluting lust indulge the flesh', Bauckham) suggests sodomy. *En epithumia miasmou* can be taken either as a Hebraism 'in their foul lust', or as an objective genitive, 'in their longing for the sordid'.

There are three ways of explaining the *authority* they are said to *despise*. It may mean some angelic hierarchy (as in Eph. 1:21; Col. 1:16, and perhaps the parallel passage in Jude 7–8; in all these passages *kuriotēs*, 'lordship', is used, as it is here). Alternatively, Peter may be returning to the theme of verse 1, and indicating that the false teachers despise the lordship of Christ (as in *Didache* iv. 1[1]). It is also possible that by *kuriotēs* Peter means church leadership, that is to say the 'authority' of Peter and the officially constituted presbyterate in their locality. A similar instance of this sort would be the situation in 1 *Clement* and in 3 John. The second of these explanations is the likely. There is little enough evidence to show that these libertines were interested in the different ranks of angels; on the contrary, they seem to have been very materialistic in their world view. But their dissolute behaviour is an insult to the Lord.

Peter faced a curiously modern predicament. There were people in the church who lived sensual lives and justified it. The infection was spreading. They did not believe in the notion of judgment and they laughed at the parousia. In this paragraph Peter confines himself to asserting solemnly that judgment will come: he will deal with the delay in the parousia in chapter 3. Judgment is certain, and he underlines it by three Old Testament examples which show the inevitability and universality of judgment. The false teachers, like their Old Testament counterparts, surrendered to sexual licence and laughed at the prospect of the judgment of God. People cannot do that and get away with it in God's world. Alongside this dark thread of sin and its doom runs a silver thread of God's rescue of any who, like Noah and Lot, turn to him and call for his rescue. The God of justice cannot be flouted. The God of grace can be relied on.

C. THE INSOLENCE OF THE FALSE TEACHERS (2:10b–11)

10b. At this point Peter pauses to give a further description of the false teachers. They are *bold and arrogant*. The former word,

---

[1]Clement of Alexandria in the *Adumbrations*, 1008, so interprets the parallel passage in Jude 8. His comments on 2 Peter unfortunately have not survived.

tolmētēs, smacks of the reckless daring that defies God and man. The latter word, *authadēs*, is used for an obstinate fellow who is determined to please himself at all costs. The next phrase may mean that they 'slander celestial beings', or that they 'speak disrespectfully of church leaders'. It all depends on the meaning we assign to *doxai* and *kat' autōn*. Assuming the *doxai* to be celestial beings they could be theoretically either good angels or demons. If the former, then the *kat' autōn* will refer to the false teachers. If the latter, the *kat' autōn* will refer to these *doxai*. It is, however, exceedingly difficult to maintain the hypothesis of evil angels here, despite the parallel passage with Michael and Satan in Jude, because *doxai*, a word full of the imagery of light, is totally inappropriate to demonic beings. The *doxai*, must be the angels, and the *autōn* the false teachers, on whom the angels pronounce God's judgment – in temperate terms.

Assuming, then, that Peter is thinking of the slandering of angels, the phrase could be taken in two ways. Either they 'made light of' the unseen powers, in the materialistic attitude of which verse 12 complains, when it likens them to brute beasts; or else they 'spoke disrespectfully' of angelic beings. This is the meaning in Jude, and perhaps here too. It could well be that the false teachers justified their licentious ways by citing the example of the 'sons of God' who mated with the daughters of men (Gn. 6:1ff.). There was considerable rabbinic argument as to whether these 'sons of God' were men or angels. If the false teachers took the latter view, and quoted the angels in justification of their immorality (and Cyril of Alexandria inveighed against people in his day who did just that with the Genesis story), they would indeed be blaspheming (lit. 'speaking harm of') the angels and bringing them into disrepute.[1] In favour of this interpretation, it could be urged that Paul uses both *doxa* and *kuriotēs* of the angelic powers, and the present context makes such an interpretation probable. However, in the light of verse 12 with its insistence on the crass materialism of the heretics, we cannot rule out Bigg's understanding of the phrase as referring to church leaders, against whom the false teachers

---

[1]Plato attacked the Homeric sages for this very reason, that in their tales of amours between the gods and men, they were slandering the Divine.

were insubordinate. 'The rulers of the church would naturally rebuke the false teachers, and these would naturally reply in unmeasured language' (Bigg).

This, then, is the character of the false teachers as set out so far. They are dominated by lust; their passions are given free sway, with the result that they behave like animals, while the mental and spiritual sides of their humanity suffer atrophy. They are headstrong, rebellious against the will of God, and reckless of the consequences. They are contemptuous of other people, be these human or celestial. They are self-willed; the sensual man always is, for in the last analysis self is all that matters to him. His hell is this, that his world contracts until the only thing he has left is the self he has corrupted. Who can say that 2 Peter is irrelevant to our generation?

11. In contrast to these headstrong fellows, the angels, though *stronger and more powerful* do not use insults when pronouncing judgment on them from the Lord. The argument is *a fortiori*. The false teachers do not hesitate to bring vituperative accusations against their superiors; whereas the angels do not even dare to impugn their inferiors in such terms in the Lord's presence.

Such I take to be the general meaning of the verse, but the passage is exceedingly difficult, not only because the background is uncertain, but also because the Greek is ambiguous. Thus, to whom are the angels superior? Does he mean the *doxai* of the previous verse, in which case they would either be church leaders or (inferior) angels? Or does he mean simply that the angels are vastly superior to the blasphemous false teachers?

A further complication is whether the phrase *in the presence of the Lord* should be omitted, along with Jude 9 and several MSS here. No. On intrinsic grounds the different reading is to be preferred, and it has better attestation than the omission. In the context, too, it fits well. Unlike the false teachers who are careless of the lordship of Christ and are free with their insults, the angels so revere their Lord as they live all their lives in his presence, that no insulting language is allowed to pass their lips, even though it would be richly deserved.

So much for the complexities of the syntax of this passage. On its meaning commentators differ according to the background which they postulate. Some regard Peter's words as a generalized edition of Jude 9, and accordingly see the background as the conflict between Michael and the devil which is referred to there. The devil claimed the body of Moses, when Michael was about to bury him, on the grounds that Moses had murdered the Egyptian. The archangel, instead of bringing a stinging charge against Satan, left the matter in God's hands with a simple 'The Lord rebuke you'. However, there is no explicit reference to this story here, and it may be gratuitous to assume it. Others, therefore, turn to *Enoch* ix for illumination. Here the archangels lay complaints against evil angels before the Lord, but do not take it upon themselves to condemn them. They leave the matter with God.[1] Either this or the previous story would form a fitting contrast to the indisciplined and irreverent tongues of the false teachers, and it may well be that some such apocryphal embellishment of Zechariah 3:1–2 lies behind what Peter says here. The background would obviously be apparent to the readers, though it is obscure to us, and it may be for this reason that Peter is not more specific, though it is equally possible that he is not anxious to quote the Apocrypha. One other possibility is worth mentioning. Conceivably the heretics were libertines with a definite grudge against the angels. For, according to Jewish tradition, the angels were instrumental in the handing over of the Law to Moses (see also Gal. 3:19; Heb. 2:2). Now the Law contained the seventh commandment! Could it be that these errorists regarded licence as having positive religious value (*cf.* sacred prostitution in many religious systems)? Is *that* why they insulted angels? It is impossible to be certain. In any case, Peter is asserting that these men were more free with their language than the angels themselves, and it would be no bad thing if Christians remembered that any condemnations of others are necessarily uttered 'before the Lord'. Consciousness of his presence tames the tongue.

---

[1] In *Enoch* lxviii Michael and Raphael, the archangels, stand appalled at the majesty of God and the wickedness of the sinful angels. If this were in Peter's mind, it would afford a healthy contrast to the attitude of the false teachers.

D. THEIR ARROGANCE, LUST AND GREED (2:12–16)

12–13a. Peter now launches out in a direct assault on the false teachers; he glows with moral indignation. These men, so far from possessing angelic restraint, live *like brute beasts* at the dictates of their passions, or as RSV translates, 'like irrational animals, creatures of instinct', in contrast to the rational being, man. But these folk have neglected their rationality and followed their passions. Very well, their end will be like an animal's too. They will be *caught and destroyed*. What a graphic indictment of the effect on a man of living like a beast! First he gets captured and then he gets destroyed by his passions. As Barclay points out, sensuality is self-destructive. 'The aim of the man who gives himself to such fleshly things is pleasure; and his tragedy is that in the end he loses even the pleasure.' What is more, he goes on, 'for a while he may enjoy what he calls pleasure, but in the end he ruins his health, wrecks his constitution, destroys his mind and character and begins his experience of hell while he is still on earth'.

Their mistake is to confuse the thrill of animal instinct with the presence of the Holy Spirit – for it is very likely that these advocates of Christian liberty were loud in their claims to fullness of the Holy Spirit. Käsemann has very acutely noticed (though the conclusion he draws is bizarre) that both the heretics and Peter make essentially the same claim against the other. The heretics claimed to have 'knowledge', to have the Spirit who gave them liberty (both from ecclesiastical discipline and moral restraint) which they prized; they regarded the orthodox as devoid of the Spirit. On the contrary, Peter seems to say, the Spirit manifests his presence not by ecstatic thrills and insubordinate action but through moral renewal. It is you heretics who are devoid of the Spirit; you behave like dumb beasts on the level of your instincts, and you will end up, like them, in the slaughter-house! Peter, like the rest of the New Testament writers, emphasizes that Christianity is inescapably ethical. You cannot have relationship with a good God without becoming a better man.

The next phrase, *blaspheme in matters they do not understand*, is obscure in the Greek. 'Cursing away in matters of which they are ignorant' (Funk-Debrunner, p. 84), or 'they pour abuse on things they do not understand' (NEB), are feasible. Possibly *en hois, of the things*, may mean 'because' as it sometimes does in late Greek; thus 'they blaspheme because they do not understand'. Does Peter refer to their cursing of the angels, if angels is what is meant by the *doxai* above? If so, Mayor's quotation of the *Testament of Asher* vii. 1 is apt: 'Do not become like Sodom, which failed to recognize the angels of the Lord, and was destroyed for ever.' But more probably Peter refers to their immorality. They pour abuse on the way of Christian restraint, which they do not, in any case, understand.

What will be the fate of these men? They *will perish* and be done out of the wages of their wrongdoing. Such is Peter's grimly sardonic conviction. Theoretically, *en tē phthora autōn kai phtharēsontai* could mean 'they will even be corrupted by their corrupt living'; it will be the end of them. But the comparison with the *phthora* of the animals (v. 12) makes it clear that destruction, not corruption, is meant. The false teachers will perish with the animals they emulate. The Greek here has interesting features. The first phrase is another Hebraism, 'they shall, in their destruction, certainly (*kai*) be destroyed', and Bigg sees here three indications of the priority of Peter over Jude (*cf.* Jude 10). The Hebraism is characteristic of him, so is the repetition of the word (*phthora phtharēsontai*), while it is also clear that *pthora* is one of Peter's favourite words, for four out of the eight New Testament occurrences come in this Epistle. The second phrase, *adikoumenoi misthon adikias* can be taken in either of two ways. Either, 'suffering the recompense for their wrongdoing' (*they will be paid back with harm for the harm they have done*) which is possible, but strains the *adikoumenoi*. Alternatively, it may mean 'done out of the profits of their evil-doing', 'defrauded of the wages of fraud'. That this is the likely meaning is suggested by *Pap. Elephant.* 24 and 27, where we read, 'When this has been done (in the context, 'when a receipt has been given'), we shall not be defrauded (*ēdikēmenoi esometha*).' So it appears that Peter is using a highly evocative commercial metaphor to stress that immorality is not worthwhile. In the end it will rob you, not pay you.

13b. Here NEB is clear in giving the main thrust of Peter's powerful denunciation: 'To carouse in broad daylight is their idea of pleasure; while they sit with you at table they are an ugly blot on your company, because they revel in their own deceptions.' But once again the details are uncertain. In addition to the problems over *apatais* (*pleasures*; see below), *hēdonē* can mean good or bad pleasure, *truphē* delicacy or revelling, while *en hēmera* (*in broad daylight*) can also be variously interpreted. For *spiloi* (*blots*) Jude, in his version, has *spilades* (*blemishes*, or 'sunken reefs', Jude 12).

Daylight debauchery was frowned on even in degenerate Roman society (*cf.* 1 Thes. 5:7), and this accounts for Peter's words in Acts 2:15, indignantly rebutting the charge of daylight drunkenness. *Blots . . . and blemishes*, Peter calls them; not only blots on Christian company, but the very opposite of the character of Christ, whom he describes in 1 Peter 1:19 as 'without blemish or defect'. The church should be like her Master, 'without stain or wrinkle or any other blemish' (Eph. 5:27), but such men share nothing of this character. Peter has already shown us in the preceding verses how the heretics deny the Lord who bought them, by the insubordination of their language and the arrogance of their attitude. Now they demonstrate that denial in the uncharitableness of their behaviour.

This daylight revelry is carried on *while they feast with you*. If one well-attested reading, *agapais* for *apatais*, is accepted, it took place at the Agapae or 'love-feasts' which accompanied the Holy Communion (see 1 Cor. 11:20ff.). This is certainly the right reading in the parallel passage in Jude 12, and would make good sense here. We know from 1 Corinthians that immorality and greed had broken out at the love-feasts in Corinth in the fifties, and the dangers of this sort of abuse later led to the discontinuance of the Agapae. The surrounding words might be held to support this reading of *agapais*; thus Clement of Alexandria[1] uses *euōchia* of the Agape (*cf. suneuō-choumenoi, while they feast with*, here) and Hippolytus[2] tells us that the Agapae were conducted in daylight in order to avoid

---

[1]*Paed.* ii. 1. 6.   [2]*Apost. Trad.* xxvi.

slanderous rumours. The charge against the heretics would then be that they disgraced the sober daytime Agapae by their licentious behaviour. Even if the reading *apatais* (*deceitful pleasures*) be preferred here, as may well be right, the meaning could well be 'mock love-feasts', and the allusion would still be to the Agapae, though Peter would be using a biting play on words.

Whatever the right reading, the gravity of their debauchery is the main point, and Peter makes this acute observation. Lust is subject to the law of diminishing returns. Soon mere drunkenness fails to satisfy; it must be drunkenness in the daytime. Fornication, likewise, is not enough; it must be rape at the meal-table. Doubtless the heretics rationalized it as sacred prostitution, enacting in the cultic meal the unity between Christ and his church – but lust, naked lust, was their driving force. And lust often delights to deck itself out in religious garb.

14. Their eyes are full, says Peter in a remarkable phrase, not of *adultery* (so also RSV) but of 'an adulterous woman' (*cf.* NEB). They lust after every girl they see; they view every female as a potential adulteress. Peter makes another shrewd psychological observation. Lascivious thoughts, if dwelt upon and acted upon, become dominant. It becomes impossible for them to look at any woman without reflecting on her likely sexual performance, and on the possibilities of persuading her to gratify their lusts.

Not only does lust act as an irritant; it never satisfies. It always leaves a man restless, longing for more (which in its turn, equally fails to satisfy). These libertines had such eyes that *they never stop sinning* (*akatapaustous hamartias*). It may be that this phrase should be translated, as in NEB, 'never at rest from sin', in which case Peter would be referring not to the unsatisfactory nature of lust, but to the bondage it brings with it. There is only one way out, the way of death to sin and rising to newness of life; the only alternative to denying Christ is to be identified with him in his death and resurrection. It is this way of victorious living to which Peter refers in 1 Peter 4:1–3, 'he who has suffered in his body (*i.e.* died to sin) is done with sin'. The verb he uses for 'ceased from' in 1 Peter is cognate to the rare word *akatapaustous* here.

Peter turns to another characteristic of the libertines. They seduce the unstable. The metaphor is from fishing and recurs in verse 18; *deleazō* means 'to catch with bait'. Its use would be particularly appropriate if Peter is indeed the author of the Epistle, but the word is also found in James 1:14 (and nobody has suggested he was once a fisherman!). Xenophon speaks of men who are 'hooked' by their gluttony[1] while Demosthenes knows men who are 'hooked' by idleness and 'having it too good' *(rhastōnē)*.[2]

Unstable (astēriktoi) describes Peter's recipients. They were easily toppled over because they had not planted their feet firmly enough on Christ. That is why the false teachers represented such a danger to them. Here again the comparatively rare word *astēriktoi (cf.* 1:12; 3:16) comes most appropriately from Peter, whose own past had been so unstable, and who had been told by Jesus, 'When you have come to yourself, you must lend strength to *(stērixon)* your brothers' (Lk. 22:32).

Peter's next charge is coolly deliberate. They *are experts in greed.* They had 'trained themselves' (he uses the word from which our 'gymnasium' is derived) in avarice. *Pleonexia* (greed) is a difficult word to translate fully. It means unbridled desire for more and more things; things you have no right to, things you have no need of. It is often used of money, often of illicit or unnatural intercourse. These men had schooled themselves in the desire for forbidden things. No wonder Peter concludes with yet another expressive Hebraism, *an accursed brood.* He means 'God's curse is on them!' (NEB). There is nothing vindictive in this; it is merely descriptive. These men rest under the curse of God, as do all who fail to trust in Christ who bore man's curse (Gal. 3:10, 13). It is parallel to the 'children of wrath' in Ephesians 2:13. For the Hebraism, *cf.* 1 Peter 1:14, 'children of disobedience' – yet another subtle link between the two letters.

15. Peter explains how the errorists come to be under the curse of God. They have deliberately *left the straight way and have wandered off,* or gone astray. The right or straight way (*cf.* 'the

[1]*Memorabilia* ii. 1. 4.   [2]Demosthenes, 241. 2.

way of truth', 2:2) is a common Old Testament metaphor for obedience to God (*cf.* 1 Sa. 12:33; Ezr. 8:21), and an illuminating parallel is found in Acts 13:10, where Elymas perverts 'the straight paths of the Lord' (itself a quotation of Hosea 14:10). The result of such disobedience is that men get lost. There is a tragic irony in 'lostness' being the penalty of self-assertion.[1]

But in what way are they lost? Why are they said to resemble *Balaam*? Covetousness is the obvious point. He *loved the wages of wickedness*. A subtle development of this point by Bo Reicke emphasizes that Balaam acted as hired agent for the heathen king, Balak. He suggests that 'the seducers of the Christians act as hired agents of foreign employers', to fit in with his theory that the people denounced in this Epistle are not libertines so much as agitators for political freedom in the days of Domitian (AD 81–96). Alas, political agitators did not last long in the days of Domitian! Calvin thinks the essence of the comparison here is that the heretics 'by their teaching spread the deadly poison of godlessness', just as 'Balaam used his venal tongue to curse the people of God.'

Now it is quite true that the main point of the Balaam account in Numbers 22–24 is his avarice; but Numbers 31:16 attributes to his influence the immorality of the Israelites at Baal-Peor (Nu. 25). These two factors surely combined to make him a most useful prototype of the immoral false teacher out for gain. Such a type appears in Jude 11, where the reference to Baal-Peor is implicit (*cf.* 1 Cor. 10:8), and also in Revelation 2:15, where the same charge occurs again. The Nicolaitans, like Balaam, seem to have taught that the covenant of Yahweh with his people was so strong that nothing could impair it, certainly not some insignificant peccadillo like fornication or idolatry! All this was urged in the name of compromise, both political and social. Consequently the use of Balaam was a master-stroke against the plea for compromise, no matter how lucrative, how seductive it was made to appear. Once again we come up against this Christian insistence on the ineradicable link between right belief in the true God and right behaviour. This link the Balaam tradition sought to break.

[1]See also on Jude 11.

Some MSS call Balaam 'son of Bosor' not *son of Beor*, in this verse. If Bosor is right, it may be a grim allusion to their sins, by paranomasia with *bāśār* ('flesh'). It has also been suggested that this represents the Galilaean mispronunciation of the guttural in the Hebrew name, and as such is perhaps a pointer to Petrine authorship; for his Galilaean accent was noticeable (Mt. 26:73).

16. Peter makes a good deal of the Balaam incident in order to encourage the simple orthodox among his readers, who might easily be overwhelmed by the specious arguments of their seductive teachers. 'A dumb ass possessed sounder prophetic vision than a religious official whose moral sense had been perverted by gain from wrongdoing' (Barnett).

NIV is loose in this verse. *Elengxis* ('rebuke', 'confutation') is nowhere else used in the New Testament, nor is *paranomia*, 'disobedience'. *Phthenxamenon* ('speaking') is a word used of important, portentous utterance; the oracular speech of the (justifiably) disobedient donkey is contrasted with the madness of the (culpably) disobedient prophet. Modern readers inevitably question a donkey that talks. This was simply not an issue in the first century; nobody would have been troubled by it. The Old Testament was not a problem to the early church. It was their datum point. In any case Peter and his readers would, if they followed rabbinic precedent, regard the literal meaning as of minimal importance. It was the significance of the ass's message, rather than the mechanics of its speaking, that mattered.

The reference to 'brute beasts' in verse 12 may have led Peter to bring in the story of Balaam, the greedy prophet. Like him they have wandered from the straight path and got lost. Like him they are consumed by avarice. And like him they will receive the wages of wickedness, that is to say, their just reward. Moreover 'Balaam's judgment was so swayed by his greed that he actually thought he could succeed in his plan of opposing God's will. Similarly, the false teachers, who deny the reality of God's judgment, foolishly imagine they can sin with impunity. But in Balaam's case even his donkey knew better' (Bauckham).

E. THE EMPTINESS OF THE FALSE TEACHERS (2:17–22)

17. After his excursus on Balaam, Peter returns to the attack. The seducers are described in two brilliant metaphors.

They are *springs without water*. This describes the unsatisfactory nature of the false teaching. You come to it as to an exciting new spring – and find it has no water to offer.[1] It is only the man in touch with Christ, the water of life (Jn. 4:13–14), who will find lasting satisfaction, and, indeed, will pour out of his inner being water that will satisfy the thirsty round about (Jn. 7:38). Heterodoxy is all very novel in the classroom; it is extremely unsatisfying in the parish.

They are also *mists driven by a storm*. Aristotle (*Meteor*.1.34b) tells us that the *homichlē* is the haze which heralds dry weather, but is so easily dispersed by a sharp gust of wind. This describes the instability of the false teachers and the ephemeral nature of their teachings. You have only to visit a second-hand theological bookshop, with its piles of unsaleable rubbish, once the latest thing in theological audacity, to see the force of this. As for the darkness reserved for the heretics, Calvin writes, 'In place of the momentary darkness which they now cast, there is prepared for them a much thicker and eternal one.' Surely he has understood the link between the errorists' crime and punishment, which has escaped most commentators, who complain that darkness is a very inappropriate doom for mists or springs!

The phraseology in this verse is poetic and grandiose. It is interesting to see how many Homeric and tragic words like *zophos* ('darkness'), *phthengomai* ('to utter'), *homichlai* ('mists') passed into common use in *koinē* Greek and, indeed, have reappeared in modern Greek. The rareness of *homichlai* in the New Testament and the reading of *nephelai* in the parallel passage, Jude 12, has induced the insertion of *nephelai* for *homichlai* here in some MSS – wrongly.

18. They mouth big, ponderous words (*hyperonka, swelling*, means 'unnaturally swollen', can also mean 'bombastic, haughty') in their discourses (this is the nuance of *phthen-*

---

[1] There may be an allusion to Pr. 10:11; 13:14; 14:27; Je. 2:13 here.

gomenoi); but they are words which amount to nothing of significance (*mataiotētos* is a descriptive genitive, *empty*). Ostentatious verbosity was their weapon to ensnare the unwary, and licentiousness was the bait on their hook, *i.e. by appealing to the lustful desires of human nature, they entice . . .'. For deleazō* ('ensnare', *entice*) see on verse 14. *Aselgeiais* is extremely difficult syntactically. Is it in apposition to 'the desires of the flesh'? Or is it an instrumental dative, 'by shameless immorality'? At all events 'grandiose sophistry is the hook, filthy lust is the bait' (Bigg).

No doubt these teachers maintained that the salvation of the immortal soul was all that mattered. Once that was secured through the knowledge (*gnōsis*) which they themselves could impart to disciples, then it mattered little what a man did with his body. They may have suggested that the deeply spiritual should express their religion sexually, as some second-century heretics did. Paul had to face similar false teaching about the nature of the body in 1 Corinthians 6, and he countered it by asserting that the body does matter a great deal; it is the temple where the Spirit of God is pleased to dwell; it will rise again; and it is the purchased possession of Christ to whom it belongs. Man is a unity. What he does with his body affects the whole personality. This consideration must always set boundaries to the Christian's exercise of his liberty. See on verse 19.

But whom were they corrupting? 'Those who are just shaking themselves free of pagan associates' is the most probable interpretation, but textual problems complicate the issue. Should we read *apophugontas*, 'those who have escaped', or *apopheugontas*, 'those who are escaping' or perhaps 'are trying to escape'? Probably the latter: the aorist participle may have crept in from verse 20. If we do accept the second reading, a present participle, here, it implies a smaller degree of Christian attainment.[1]

[1] Democracie Hemmerdinger-Iliadon, writing in the *Revue Biblique*, 1957, p.399, believes that he has found the original reading of this passage in a palimpsest of Ephraem Syrus, *tous tous logous apopheugontas tous eutheis kai tous en planē anastrephomenous*, 'those who run away from straight words and those who live in error'. The Harklean Syriac has much the same, 'those who with few words run away from those who live in error.' If this is indeed the right reading, it is fascinating that it should have been preserved in the Syrian Church, where for so long 2 Peter was not recognized as canonical, and above all in Ephraem Syrus, who was previously thought not to have been aware of 2 Peter's existence!

A further problem is this. Should we read *ontōs*, 'really and truly' (so the AV with *clean escaped*), or *oligōs*, which could mean either 'for a little time' (*i.e.* very recently) or 'to a small extent'? The two readings are almost indistinguishable in uncial MSS. *Oligōs* goes better with the present participle, 'only just escaping'; *ontōs* better if we accept the aorist participle, 'clean escaped'. In any case, it is clear that the gross sin of the false teachers was to corrupt relatively new Christians, the unstable souls of verse 14. Those at the end of the verse *who live in error* must be pagans, not, as is often suggested, the false teachers. For it is the latter who are doing the corrupting; they are not the society which the orthodox have recently left.

The Valentinians, according to Irenaeus, were adept at presenting the young believers with high-sounding talk which acted as a cover for the basest of obscenity. Nor has the tendency to dress up vice as virtue died in succeeding generations. In our own generation a bishop can publicly describe the (adulterous) liaison in *Lady Chatterley's Lover* 'as in a real sense an act of holy communion',[1] and a theological don can defend fornication (in certain circumstances) as a form of charity. 'This letter can therefore be of considerable advantage to our times' (Calvin).

19. The psychological insight of this verse is profound. The false teachers *promise . . . freedom* – the very thing they have not got! In their quest for self-expression, they fell into bondage to self. To men who had begun to taste the paradox of freedom from the *phthora*, the corruption of pre-Christian days, through voluntary bondage to Christ as Lord (*cf.* 2:1), the heretics proposed a new paradox, freedom from the rules of love imposed by their new Master – only to plunge them back into the bondage in which they themselves lived. No man can serve two masters; but all men must serve one. These men were not the last to set liberty against law. Yet their vaunted liberty turned into licence, and generated a new bondage. On the other hand glad bondage to the law of Christ, which was so disparaged by

[1] Clement of Alexandria particularly attacks heretics who call their fornication 'mystic communion': *'sunt autem, qui etiam pallicam venerem pronuntiant mysticam communionem; et sic ipsum nomen contumelia afficiunt' (Strom.* iii. 4). Truly *autres temps, autres moeurs!*

the false teachers, leads in fact to an emancipation more complete than the errorists could ever have imagined. Peter has already shown, in 1:3–4, that true liberty, true escape from the relentless grip of *phthora*, comes through knowing Jesus Christ. So here he shows that precept and love, charity and chastity, law and gospel are not combatants but correlatives. It is ever the way of licence to champion gospel over law, and of dead orthodoxy to champion precept over love. Healthy Christian living comes when God's commands are seen as the kerbstones on his highway of love, the hedge encompassing his garden of grace.

Notice the subtlety of the present participles in this verse. They keep on chattering about liberty when all the time they themselves have been (and still are) in the prison-house of lust. Romans 6:6 and John 8:34 are obvious parallels. Jesus told the Jews, who prided themselves on their liberty, that they were actually the slaves of their sinful selves. Barclay quotes Seneca's apophthegm, 'to be enslaved to oneself is the heaviest of all servitudes'.

20. It is sometimes held that Peter is referring in this verse to young, unstable believers; in which case, those who are said in verses 18 and 20 to 'have escaped the pollutions (*corruption*, NIV, is inaccurate) of the world' (AV) would be the same people. But it is better to assume that the false teachers continue to be the subjects in view, since the 'for' connects this to the previous verse, where the false teachers were called slaves of corruption. The subject of the whole paragraph is then the same, and moreover those overcome in verses 19 and 20 are also the same. There can be little doubt that the false teachers had once been orthodox Christians. *Miasmata*, 'pollutions', occurs only here in the New Testament, but is found in the LXX and in Greek tragedy; it also comes in the *Apocalypse of Peter*, 9, 'the pollution of adultery'. The *world* is society alienated from God (*cf.* its frequent use in this sense in 1 John). Their way of escape was by coming to know the (some MSS read 'our') Lord. See on 1:3. Now, however, they *are again entangled* (another fishing metaphor like *deleazō* in vv. 14, 18) by these very pollutions, and *overcome* by them. Instead of looking to a deepened knowledge of . . . Christ for liberation, these people continued to talk about knowledge, but it was merely head knowledge now, held with all the arrogance and exclusiveness of a sect. They continued to talk about liberty, but for all their high-flown phrases they knew nothing of it in practice. Like the men of Hebrews 10:26 they had apostasized.[1]

Peter is convinced that the last state of such men is worse than the first. A servant who wilfully disobeys his master is far more culpable than one who disobeys through ignorance. There appears to be an allusion here to the words of Jesus in Luke 12:47f. But there is no less clear an allusion to the last state of the man who got rid of one unclean spirit only to be invaded by seven others (Mt. 12:45; Lk. 11:26). Indeed, it is almost a straight quotation. The only difference is illuminating. Jesus says 'The final condition of that man is worse than the first', and prophesies 'That is how it will be with this wicked generation'. Peter says, in effect, that Jesus' prophecy has come true: the last state of the false teachers has turned out to be worse than the first. This would be a most natural adaptation of Jesus' words if Peter is indeed the author of this Epistle; in a forger it would be a most sophisticated touch.

21. Peter pursues the theme that ignorance of *the way of righteousness* is preferable to apostasy from it. 'The Way' was, of course, the primitive name for Christianity, and Peter delights to use it and adapt it (*cf.* 'the way of truth', 2:2; 'the straight way', 2:15). 'The way of righteousness'[2] here may also be an echo of the words of Jesus in Matthew 21:32, where the same phrase is found; and it is taken up twice in the *Apocalypse of Peter*. While making 'knowledge' their motto (the root comes three times in these two verses) the heretics sinned against knowledge. To call darkness light, to call bondage liberty, is unforgivable sin, unforgivable not because God is unwilling to forgive, but because the man who persists in such self-delusion refuses to accept the forgiveness which God patiently proffers to rebels.

---

[1] On the possibility of apostasy, see my *The Meaning of Salvation*, 1965, chapter xi.
[2] This again takes us back to Proverbs (8:20; 12:28, *etc.*).

The text is in some confusion, bearing witness to three different words for 'turn back', and two (*ek* and *apo*) for 'from'. Some MSS also add 'away backwards' after 'turn'. This all makes little difference to the sense, though *ek* ('out of') implies, as *apo* ('away from') need not, that they were once within the realm of *the sacred commandment that was passed on to them* (*i.e.* Christians). However, this is small comfort to those who would dogmatically deny the possibility of a Christian apostatizing. One must still face the fact that these men are said to have known (and knowledge means personal acquaintance in Peter's usage, see 1:2; 2:20; 3:18) the way of righteousness and to have escaped, once upon a time, from the world's defilements. The parallels with 1 Corinthians 10:1–12; Hebrews 3:12–18; 6:6; 10:26, 38f.; Jude 4–6, are clear and unmistakable. Apostasy would seem to be a real and awful possibility.

It is, I think, a fair inference from the text that the first stage in their apostasy was the rejection of the category of law. Such enlightened Christians as themselves, full of a knowledge which emancipated them from the claims of morality, had no need for *the sacred commandment*. Were they the forerunners of those who, in later times, set love against law? But law is God's love-gift. *The sacred commandment* is *passed on* to man for his good by God, as the book of Deuteronomy continually stresses, 'I command you this day for your good.' Rejection of God's law is the first step to the rejection of God, for God is a moral being; he is *holy*, and so must the man be who has dealings with him (see 1 Pet. 1:15).

The precise language here is significant. By *entolē* in the singular (unusual, but paralleled in 3:2; 1 Tim. 6:14; 1 Jn. 3:23) Peter shows that it is a place for law, not the detailed prescriptions of law, that he is fighting for. His idea of law appears to be that of the moral law which Jesus underlined in his Sermon on the Mount. By *passed on* Peter means the oral tradition of primitive Christian teaching, derived from the old Jewish *halakah*, which has been the subject of much careful study in recent years.[1] There is some parallel to this phrase in Jude 3, where he speaks

---

[1] See Essays 1 and 11 in E. G. Selwyn's *The First Epistle of St. Peter* (1946), Carrington's *Primitive Christian Catechism* (1940) and O. Cullmann's essay 'The Tradition' in his book, *The Early Church* (1956).

of 'the faith once for all entrusted to the saints', though Peter
here sees Christianity more in terms of *the sacred commandment*,
whereas Jude sees it in terms of 'the faith'. Ethics and doctrine
are both crucial for new Christians.

22. Peter concludes this chapter of stirring denunciation and
strong invective with two proverbs which aptly describe the
situation of the false teachers. Their punishment is that they will
be given over to the lot they have chosen. The awfulness and
irrevocability of hell lies just here; God underwrites a man's
deliberate choice. In the end we all go 'to our own place'. The
dog which has got rid of the corruption inside it through vomit-
ing it up cannot leave well alone; it goes sniffing round the
vomit again. The pig that has got rid of the corruption outside it
by means of a scrubbing cannot resist rolling in the mud. 'The
gospel is a medicine that purges us as a wholesome emetic, but
there are many dogs who swallow again what they have
brought up, to their own ruin. Likewise the gospel is a basin
which cleanses us from all our dirt and stains, but there are
many pigs who, immediately after they have washed, roll back
again into the mud. Thus the godly are warned to beware of
both dangers if they do not want to be included in the ranks of
dogs and pigs' (Calvin).

These two similes are particularly apt, in line with the animal
theme which has been applied by Peter to the false teachers in
this chapter (vv. 12,16). But Peter also calls these expressions
proverbial. He probably took them from some popular collection. The first appears to be biblical[1] (Pr. 26:11), the second not.
It does, however, readily fit into verse, and reappears in the
Syrian story of *Ahikar*, which was certainly in existence by the
second century BC, and so may well have been known to our
author. Incidentally, in the *Ahikar* story, it follows a proverb
about a dog. 'My son, thou hast been to me like the swine that
had been to the baths, and when it saw a muddy ditch, went
down and washed in it, and cried to its companions, "Come and

---

[1]It is also quoted in *The Gospel of Truth* 33.15, 16, and this may be dependent on 2 Peter,
since the LXX translation is very different.

bathe".'[1] *Borboros, mud,* a rare poetic word, is otherwise found in the Bible only in the LXX of Jeremiah 45:6, where it describes the filth of Jeremiah's prison. But it is used in the *Apocalypse of Peter* viii for the filth of hell, and is also found in the *Acts of Thomas* lv. *Exerama, vomit,* is also a New Testament *hapax legomenon* (the word in Proverbs is *emeton*), as is *kulismos, wallowing* (not *kulisma,* as in the majority of inferior MSS). Significantly, dogs and pigs are united by Jesus, in Matthew 7:6, as pictures of mankind out of touch with God. Both were unclean animals to the Jew.

Why has Peter expended so much powder and shot on the false teachers in this chapter? Because he is primarily a pastor. He is concerned to feed his Master's sheep (*cf.* Jn. 21:15–17, 1 Pet. 5:1ff.), and he is furious to find them being poisoned by lust masquerading as religion. It is only by paying very cursory attention to the contents of this passage that Käsemann can say, 'The attack on the heretics has taken on a stiff and stereotyped character, because the writer is no longer conducting the campaign on the basis of his own experience.' It does our generation little credit that such passion for truth and holiness strikes an alien note in our minds. Peter's plain speaking in this chapter has a very practical purpose, just as Jesus' warnings had: 'What I say to you I say to everyone: "watch"!' We would be mistaken to assume, 'It could never happen to us.' Both Scripture and experience assure us that it could. 'So, if you think you are standing firm, be careful that you don't fall' (1 Cor. 10:12). Covetousness, sophistical arguments, pride in knowledge, gluttony, drunkenness, lust, arrogance against authority of all kinds, and, most of all, the danger of denying the lordship of the Redeemer – are these not all the paramount temptations of money-mad, sex-mad, materialistic, anti-authoritarian, twentieth-century man?

---

[1]*Ahikar* viii. 18. The Arabic recension is somewhat closer to 2 Peter: it reads, 'went into the hot baths with people of quality, and when it came out of the hot bath it saw a filthy hole and went down and wallowed in it' (viii. 15).

CHAPTER THREE

A. THE PURPOSE OF THE LETTER REITERATED (3:1–2)

1. In this chapter Peter returns from harrying the heretics to encourage the faithful. He calls them *dear friends* as he summons them to *recall*. Jude also marks his switch from attack to encouragement by calling his readers 'dear friends' (v. 17). The title comes three times in this last chapter of 2 Peter in significant contexts: 'Dear friends, recall' (v. 2); 'Dear friends . . . make every effort . . .' (v. 14); 'Dear friends, be on your guard' (v. 17).

The vehemence of his attack in the last chapter, and the repetition of his reminders here, alike spring from a pastoral heart of love towards his flock. On the theme of reminding, see on 1:12–13. Moffatt aptly cites Dr Johnson, 'It is not sufficiently considered that men more frequently require to be reminded than informed.' *Wholesome thinking* translates *eilikrinē dianoian*, a phrase used by Plato to mean 'pure reason', uncontaminated by the seductive influence of the senses. Did Peter take over what may well have become a catchword, and encourage his readers by telling them that he believed that their minds were uncontaminated by the lust and heresy all around them? Certainly the affection he showers on them, the compliment he pays them and the confidence he expresses in them are marks of the wise and shrewd Christian pastor at work among his flock.

This second letter most naturally suggests that its predecessor was 1 Peter. Certainly this would be in the author's mind if 2 Peter is pseudonymous; it would be the plainest mark of the forger seeking to father his work on the apostle. However, it can hardly be said that 1 Peter is primarily a letter of reminder, still less a dissuasive against heresy, which seems to be implied in these two verses. Furthermore, while the author of 1 Peter clearly had no close personal link with the far-flung circle of his readers in five different provinces of the Empire, our present writer knows his readers well. It is probably best, then, with Zahn and Spitta, to suppose that if this letter is indeed Petrine, it refers not to 1 Peter but to a previous letter of his to the same readers. This must have suffered the fate of the majority of the apostolic correspondence and been lost to posterity.[1]

Robinson thinks Jude wrote both the Epistle of Jude and (as Peter's amanuensis) 2 Peter, so the reference here alludes to that Epistle (Jude 3). Bauckham thinks 1 Peter is meant, and that Peter's follower, who wrote 2 Peter, needs to re-establish that he is writing in Peter's name after the polemics of chapter 2.

2. The continuous procession of genitives which marks this verse in Greek is extremely harsh. It appears to mean 'the commandment of the Lord and Saviour through your apostles' and the construction seems to be a double possessive genitive: the command is the apostles', and they are Christ's. Bigg may be right in taking the final phrase as an afterthought, 'the commandment of your apostles, or rather, I should say, of the Lord'. At all events, the meaning is clear enough, and stresses the link between the prophets who foreshadowed Christian truth, Christ who exemplified it, and the apostles who gave an authoritative interpretation of it.[2] God's self-disclosure was to be seen in the written word of God through the prophetic scriptures, and the spoken message through the apostolic proclamation (see Eph. 2:20; 3:5). The source of their authority was the Spirit who inspired both (Eph. 3:5; 1 Pet. 1:10–12; 2 Pet. 1:16–21). Peter has already in 1:16 stated that under the influence of this same Spirit of God both apostles and prophets bear testimony to the 'power and coming of our Lord Jesus Christ'. It is clear that the heretics have questioned both these attributes. In chapter 2 they are taken to task for denying the authority of the Lord who bought them, and for despising his power. In chapter 3 they will be reproved for doubting the reality of his parousia.

What, then, was the *command*, in which Old Testament

---

[1]*Cf.* 1 Cor. 5:9, where Paul refers to a letter of his which almost certainly does not survive. See Introduction, p.39ff.

[2]A particularly illuminating example of the subapostolic attitude to the place of the apostles and prophets in the unity of scriptural revelation is Polycarp's *Ep.* vi: 'Let us so serve Jesus with all reverence and fear, as He Himself gave commandment and the apostles who preached the gospel to us, and the prophets who proclaimed beforehand the coming of the Lord.' Similar passages setting the prophets and apostles side by side as an authority are common: see 2 *Clem.* 14.2, Ignatius *Philad.* 5 and 9.

prophets, New Testament apostles and the Lord himself concur? There can be no doubt that it is to live holy lives in the light of the Saviour's return at the end of history. Peter wishes to remind his readers of the teaching about the parousia and the moral requirements of the gospel. Note that Peter again uses the full title *Lord and Saviour*, probably because he is about to emphasize the future element in salvation which the scoffers ridicule. Jesus is not only Saviour from the past (1:1–4), and in the present (2:20), but for the future as well. To deny the second coming of Jesus is to deny Jesus as Saviour.

The use of *holy* with *prophets* is widely taken as a mark of inauthenticity. By the time this forger wrote, it is said, the prophets have become stylized as holy. However, 'holy prophets' is found in the *Benedictus*, which is universally agreed to be a very early Christian hymn (Lk. 1:70), and, so some scholars believe, may be adapted from a song of Maccabaean times. In any case the phrase has reputable antecedents, and need occasion no surprise here. Prophets were traditionally holy men in Israel; they were in a special sense set apart for God and in touch with him. Thus the prophets of 1:19, 21 are appropriately called 'holy' in many manuscripts. If the whole people of God can be called *hoi hagioi* ('the holy ones' or 'the saints') in both Old and New Testaments, it is hard to see why the epithet should be denied to the prophets and apostles.

Your apostles does not merely mean 'your missionaries', the folk who evangelized you. When the New Testament writers mean merely 'church emissary' by *apostolos*, they say so, or the context makes it plain (Phil. 2:25). Peter is referring here to the 'apostles of Jesus Christ'. It is they and they alone who are put on a level with the Old Testament prophets. There is no need to regard the phrase 'your apostles' as proof of a forger. Far from it. Such a view of the function of the apostolate is strictly in line with the primitive conception of the ministry, as men primarily called to serve, not to dominate (*cf.* 1 Cor. 3:21ff.).[1] This concept speedily disappeared (it is almost gone by the time of Ignatius in the first years of the second century), and this in itself makes a late date for this Epistle unlikely. The phrase is particularly

[1]See chapter 2 of my *Freed to Serve*, 1983.

apposite here. ' "Your apostles" are the men you ought to trust; do not listen to the false teachers with whom you have neither part nor lot' (Bigg). The most natural meaning of *your apostles* is those apostles who preached the gospel to you and founded the churches in your area. This means, of course, that 2 Peter was not a general letter, but sent to specific churches. Clement in *1 Clement* xliv:1 speaks of 'our apostles' when he means those who founded the Roman Church. Instead of cleverly devised myths, the apostles pass on the truth of God (1:16).

B. THE TAUNTS OF THOSE WHO SCOFF AT THE SECOND COMING (3:3–4)

3. *First of all, you must understand.* Peter has used this phrase in connection with prophecy (1:20); now he repeats it in the context of an apostolic warning. It was important for them to know that the activities of the mockers were not unexpected by the apostles. Acts 20:29–31 gives one such example of apostolic warning; 1 Timothy 4:1ff. another. The grammar seems loose here, but probably the nominative participle ('knowing') agrees with the *dear friends* of verse 1. Alternatively the participle may stand for an imperative (so NEB, 'note this first').

A skilful contrast is implied in verses 2–4 between the readers who remember the predictions of the prophets and the command to live a holy life, and the scoffers who reject the commandment by indulging their own lusts, and flout the predictions of the prophets by mocking the parousia hope.

The *scoffers* were, of course, already present, but the apostles had given prior warning of their arrival (hence the use of the future tense) *in the last days*. This is a fascinating description of the Christian era, and preserves the tension between what is already realized in Christ and what lies ahead. His coming to the world was the decisive event in human history. It was 'when the time had fully come' (Gal. 4:4), 'these last days' (Heb. 1:2). With the advent of Jesus the last chapter of human history had opened, though it was not yet completed. In between the two advents stretches the last time, the time of grace, the time, too, of opposition. For the prediction of false teachers in the last days, see Matthew 24:3–5, 11, 23–26; 2 Timothy 3:1ff.; James 5:3; Jude 18. Such false teaching and apostasy were seen as part of the necessary birth-pangs before the messianic age in all its fullness was born.[1]

The false teachers are described by a pleonastic Hebraism, 'scoffers . . . with scoffing' (RSV; Jude 18 omits the 'with scoffing'). These men mock at the parousia and at the same time 'live self-indulgent lives' (NEB). Cynicism and self-indulgence regularly go together. The renewed emphasis on the lust of those he is opposing makes it almost certain that Peter has the same men in mind here as in chapter 2; they are not two different sets of opponents. These men do not mock merely because the second coming has delayed; they laugh at the very idea. If we are right in seeing something of a proto-Gnostic flavour in this heresy, this particular characteristic would fit well with what we have already seen in chapter 2. Intellectual arrogance, social snobbery, contempt for the physical and the sensuality that so often accompanies such an attitude – all this would make them as opposed to the notion of judgment, inherent in the parousia, as their counterparts at Corinth were to the idea of bodily resurrection. Anthropocentric hedonism always mocks at the idea of ultimate standards and a final division between saved and lost. For men who live in the world of the relative, the claim that the relative will be ended by the absolute is nothing short of ludicrous. For men who nourish a belief in human self-determination and perfectibility, the very idea that we are accountable and dependent is a bitter pill to swallow. No wonder they mocked! For an Old Testament example of a similar situation and message see Isaiah 28:14–22.

4. They scoff at Christ's return because years have passed and it has not happened – *everything goes on as it has since the beginning of creation.* So they maintain that God's promise is unreliable, and that God's universe is a stable, unchanging system where events like the parousia just do not happen. Peter answers their objections in reverse order. This attitude to the

---

[1] As Fornberg acutely observes, there is an 'ironic ring to the passage. The adversaries who denied the parousia were themselves a proof of its imminence.'

second coming does not help us to date the letter precisely, but for what it is worth it supports an early rather than a late date. By the middle of the second century, to which many wish to assign the Epistle, this complaint must surely have been somewhat overdue! We know from 1 Thessalonians 4 and 1 Corinthians 15 that the issue was an acute one in the fifties of the first century. Mayor points out that there are signs of impatience at the delay in New Testament documents of roughly this period, and cites Luke 12:45; Hebrews 10:36f.; James 5:7f. Doubt must have arisen as the first generation began to die off, in view of Jesus' words in such passages as Matthew 10:23; 16:28; 24:34. That such complaints as this were common enough is made clear by a quotation from what 1 *Clement* xxiii calls 'Scripture' (*graphē*) and 2 *Clement* xi 'the prophetic word'. The quotation runs as follows. 'Wretched are the double-minded who doubt in their soul and say, "These things we heard in the days of our fathers (*paterōn*) also; and, behold, we have grown old and none of them has befallen us" ' (or, as the 2 *Clement* version concludes, 'and we, though expecting them day after day, have seen none of them'). Evidently they both quote some sort of early Christian prophecy or apocalypse which has not survived, but which was created in order to deal with this pressing problem of the delay of the parousia. M. R. James cites a rabbinic comment on Psalm 89:50, 'They have scoffed at Messiah's coming' and 'He delays so long that they say "He will never come" '. This shows us that the topic was alive in Jewish as well as Christian circles.

The scoffers supported their scepticism that God would break decisively into history at the return of Christ, by emphasizing the immutability of the world. Had they been alive today, they would have talked about the chain of cause and effect in a closed universe governed by natural laws, where miracles, almost by definition, cannot happen. 'The laws of nature', one can almost hear them saying, 'disprove your *deus ex machina* doctrine of divine intervention to wind up the course of history.' Their mistake was to forget that the laws of nature are God's laws; their predictability springs from his faithfulness.

Our fathers is taken by many to mean 'the first Christian generation'; and among these, some see it as a gross anachron-

ism, the slipping of the forger's mask. Others point out, however, and justly, that the death of such 'fathers' as Stephen,
James the son of Zebedee, James the Just and other Christian
leaders (*cf.* Heb. 13:7) would make excellent ground for such a
taunt by the mid-sixties. This meaning of 'fathers' is possible
here, and could well be the right one in the passages in *1* and
2 Clement cited above. However, since every other reference to
'the fathers' in the New Testament (*cf.* Acts 3:13; Rom. 9:5; Heb.
1:1, *etc.*) means 'the Old Testament fathers', such I take to be the
probable meaning here. For it is not said that things continue as
they have done since the coming of Christ, but since *the beginning of the creation*. The mockers were twisting the Old Testament Scriptures; it is, appropriately, out of the Old Testament
that Peter confounds them.

Notice the lovely word for death, so characteristic of the
post-resurrection perspective, and so remarkable in a world that
as a whole was hagridden with the fear of death. The fathers
'fell asleep' (Gk). That is how Jesus had talked of death – the
suspended animation of sleep (Mk. 5:39; Jn. 11:11). So when
Stephen died, he is said to have fallen asleep (Acts 7:60). When
Thessalonians died, Paul describes them as being 'asleep in
Jesus', and 'with Jesus' (1 Thes. 4:13–14). This confidence in the
face of death arose solely from the victory that Jesus had won
over the last Enemy. Even the word cemetery (derived, as it is,
from this Greek word *ekoimēthēisan* 'to sleep') should remind us
that death's fangs have been drawn, through the triumph of the
risen Christ.

C. PETER ARGUES FROM HISTORY (3:5–7)

5. Peter takes their last argument first. Their premise (that
this is a stable, unchanging world) is false; hence their conclusion (that it will remain so, and there will be no parousia) is
false also. They wilfully neglected the flood, when God *did*
intervene in judgment. The lesson taught by the flood was that
this is a moral universe, that sin will not for ever go unpunished;
and Jesus himself used the flood to point this moral (Mt. 24:37–
39). But these men chose to neglect it. They were determined to

lose sight of the fact that there were heavens in existence long ago, and an earth which was created by the divine fiat out of water, and sustained by water. Such seems to be the meaning; but it is a difficult verse. Peter refers, of course, to the watery chaos (Gn. 1:2–6) out of which the world was formed at God's repeated word, 'Let there be . . .'. It was from water that the earth emerged; it was *with* (*i.e.* by means of) *water* (rain, *etc.*) that life on earth was sustained; and yet this same water engulfed it, when God's word of judgment went forth at the flood. Many commentators take *by God's word* to refer both to the divine fiat, the *debar Yahweh*, which was active in creation, and also to the Eternal Word through whom creation was accomplished (Jn. 1:3; Heb. 1:2). The same ambiguity can be found in Hebrews 11:3. I doubt whether this double meaning was intended in this context, thought it was undoubtedly a commonplace in Jewish Wisdom literature (Pr. 8:23–31). Peter means that the world exists only because God commanded that it should (see Gn. 1:3–30; Ps. 33:6; 148:5; *Wisdom* ix:1).

The emphasis in this verse on God's fiat in creation is important to Peter in arguing against the false teachers who apparently held the self-sufficiency and immutability of the natural order. On the contrary, he insists, the course of history is governed by the God who is both Creator and Judge of his world. 'The words are a protest against the old Epicurean view of a concourse of atoms, and its modern counterpart, the theory of a perpetual (*i.e.* unbroken) evolution' (Plumptre).

6. The connecting particle *di' hōn* in the Greek is full of ambiguity. More precisely it means 'and through these things'. The plural could mean water and water (mentioned twice in the previous verse); or water and God's word; or the two regions where the waters were sometimes thought to be stored (*cf.* Gn. 7:11) or the heavens (it was by means of these that the old world was deluged: so M. R. James). J. B. Mayor's way out is to read with a single MS *di' hōn*, 'because of which'; 'which' would then refer to its antecedent, the word of God. The second alternative above is preferable. It stresses, over against these upholders of the independence of nature, the truth that 'nature is not enough to support and maintain the world, but rather it contains the material for its own ruin whenever it may so please God' (Calvin). At God's decree, the very element from which this earth had its origin, by which it was maintained, was used to destory it.

There is thus a neat parallelism in these three verses. By his word and by means of water God created the world (v. 5); by his word and by means of water, he destroyed it (v. 6); by his word and by means of time he will destroy it in future judgment (v. 7).

Commentators have made heavy weather of the statement that *the world of that time was . . . destroyed*. They have wondered whether this meant the heavens as well, and whether there is any reference here to the collapse of the heavens in *1 Enoch* lxxxiii. 3. But *kosmos* means primarily 'order' as opposed to primordial chaos, and Peter may mean no more than that the orderliness, the continuity of nature, was broken up by the flood. Perhaps *kosmos* simply means 'the world of men', as it does in an identical context in 2:5. Peter would then mean that human life perished. There is nothing here to suggest that the whole earth was destroyed by the flood, let alone the heavens as well.

In the first century AD a great deal was made of the flood as a warning to the wicked, and as a sign of the breaking in of the new age.[1] It is several times so used by Jesus, and, of course, it is stressed in 1 Peter 3:9 – yet another link between the two Epistles.

7. Once again there are two different ways of taking this verse. With AV and RSV we may take the *de* as adversative, and translate *but*. The present heavens and earth would then be contrasted with the previous ones. It is just conceivable that our author believed that the whole universe had been renewed since the flood, particularly if this Epistle is a pseudepigraphic work influenced by stoic belief in the periodic destruction and rebirth of the world. But it is preferable to follow NEB and to take the *de* as a connecting particle and translate 'and'. In this case, the contrast will not be with some antediluvian heavens and earth, but with the new heaven and earth to which Peter looks forward

---

[1] See Philo, *Vit. Mos.* ii. 12; *Sib. Orac.* vii. 11; 1 *Clem.* ix. 4.

(3:12–13) after the parousia. NIV inexcusably omits the *de* altogether.

The main point in this verse should not be obscured by problems over the details. It is that 'the God who created the beginning of all things has power to end them' (*Keryg. Petr.* in Clem. Alex. *Strom.* 6.5.39). 1 *Clement* (xxvii.4) asserts robustly 'By a word of his majesty he created all things, and by a word he can destroy them'. Bauckham argues quite convincingly for a Jewish apocalyptic source underlying 2 Peter and these two allusions in *1 Clement* and *Kerygma Petrou*, probably the same source that can be inferred from verse 4 together with *1 Clement* xxiii.3 and *2 Clement* xi.2.

Does Peter teach that the whole world will be destroyed by fire? There is no *a priori* reason why he should not. Some Jews, at least, believed in a dual cataclysm of the world, by water and by fire, and attributed this idea to Adam![1] It had a respectable ancestry in the Graeco-Roman world, though the stoic conception, which is usually quoted,[2] is not strictly parallel, for it anticipates the alternate destruction and renovation of the world through the cataclysms of fire and water, not, as Peter does, the consummation of all things. Moreover, the stoic programme was pantheistic, Peter's monotheistic; the Stoics looked for a fresh world to emerge from the conflagration, but a world of the same quality as the last, while the Christian hope was for a transformed world, the necessary complement to their belief in the resurrection of the body and the redemption of the created order.

It seems, then, that 2 Peter owes little if anything to Stoicism here, as Origen perceived in his *Contra Celsum* iv:11ff. The concept of fiery judgment is to be found throughout the Old Testament. God himself is spoken of as a consuming fire (Dt. 4:24; *cf.* Mal. 4:1), who will in the last day consume what is wicked and refine what is good.

The classical Old Testament paradigm for this is, of course, Sodom and Gomorrah which were burnt to ashes in the judgment of God (2:6), and the idea becomes common in the Old

---

[1]Josephus, *Antiq.* i. 2. 3.
[2]Seneca, *Nat. Quaest.* iii. 29; Diog. Laert. vii. 134; Plutarch, *Moral.* 1077D.

Testament (*e.g.* Dt. 32:22; Ps. 97:3; Is. 30:30; 66:15f.; Ezk. 38:22; Am. 7:4; Mal. 4:1). It was one of the main expectations in intertestamental times (*e.g.* IQH 3:19–36, *Sib. Orac.* 3:54–87; 4:173–81, Josephus *Ant.* 1:70, *Adam and Eve* 49:3) and became a commonplace in subapostolic times (Hermas *Vis.* 4:3; Justin *1 Apol.* 20:1, 2, 4 and 60:8, *2 Clem.* 16:3, Theophilus *Ad Autol.* 2:38). We do not need to look to Iranian or neoplatonic parallels when there is this unbroken line of biblical expectation. If Peter was aware of the pagan parallels he is not likely to have been very concerned with them. He believed that the world was 'reserved for fire' *by the word of God*, *i.e.* by the biblical revelation. God had spoken. Deuteronomy 32:22 was basic for this conviction, and was cited by Justin in his discussion of the destruction of the world by fire (*1 Apol.* 60:8). Other key verses were Isaiah 34:4 (LXX, to which Peter alludes in 3:10) Malachi 4:1 (cited in *2 Clem.* 16:3) and Isaiah 66:15f., Zephaniah 1:18.

The whole idea of cosmic conflagration belongs to apocalyptic imagery, and that is a sphere where literalism is always dangerous: Origen, for instance, was at pains to deny that literal fire is intended. Judgment by fire is one of the great Old Testament pictures of the Day of Yahweh;[1] the same holds good of intertestamental literature[2] and the New Testament.[3] It means purification and the destruction of evil when God comes to judge his world. And so here, while we may not exclude the possibility that Peter is envisaging the fiery destruction of the whole universe (by no means incredible to a generation which lives after Hiroshima), all that he actually says is that the heavens and earth are kept in store for fire in anticipation of the judgment of ungodly men.

But whether Peter intends to speak of the fiery transformation of the whole universe or of the impending judgment of sinful men, the theology is distinctively Christian, and is not to be confused with Stoicism, for which it could superficially be mistaken. Justin pointed out the contrast, 'Whereas they think God Himself shall be resolved into fire . . . we understand that God, the Creator of all things, is superior to the

[1] Ps. 1:3; Is. 13:9–13; 29:6; 30:30; 64:1–2; 66:15–16; Dn. 7:9–11; Na. 1:5–6.
[2] *E.g.* 1 QH iii. 19–36; *Sib. Orac.* iii. 71–87; *Enoch* x. 3.
[3] *E.g.* Mt. 3:11; 1 Cor. 3:13; 2 Thes. 1:8; Heb. 12:29; 1 Pet. 1:7 and Rev. *passim*.

things that are to be changed.'[1]

By the same word (reading *tō autō*, not *tō autou*, 'his word'). The Old Testament, which spoke of a flood in the past, speaks often of a fiery crisis in the future. But this, too, *they deliberately forget* (v. 5). The parallel between flood and fire is emphasized by the use of the same root in each case for *destroyed* (v. 6) and *destruction* (v. 7). Plumptre aptly quotes Mclito of Sardis, who wrote towards the end of the second century AD, 'There was a flood of water . . . There will be a flood of fire, and the earth will be burnt up together with its mountains . . . and the just will be delivered from its fury as their fellows in the Ark were saved from the waters of the Deluge.' It is interesting to find in the Qumran literature much the same view.[2]

This passage poses many hermeneutical problems for modern people. We find difficulty in the creation of the world from water, the flood, and the possible destruction of the world in a fiery conflagration. But the imagery is as relevant and powerful today as it was then. Mankind cannot presume on the stability of the world. We cannot take for granted that our environment will continue to make possible human life. The forces of nature retain their primeval destructive power: nuclear weaponry makes the literal fulfilment of Peter's apocalyptic picture of cosmic conflagration not only possible but the daily background of our lives. And Peter's assurance that these things are not governed by rationalistic presumption or chance, but by divine control is the ultimate justification for retaining hope in the midst of a crazy world. God is in control. Final doom is no more inevitable for our world than it was for Nineveh, if, like the men of Nineveh, we humble ourselves and repent.

D. PETER ARGUES FROM SCRIPTURE (3:8)

Peter now turns his attention to the faithful. Although the heretics may remain wilfully ignorant, at least let his beloved readers not miss the important truth that time is not the same to God as it is to man. In providing them with ammunition to meet

[1] *1 Apol.* i. 20.   [2] 1 QH iii. 28 ff.

the scoffers' scorn at the parousia's delay, the writer emphasizes first the relativity of time, and secondly the loving forbearance of God.

In *a day is like a thousand years* he quotes Psalm 90:4, 'a thousand years in your sight are like a day that has just gone by, or like a watch in the night'. What man regards as a long time is like a mere day in God's reckoning of time. Peter has been accused of 'selling the pass' and getting out of the difficult doctrine of the parousia by maintaining the relativity of time. On the contrary he stands within a Jewish exegesis of Psalm 90:4 which is apparent, *e.g.*, in 2 *Baruch* 48. 12–13, 'with thee the hours are as the ages, and the days are as the generations.' He is asserting God's sovereignty over time. The delay in the parousia may seem long to us: in God's eternal perspective it may be short. Peter is urging his readers 'when the coming of Christ is talked about, to raise their eyes upwards, for by so doing they will not subject the time appointed by God to their own ridiculous wishes' (Calvin). God sees time with a *perspective* we lack; even the delay of a thousand years may well seem like a day against the back-cloth of eternity. Furthermore, God sees time with an *intensity* we lack; one day with the Lord is like a thousand years. 'On this account men ought constantly to be on the alert, for the end may come at any time' (Reicke). Time is God's gift, and he has bidden us to watch, pray and work.

It is interesting that, whereas the psalmist emphasizes only the insignificance of time in comparison with God's ways, Peter also stresses the significance of time, and its value to the God who has, through the incarnation, for ever immersed himself in human history. And whereas Psalm 90 contrasts the eternity of God with the brevity of human life, 2 Peter contrasts the eternity of God with the impatience of human speculations. God is *patiens quia aeternus* (Augustine).

The delay of the Day of Yahweh was a problem the prophets had to face (Hab. 2:3) and one which concerned the men of Qumran as well (1 Qp Hab. vii:6–14), both of which assert that, despite the delay, the Day will come. Peter also makes this point, after asserting that the delay only seems long because of our time perspective, and that it provides further opportunities for men to repent and be saved.

'Faith', writes Barnett, 'orients man to eternity, whereas scoffers remain children of time.' God knows the end from the beginning; all is present with him, including 'the imminent end of all things' (1 Pet. 4:7). There may be a further allusion to the words of Jesus recorded in John 21:18–23 (see on 1:14). Peter had been warned that he would not live to see the parousia; accordingly, he displays no interest in any signs preceding it. One wonders if a pseudepigrapher would have been so reticent.

This verse, of course, had a great influence on second-century chiliasm, the view that there would be a thousand years of rule by the saints in an earthly Jerusalem when the Day of the Lord dawned at the parousia. It appears to be cited along with Revelation 20:4–5 in Justin's *Dialogue* lxxxi, where Justin, an enthusiastic chiliast, claims 'We have perceived that the expression "The day of the Lord is as a thousand years" is connected with this subject', and is certainly alluded to in Barnabas (*Ep.* xv.4) and Irenaeus (*A.H.* v. 23.2 and v. 28.3). If this Epistle had been written in the second century, when this doctrine was so widespread that it almost became a touchstone of Christian orthodoxy, is it likely that the author could have refrained from making any allusion to it whatever when quoting the very verse which gave it birth? The apostles respected Jesus' command not to speculate about the time of the end, but that reserve did not persist into the second century. This verse was taken by Barnabas and Irenaeus to support the belief that the world would last for as many thousand years as there were days in creation, since a day equalled a thousand years! The intertestamental books *Jubilees* (iv.30) and 2 *Enoch* (xxxiii) take a similar line.[1] Once again one is struck by the reserve of our author. He is guided by the Old Testament and its corollaries, and has no truck with speculative time-charts.

---

[1] D. S. Russell (*Method and Message of Jewish Apocalyptic*, 1964, p.212) points out how difficult it was for writers of this period to express a supratemporal idea like eternity. They oscillated between such statements as *Jubilees* iv. 30, 'One thousand years are as one day in the testimony of the heavens' and the *Apocalypse of Abraham* xxviii, 'One hour of the Age, the same is a hundred years', and *Enoch* xci. 17, where eternity is described as 'many weeks without number for ever'. Eternity, in either case, is not other than time. It is the totality of time.

E. PETER ARGUES FROM THE CHARACTER OF GOD (3:9)

Peter's third refutation of the scoffers is drawn from the nature of God and has many antecedents in Jewish apocalyptic thought. It is not slowness but patience that delays the consummation of all history, and holds open the door to repentant sinners, even repentant scoffers. Not impotence but mercy is the reason for God's delay. God has always been 'slow to anger' (Ex. 34:6). 1 Peter 3:20 speaks of the patience of God in relation to the flood; here it is in relation to the judgment – yet another slight indication for common authorship. God does not wish any man to perish: he wants all men to be saved (1 Tim. 2:4). He is ready to show his mercy upon all (Rom. 11:32). He has no pleasure in the death of the wicked – but rather, he waits for the wicked to turn from his ways, and live (Ezk. 18:23).

There was a lot of discussion in late Judaism of the problem of eschatological delay, as Strobel has exhaustively demonstrated. The *locus classicus* was Habakkuk 2:3, to which Peter probably alludes here. Delay does not mean non-fulfilment. The Lord is sovereign over time, and defers it for good reason. The forbearance of God, the opportunity to repent and the certainty of the day of the Lord were all hot issues in Judaism at this time (see Bauckham's *Commentary* p. 306–314). Indeed they continued to be. In AD 260 Rabbi Samuel b. Nahmani said 'Blasted be the bones of those who calculate the end. For, they say, since the predetermined time has arrived, and yet he has not come, he will never come.' This is a position which the good rabbi set out to demolish!

Whereas some, like Barclay, see a hint of universalism here (how can he in view of v. 7?) and others, like Calvin, posit a 'secret decree of God by which the wicked are doomed to their own ruin', the plain meaning is that, although God wants all men to be saved, and although he has made provision for all to be accepted, some will exercise their God-given free will to exclude God. And this he cannot prevent unless he is to take away the very freedom of choice that marks us out as men. Some will indeed perish (v. 7), but this is not because God wills it.

The logical corollary of this verse is that Christians should use the time before the advent for preaching the gospel. The word of evangelism always belongs to the word of the end (Mk. 13:10). For the gospel concerns a Person whose first coming ushered in the last days, and whose return will seal them. Its proclamation issues from the command of this Person and is empowered by his Spirit. The preaching of the gospel is eschatological through and through.

F. PETER ARGUES FROM THE PROMISE OF CHRIST (3:10)

Although the parousia may be deferred in God's patience with sinners, that patience is not inexhaustible. The Day will come. Therefore those who have succumbed to the blandishments of the false teachers should hasten to repent.

Peter, never reluctant to remind his readers of what they already knew, here follows his own precept, and once again reverts to a saying of Jesus, one which made a great impression on the early church. *The day of the Lord will come like a thief* (see Mt. 24:43–44; Lk. 12:39–40). The parousia will be as sudden, as unexpected, as disastrous to the unprepared, as a nocturnal burglary. Paul speaks of the suddenness and decisiveness of the advent in the same terms (1 Thes. 5:2), and the saying was well known in the Asian churches (Rev. 3:3; 16:15). In the former passage the analogy is particularly apt, for Sardis had twice in its history been overcome through failure to watch, and the enemy had scaled the precipitous sides of the Acropolis and broken in like a thief. Here, as throughout the early Christian tradition, a saying of Christ was treasured because it dealt with a living problem, the date of his return. It was useful to the early leaders in curbing the apocalyptic excesses of the enthusiasts who were always fixing dates for the end. Jesus had said that he did not know the date (Mk. 13:32), and he had told his followers not to speculate about it (Acts 1:7), for the coming of the Son of man would be like that of a thief in the night. Verses 8–9 counter Christian apathy about Christ's return; verse 10 counters excessive enthusiasm. We must leave the time to God, but we must watch.

Despite the delay, the Day of the Lord *will* come. It will mark

149

the end of God's forbearance, and so it threatens the impenitent. And Peter goes on to describe it in apocalyptic language culled from the Old Testament, the words of Jesus, and non-biblical material. Jesus had spoken of 'signs in the sun, moon, and stars. On the earth, nations will be in anguish and perplexity' (Lk. 21:25),

'the sun will be darkened,
and the moon will not give its light;
the stars will fall from the sky,
and the heavenly bodies will be shaken.'

. . . 'heaven and earth will pass away, but my words will never pass away' (Mt. 24:29, 35). Peter recalls and adapts the language of Jesus about the cosmic destruction at the parousia; he recalls, too, the permanence Jesus attributed to his own words by alluding to the reliability of the promise of the Lord (vv. 9–10). And in the light of these words of Jesus, Peter turned to his Old Testament for further illumination. Passages such as Isaiah 13:10–13; 24:19; 64:1–4; 66:16; Micah 1:4 would have come to mind, so would Isaiah 34:4, 'All the stars of the heavens will be dissolved and the sky rolled up like a scroll' (a verse which reappears in the *Apocalypse of Peter*, v). But the coming of Jesus into the world split the unitary conception the prophets had had of the Day of Yahweh. Since then, part had been fulfilled, and part still lay in the future. In particular, fire, judgment and so forth belonged to his second coming.

Peter's language is not entirely clear in detail, which is hardly surprising. He is using the language of apocalyptic in the attempt to describe the indescribable. His main purpose is to lift up the eyes of his readers to the climax of history. He makes three points.

First, *the heavens* (*i.e.* the sky, thought of as an envelope above the world) *will disappear with a roar*. *Rhoizēdon* is a New Testament *hapax legomenon*. It is a colourful, onomatopoeic word which can be used of the swish of an arrow through the air, or the rumbling of thunder, as well as the crackle of flames, the scream of the lash as it descends, the rushing of mighty waters, or the hissing of a serpent. 'He has chosen it', writes Lumby, 'as if by it he would unite many horrors in one.' That fire is uppermost in Peter's mind in this instance is clear from verse 7; for the idea, *cf.* Revelation 20:11; for the language, *cf.*

Mark 13:31; for Peter's fondness for 'fire', *cf.* 1 Peter 1:7; 4:12.

Secondly, the physical *elements* (*stoicheia*) *will be destroyed by fire* (*luthēsetai*). The *stoicheia* could mean the physical elements of earth, air, fire and water, out of which all things were thought to be composed. Alternatively it could mean the heavenly bodies, sun, moon, stars (so Justin, *Apol.* ii.5 and most of the Greek Fathers). For a partial parallel, *cf.* Mark 13:24–26. The view of Spitta that Peter means the spirits in charge of the powers of nature, though this was indeed a Jewish and probably a Pauline belief (*Enoch* lx. 12; *Jubilees* ii. 2; Gal. 4:3, 9; Col. 2:8, 20), does not fit the present passage.

Thirdly, Peter anticipates the disappearance (*aphanisthēsontai*), the burning up (*katakaēsetai*), or best the disclosure, the laying bare (*heurethēsetai*)[1] of the earth and all its works. The latter may mean either its fine buildings or the deeds of men.[2] The text is in considerable disarray but the expectation had considerable backing. It originated with Malachi 3:19 (LXX) 'For the day of the Lord is coming burning like an oven' and Isaiah 34:4 (LXX) 'and all the powers of the heavens will melt', which has influenced not only 2 Peter but 2 *Clement* 16.3 'But you know that the day of judgment is now coming like a burning oven and some of the heavens will melt and all the earth be like lead melting in the fire, and then the secret and open works of men will appear.' It may even be, as Bauckham thinks, that these references point to the existence of a Jewish apocalyptic source which dealt with the problem of delay in the end.

Bo Reicke comments, 'The solar system and the great galaxies, even space-time relationships, will be abolished . . . All elements which make up the physical world will be dissolved by heat and utterly melt away. It is a picture which in an astonish-

---

[1] This reading is rightly defended by F. W. Danker in *ZNTW*, 1962, pp.82–86 and adopted by NIV. It is the most difficult reading and explains all the variants. By comparison with another occurrence of the word in *Psalms of Solomon* xvii. 10, he concludes that the meaning is 'judicial enquiry culminating in a penal pronouncement'.

[2] So H. Lenhard takes it (*ZNTW*, 1961, pp.128 f.). Both the earth (mankind) and the deeds done upon it will be manifest before God's tribunal. The whole world will pass away, and only man be left to give account of himself to his Maker. Bauckham provides a full discussion and comes up with a similar conclusion. The earth and its works will be *found* (guilty) by God in contrast to believers who will be *found* spotless, blameless and at peace with him at the parousia (v. 14).

ing degree corresponds to what might actually happen according to modern theories of the physical universe.' In any case, the main point of it all is not the apocalyptic imagery which may or may not be literally fulfilled, but the moral implications of the parousia, to which Peter now turns his attention.

G. THE ETHICAL IMPLICATIONS OF THE SECOND COMING (3:11–14)

11. As always in the New Testament, the moral imperative follows the eschatological indicative. The expectation of the Lord's return always inspires Christians to a holy life (*cf.* 1 Jn. 2:28). Disbelief in the Lord's return all too often produces indifferentism in behaviour, as it had with these errorists. There is an indissoluble link between conduct and conviction. Barclay gives three superb examples from the inscriptions on heathen tombs of what happens when men reject the teleological view of history, the belief that creation has a goal, a climax, which is one of the main themes of the doctrine of the advent. It leads to *hedonism*: 'I was nothing; I am nothing; so thou who art still alive, eat, drink, and be merry.' It leads to *apathy*: 'Once I had no existence; now I have none. I am not aware of it. It does not concern me.' It leads, finally, to *despair*: ' "Charidas, what is below?" "Deep darkness." "But what of the paths upward?" "All a lie" . . . "Then we are lost." ' Barclay concludes, rightly, that without the truth, embodied in the second coming doctrine, that life is going somewhere, there is nothing left to live for.

In the midst of a precarious existence in a precarious world, it is important to remember, as this verse reminds us, that people matter more than things. This we tend so easily to forget. We slip into the habit of thinking of the world as more enduring than its inhabitants. Peter denies this. People are more important and more enduring than things. In an unstable and perishable universe the one stable and imperishable factor is human personality. It is with this that God is primarily concerned. A man's character is the only thing he can take out of this life with him. Therefore, whether we choose to consider dissolution in personal or cosmic terms, the quality of the lives we lead in the light of this coming dissolution is of supreme importance. Peter, wise pastor that he is, urges his readers to reflect, and apply to themselves the truths he has just enunciated. Holiness of life, worship of God and service to men are the three practical conclusions he draws from this study of the advent. These qualities are meant to be permanently present (*huparchein*) in our lives, in contrast to the unpredictability of our circumstances in a world where all things may be dissolved.

12. Christians are expected to look for the coming of the Lord; had not Jesus himself told them to watch? But this does not mean pious inactivity. It means action. For, wonderful as it may seem, we can actually 'hasten it on' (NEB) (not 'hasting unto' as in AV).[1] In other words, the timing of the advent is to some extent dependent upon the state of the church and of society. What a wonderfully positive conception of the significance of our time on earth. It is no barren waiting for *Finis* to be written. It is intended to be a time of active co-operation with God in the redemption of society. Our era between the advents is the age of grace, the age of the Spirit, the age of evangelism.

Evangelism is one way in which we can be said to hasten the coming of the Lord (*cf.* Mk. 13:10), but we cannot confine our preparations to evangelism. We cannot exclude the prayer, 'Your kingdom come' (*cf.* Rev. 8:4); nor Christian behaviour (verse 11, and see 1 Pet. 2:12); nor repentance and obedience (Acts 3:19–21). All these contribute towards the ultimate goal. The Rabbis had two apt sayings: 'It is the sins of the people which prevent the coming of the Messiah. If Jews would genuinely repent for one day, the Messiah would come', and 'If Israel would perfectly keep the Torah for one day, the Messiah would come'. It is Christian listlessness, disobedience and lovelessness which delay *the coming of the day of God*. The remarkable expression for the usual 'day of the Lord' (attested here in some MSS) smacks of the Old Testament 'Day of Yahweh', as does the only other New Testament occurrence, Revelation

---

[1]There is much in the Old Testament (*e.g.* Is. 10:23; 60:22, LXX) and the intertestamental books (*e.g. Sirach* xxxiii:8; 2 *Baruch* xx:1–2; lxxxiii:1) about God's hastening the end in response to Israel's good works or repentance. 'This does not detract from God's sovereignty in determining the time of the End, but means only that his sovereign determination graciously takes human affairs into account.' (Bauckham).

16:14. The return of Jesus Christ *is* the *day of God*.

The judgment is again seen in terms of fire, fire which destroys dross (v. 10) and purifies gold (*cf.* 1 Pet. 1:7). There was plenty of Old Testament precedent for this (see, *e.g.*, Mal. 3:3; 4:1). The Christian who is living in touch with Christ can face the thought of the dissolution of all things without dismay – even with joy. This is how the fire which strikes terror into the heart of the mockers can here be adduced as an incentive to the faithful (*cf.* Dn. 3). Paul makes precisely the same use of it in 1 Corinthians 3:10ff.

The Greek *di' hēn*, 'because of which', is neatly paraphrased in the NIV, *That day will bring about* the destruction. It takes place because God's 'day' has arrived. The prophetic present, *tēketai*, is combined with a future participle, *kausoumena*, to mean *will melt in the heat*, though once again the text is corrupt. The word occurs in the LXX of both Micah 1:4 and Isaiah 34:4, both of which passages have influenced Peter's whole treatment of the forthcoming fire. He repeats the description of the fire, in order to prepare for verse 13.

13. Once more Peter returns to the Old Testament for his description of the Christian hope. He is true to his own teaching that the 'word of prophecy' is more sure than anything else (1:19) and looks forward to the fulfilment of God's ancient promises. Sin, which has marred God's world, will not be permitted to have the final word. In a renewed universe the ravages of the fall will be repaired by the glory of the restoration. Paradise Lost will become Paradise Regained, and God's will shall eventually be done alike in earth and heaven. Isaiah 65:17; 66:22, which Peter quotes, formed the basis for the eschatological hopes of Judaism and were widespread. They 'emphasise the radical discontinuity between the old and the new, but it is nevertheless clear that they intend to describe a renewal, not an abolition of creation' (Bauckham).

Peter knew no more than did the Old Testament prophets about the way this would be accomplished. Nor are we any wiser today. We have no means whatever of conceiving what a resurrection body or what a restored universe will be like. Those who think they can map out a detailed programme of what will happen at the second coming should remember that, despite the prophecies of Scripture, nobody got the details of the first coming right! The language of this passage is figurative. It is an attempt to convey in the language of this world something of the wonder of the next. But it is not so much concerned to describe the indescribable, as to act like a *Sursum Corda*, to prevent us getting earthbound, to assure us that God has a purpose and a future not only for our souls but for our bodies, not only for redeemed individuals but for a redeemed society. There is such a thing as human solidarity, alike in creation, in fallenness, and in restoration.[1] That is why the New Testament does not represent the resurrection of the body as happening until the last day (although it makes it quite clear that the Christian dead are with the Lord and are, indeed, better off than the living). Full bliss will be possible for *any* only when it is possible for *all*. Thus Isaiah (*e.g.* 60:19–20), Revelation (21:27), and Peter here, all stress that the new heavens and earth will be the permanent home (*katoikei* not *paroikei*) of righteousness.[2] All evil will have been destroyed. The nations of the saved will have no desire but to do their heavenly Father's will.

Jesus taught the same about the effects of his return. The wicked would be destroyed, and the righteous would shine like the sun in the kingdom of their Father (Mt. 13:41–43). Again, in the apostolic *kērygma* we see the same pattern; the destruction of the wicked, the bliss of the saved, and the restitution of all things at the return of Jesus Christ (Acts 3:19–23). It is the profound moral consequences of the parousia that particularly concern Peter. It is because the ultimate destiny of men will be determined by the second coming, that he urges his readers to hasten the day of God by holy lives of service.

14. Because it is only righteousness that will survive in the new heaven and new earth, it is imperative that Christians live righteously. The look of hope must produce the life of holiness. Such is always the requirement of biblical, ethical monotheism.

[1]Thus *palingenesia*, 'new birth', is used both of personal regeneration and of cosmic renewal (Mt. 19:28; Tit. 3:5).

[2]*Katoikein* is used in Greek to denote permanent residence; *paroikein* is used for temporary residence.

It was the link between belief and behaviour that the false teachers had broken. Their hopes were earthbound; their lives immoral. Peter never tired of stressing the this-worldly consequences of the other-worldly 'look'. Three times in three verses he uses this word (*prosdokaō*), just as his Master before him had repeatedly urged his followers to 'watch'. For *dear friends*, see on 3:1, and compare Jude's final appeal to the faithful (Jude 20).

The most important thing about the parousia is that Jesus himself will return. It is the Man Christ Jesus who will confront us. He is the standard of human life by which we will be judged; he is also the compassionate one who understands our frailties. The relationship with Jesus Christ is both the initial and the final thing in a man's Christian pilgrimage. 'How will he find me?' is a very searching question for the Christian to ask himself, whether death (*cf.* 1:14) or the parousia be uppermost in view.

And just as confrontation with Christ will be the Christian's test, so conformity with Christ will be the Christian's standard. We are to *make every effort* (*spoudasate* is the same word as in 1:5), to reflect Christ's own character. The false teachers were 'blots and blemishes' (*spiloi kai mōmoi*, 2:13); the Lord Jesus was 'without blemish or defect; (*aspilos kai amōmos*, 1 Pet. 1:19). True Christians must conform to the spotless, blameless pattern of God's Son, and the parousia hope is a powerful spur to keep us abiding in him, 'so that when he appears we may be confident and unashamed before him at his coming' (1 Jn. 2:28). All down the ages it has normally been the case that men who have their hope set on the returning Christ have lived holy, attractive lives (1 Jn. 3:3, so also Jude 24).

There is, moreover, one further quality which the expectation of Christ's return should bring, a deep sense of *peace*. The parousia will be the day of vindication. It is by allowing his mind to dwell on the return of Christ that the Christian will regain a sense of balance and proportion, however difficult his present circumstances, and the peace which passes understanding will take root deeply in his heart. I remember a Bantu woman telling me in South Africa that she could face the humiliations to which her colour daily made her liable without rancour or bitterness because she knew that the Lord Jesus would return one day, and then all wrongs would be righted. Such an attitude can, of course, easily lead to a quite un-Christian quietism; religion can become the opiate which dulls the people to acquiesce in injustice. But the parousia hope can both spur men to Christian action here and now, and also give a due perspective to those enigmas which, in this life, are never resolved.

H. PETER QUOTES PAUL FOR SUPPORT (3:15–16)

15. The false teachers reappear in Peter's sights for a moment. They have impatiently put down the delay in Christ's return to slackness and assert it will bring disillusionment. Peter reiterates that it is due to *patience* and is conducive to *salvation*. The contrast could not be more sharply marked. The difference in attitudes is determined by the single word *our* Lord. The false teachers had denied the Lord who bought them. Naturally, then, they were anxious to discredit his return. The genuine Christians sought to grow in the knowledge of their Lord. Naturally, then, they eagerly anticipated his return.

On *salvation* (and *Saviour*) here, see my *The Meaning of Salvation*, pp. 194–197. The point in this verse, as in verse 9, is that the patience of the Lord displayed in the merciful delay of the parousia, is designed to lead men through repentance and faith to salvation. When the parousia dawns, the day of opportunity will be closed.

The reference to *our dear brother Paul* is fascinating. It is taken as the conclusive proof that this letter is non-Petrine by those who look at the New Testament through Tübingen spectacles, and see everywhere signs of a radical split between Jewish Christianity headed by Peter and Gentile Christianity headed by Paul. On such a view this verse, like the whole of the Acts of the Apostles, must be taken as a mid-second-century attempt to paper over the cracks and read Catholicism back into the first century. This view, however, can scarcely stand today.[1] The Acts is at pains to point out parallels between Peter and Paul, and represents Peter as supporting Paul's denial of the need for

---

[1] For a powerful dismissal of it, see J. Munck, *Paul and the Salvation of Mankind*, 1959.

Gentile circumcision (Acts 15:7–11). The same picture of amity between them emerges from Galatians 2:8–10. The only disagreement we know of between them seems to have been of short duration, when Paul publicly rebuked Peter for not being consistent with his own principles about table-fellowship with Gentiles (Gal. 2:14). It is a gratuitous assumption, and one that runs counter to the whole Christian emphasis on brotherly love and forgiveness, to suppose that the split was permanent, and that Peter could never have spoken, therefore, in such warm terms of Paul as he is made to do here. Indeed, I find it hard to imagine a pseudepigrapher managing to strike quite this note. In the second century one tended either to think of Paul as an arch-villain or as the apostle *par excellence*, not as a *dear brother*. That is, however, exactly how the first-century Christian leaders spoke of one another (1 Cor. 4:17; Eph. 6:21; Col. 4:7, 9; Phm. 16; *etc.*), and would be a very natural phrase for Peter to use of Paul.[1]

But what exactly is Peter alluding to? Is it the fact that Paul teaches, as he does, that God delays the parousia out of motives of mercy, so that more may come to repentance? That is the point of Romans 2:4 (*cf.* Rom. 3:25; 9:22; 11:22). Older commentators either assumed from this that our letter was addressed to Rome (which would not fit 3:1 if it refers to 1 Peter) or, taking it to be directed to Asia Minor, like 1 Peter (*cf.* 3:1), found it hard to discover this teaching in any of Paul's surviving letters to Asian churches. However, it is now seen to be quite probable that Romans was a circular letter,[2] at least one edition of which went to Ephesus, so even if 3:1 did oblige us to regard 2 Peter as addressed to the Asiatic recipients of 1 Peter, there would be no difficulty in the assumption that they were familiar with the teaching of Romans.

On the other hand, Peter may be alluding simply to Paul's constant teaching in all his letters about the need for holy, patient, steadfast, peaceable living (especially in the light of the

---

[1] As Lindemann has shown (*Paulus* p.95 f.) there is no justification for supposing that 2 Peter 3:15–16 is an attempt to rehabilitate Paul in orthodox circles, which had viewed Paul's letters with suspicion because Gnostics had made use of them. Paul never needed any rehabilitation among the orthodox (see 1 Clement, Ignatius and Polycarp).

[2] See T. W. Manson, 'St. Paul's Epistle to the Romans – and Others', *BJRL*, Nov. 1948.

parousia). These are, of course, the very subjects Peter himself has just been discussing. This seems the simplest solution. The exact location of Peter's recipients then becomes immaterial. They had received one or more letters from Paul, with which Peter also is familiar, and to which he here alludes.[1] There is no difficulty in supposing him to have accurate knowledge of Paul's correspondence, particularly if, as 1 *Clement* v suggests, they worked together in Rome at the end of their lives.

Notice how Peter admires Paul's wisdom – not without reason! Yet this is a gift from God, as Paul was the first to admit[2] (1 Cor. 3:10; 2:6, 16). Polycarp writes in the same vein (*c.* AD 115), 'Neither I nor anyone like me can attain to (lit. 'keep up with') the wisdom of the blessed and glorious Paul, who also, when he was absent from you, wrote you letters.'[3] It is interesting to see the difference here between the first- and early second-century references to Paul. To Peter he is a 'beloved brother': to Polycarp, though himself one of the most distinguished of subapostolic bishops and a sufferer for the faith, he had already become 'the blessed and glorious Paul'. If 2 Peter is a pseudepigraph, it is a very good one!

16. It is comforting to think that Peter, too, found Paul's letters *hard to understand*, *i.e.* 'obscure', or 'ambiguous'. *Dusnoētos* is a rare word, with a nuance of ambiguity about it. It was applied in antiquity to oracles, whose pronouncements were notoriously capable of more than one interpretation. There are, says Peter, such ambiguities in Paul's letters, which *ignorant* (better 'uninstructed') *and unstable people distort* or 'twist' (a delightful word *streblootō*, meaning literally to 'tighten with a

---

[1] It need not surprise us that Peter had read a good many of Paul's letters. It would be more surprising if he had not. 'We may assume that the early Christian teachers would naturally communicate their writings to one another, and that these would be read as containing the teaching of the Spirit for the church at large' (Mayor).

[2] Paul often refers in his letters to the grace given him by God to have a deep understanding of the mysteries of God in the gospel (*e.g.* Rom. 12:3; 15:15 f.; 1 Cor. 2:6–13; Eph. 3:2–10; Col. 1:25. The inspiration of Paul's letters cannot be called 'a later ecclesiastical idea' (Knoch). It is precisely the gift of wisdom which Paul claimed – and Peter recognized – came from the Holy Spirit.

[3] *Philippians* 3.

windlass') *to their own destruction.* Peter probably[1] is alluding to Paul's doctrine of justification by faith which was, we know, twisted by the unscrupulous to mean that once justified a man could do what he liked with impunity. Indeed, the more he sinned the better, for it afforded a greater opportunity for the grace of God to be displayed (Rom. 3:5-8; 6:1). Paul's insistence that the Christian is free from legal rules (Rom. 8:1-2; 7:4; Gal. 3:10) was twisted to mean that he condoned licence. One can almost hear his own libertarian war-cries being quoted back at him in 1 Corinthians 6:12, 'Everything is permissible for me' and in Galatians 5:13, 'You, my brothers, were called to be free'. Such was the cry of the false teachers (2:19).

Barclay reminds us, most appropriately, of G. K. Chesterton's famous picture of orthodoxy. 'Orthodoxy, he said, was like walking along a narrow ridge, almost like a knife-edge. One step to either side was a step to disaster. Jesus is God and man; God is love and holiness; Christianity is grace and morality; the Christian lives in this world and in the world of eternity. Overstress either side of these great truths, and at once destructive heresy emerges.' Such was the case here. The false teachers no longer submitted their actions to the scrutiny of Scripture; they made Scripture the justification for what they wanted to do.[2]

Peter gives a very high place to Paul's writings. They are placed alongside *the other Scriptures.* This phrase, *tas loipas graphas,* can be taken in two main ways.

(i) It may possibly *distinguish* Paul's letters from Scripture. See Bigg's note *in loc.* Thus in 1 Thessalonians 4:13 *hoi loipoi* means 'others who are not Christians', not 'other Christians'. This makes good sense. The false teachers twist Paul: they also twist the other Scriptures, *i.e.* the Old Testament. It is certainly implied, as in any case we know, that Paul's letters were held in such high esteem that they were read in church. In the Jewish synagogue, on which the church was based, there were probably two readings, one from the Pentateuch and one from the

---

[1] Alternatively they may have argued that Paul taught an imminent parousia (*e.g.* Rom. 13:11-12; 1 Cor. 7:29; 1 Thes. 4:15); that it had not happened; and that therefore it would not happen.

[2] Clement of Alexandria alludes to this verse, 'others, giving themselves to pleasures, wrest Scripture in accordance with their lusts' (*Strom.* vii. 16).

Prophets.[1] On occasion, letters from important leaders of Jewry were also read in synagogue.[2] In the Christian church, equally, there will have been two or perhaps three readings, from the Old Testament (? Law and Prophets) and from apostolic writings. See Colossians 4:16. These Christian writings were kept in the church chest, and there is ample evidence that these apostolic writings were held in the highest respect, though rarely, for half a century, specifically called Scripture.

(ii) Alternatively, it may *include* Paul's letters in Scripture. This is an easier interpretation of the Greek. If so this need not demand a late date for the Epistle. Sometimes *graphē*, 'Scripture', was used in a broad sense (*e.g.* Jas. 4:5; 1 *Clem.* xxiii. 3) to refer to material which does not appear in the Canon of the Old Testament, but was hallowed by long usage. There can, in any case, be no question that long before AD 60 Christian writings were being read in church alongside the Old Testament, and consequently were well on the way to being rated as equivalent in value to it.[3] 1 Timothy, 1 *Clement* and *Barnabas*,[4] all probably deriving from the first century, quote a combination of Old Testament and New Testament texts as 'Scripture'. The point was this. The apostles were conscious that they spoke the word of the Lord (1 Thes. 2:13) as surely as did any of the prophets. There is nothing, therefore, unnatural about their placing each other alongside the Old Testament prophets.[5] The same Holy Spirit who inspired the prophets was active in themselves. That is quite enough to explain how Peter could have put Paul alongside the Old Testament writers in this verse. Bigg remarks that, so far from having an inferiority complex about Moses and the

---

[1]See C. W. Dugmore, *The Influence of the Synagogue upon the Divine Office*, 1964, pp.1–25, and A. Guilding, *The Fourth Gospel and Jewish Worship*, 1960, pp.6–24.

[2]Eissfeldt, on the basis of *Baruch* i. 14 and the *Apocalypse of Baruch*, says 'It must therefore have been normal . . . to read aloud in the synagogues written missives from notable leaders of the community' (*Old Testament Introduction*, E.T. 1965, p.24).

[3]Boobyer appears to accept this. 'This (sc. calling Paul's writings *graphai*) does not necessarily place the Pauline letters fully on a par with the Old Testament in scriptural authority. "Scriptures" could have meant both the Old Testament and other writings venerated and used in the church's teaching and worship, and thus being at least on their way to equal recognition with the Old Testament as canonical scripture.'

[4]1 Tim. 5:18, citing Dt. 25:4 and Lk. 10:7; see 1 *Clem.* chapters xxiii, xxx, xxxiv, xxxvi; *Barnabas* xiii. 7; 2 *Clem.* 2.4; Polyc. *Ep.* 12.1.

[5]On the problems connected with this verse, see further, Introduction, pp.30f.

prophets, the apostles believed themselves to be even higher in the purposes of God. 'St. Paul sets apostles before prophets (Eph. 4:11) . . . And it follows from 1 Pet. 1:12 that the Christian evangelist was superior to the old prophets, as Christ himself was greater than Moses.'

There is, of course, no hint here that the Pauline Corpus had been collected, still less that the Canon had been formulated, though both these gratuitous assumptions are often made by commentators.

To their own destruction. Peter is very firm. The action of the false teachers in twisting Paul to justify their own libertinism and rejection of the parousia is so serious as to disqualify them from salvation. God will not have his grace turned into licence nor his moral authority mocked. *Their own* is emphatic, as in 1:20. Was Peter about to say that they twist Scripture to their own *interpretation*, as in that passage? And then he drew the implications with more biting irony: such action amounts to their own *destruction*.

I. CONCLUSION (3:17–18)

17. Once more Peter addresses them as *dear friends*. It is because of his love that he has spoken so plainly; that same love now prompts a final charge.

He picks up the theme of verse 14 from which he had been side-tracked. They *know this*, *i.e.* that false teachers are to be expected. And to be forewarned is to be forearmed. Plain speaking about Christian deviations is incumbent upon the Christian pastor who wants to lead his flock along the way of truth. That is why Peter has reminded them time and time again of the wrong and the right paths, and their respective destinations. The responsibility now lies with them to watch, to guard themselves against the specious arguments of the wicked (*athesmōn*, *i.e.* men who live without law). The remarkable compound, *sunapachthentes, carried away by* (used in connection with Barnabas's defection in Gal. 2:13) suggests that if they keep too close company with such people they will be led away from Christ. Peter, of all men, had good cause to recognize such a danger, for he had succumbed to it and denied his Master (Mk. 14:54, 66–72). There is no excuse for complacency in Christians: error has many attractive faces by which even the most experienced may be beguiled. Jesus himself had given similar warnings, not least in connection with the second coming: 'Watch out that no-one deceives you. . . . You must be on your guard. . . . Be on guard! Be alert!' (Mk. 13:5, 9, 33). Otherwise it is possible, even after for a while having remained firm, to come to a disastrous end (*ekpiptō*, the verb used here for *fall*, is used of apostasy in Gal. 5:4, 'fallen away from grace', and of shipwreck in Acts 27:26, 29).

Once again in this verse Peter stresses the relationship between knowledge and behaviour. He does not fight shy of 'knowledge' on the ground that the false teachers are making such play with it. The fact is that faith without knowledge degenerates into pietism; purely emotional religion leads, often enough, to immorality, which militates against stability as almost nothing else does. The word for 'steadfastness' (NIV *secure position*) *stērigmos*, occurs only here in the New Testament,[1] but is from the same root as the verb Jesus had used in Luke 22:32, 'When you have turned back, strengthen (*stērixon*) your brothers'. This is a command which, throughout this Epistle, Peter has been seeking to obey. It is not surprising that he who had been so mercurial and had been changed by the grace of God into a man of rock should be so concerned about stability.[2]

18. Peter's own steadfastness is shown by the fact that he ends his letter as he began it, on the subject of growth (*cf*. 1:5). The Christian life, it has been said, is like riding a bicycle. Unless you keep moving, you fall off! No true Christian thinks, as the false teachers seem to have done, that he has 'arrived'. Peter and Paul (Phil. 3:13f.) both urge others to press on as they themselves do. The Christian life is a developing life, for it consists in getting to know at ever greater depth an inexhaustible Lord and Saviour.

There are two ways of taking this parting injunction. First, we

---

[1] Elsewhere it is used of the fixed position of the stars and the steadiness of a beam of light.

[2] Peter uses the verb again in 1:12 (q.v.) and 1 Pet. 5:10.

can translate 'Grow in the grace and knowledge of . . .'. Here both *grace* and *knowledge* are regarded as qualities which Christ bestows. In this case, *gnōsis* will refer to spiritual understanding, as in 1:5–6, and the meaning will be that they must grow in knowledge about Christ, for this is the bulwark against being beguiled like the unstable of verse 16. Alternatively, we can render it 'Grow in grace and in knowledge of . . .'. In this case *gnōsis* would be used in the sense of *epignōsis* (1:2–3, 8; 2:20), personal acquaintance with Jesus Christ. It is through personal encounter with Jesus as Saviour and Lord that the Christian life begins. It is through constant contact with him in both those capacities that Christian character develops. This latter under-standing of the clause would be easier Greek, but it confuses *gnōsis* with *epignōsis*, which 2 Peter seems to distinguish.

This emphasis on knowledge, whichever of these two transla-tions be preferred, is important. It provides a goal for Christian development, the day when we know even as we are known (see 1 Cor. 13:12), and at the same time a warning against 'what is falsely called knowledge' (1 Tim. 6:20) which the heretics professed. Knowledge *of* Christ and knowledge *about* Christ are, if they keep pace with one another, both the safeguard against heresy and apostasy and also the means of growth in grace. For the more we know Christ, the more we will invoke his grace. And the more we know about Christ, the more varied will be the grace we invoke.[1]

To him be glory both now and for ever (lit. 'to the day of the age'; the *Amen* is textually doubtful).[2] What a telling final ejaculation! It reveals the mainspring of Peter's Christianity. Christ the Saviour; Christ the Lord; to Christ belongs glory for ever. In this incidental phrase we have the highest possible Christology. For glory belongs to God (Rom. 11:36; Jude 25). But Peter had learnt that all men should honour the Son even as they honour the Father (see Jn. 5:23). The false teachers detracted from Christ's glory *now*, by a wicked life, and from His glory *then*, by denying the parousia. Peter is determined to reverse both trends. He may well have succeeded. For it was in the Asiatic churches of

[1]See 1 Pet. 4:10 for the 'many-sided grace of God'.
[2]On the question of whether this ascription of glory is a prayer or rather a statement, see on Jude 25.

Bithynia, to which 1 Peter (1:1) and perhaps 2 Peter were written (if we are to infer from 3:1 that it was sent to the same destination), that the Roman governor, Pliny, about AD 112 noticed that Christians 'sing a hymn to Christ as God' (*Ep*. x. 96).

On the meaning of 'glory' see on Jude 25. The phrase 'the day of the age' is remarkable. Peter had spoken of that day in 3:7, 10, 12; it was the day of judgment, the day of the Lord, the day of God, *i.e.* the second coming. That 'day' would usher in eternity. Bigg remarks that this unusual form of the doxology (indeed, it is without parallel in the surviving literature of the second century, though something similar occurs in *Ecclus*. xviii. 9–10) 'cannot have been written after liturgical expressions had become in any degree stereotyped'. This was fairly early: by the end of the first century, *eis tous aiōnas*, a primitive addition to the Lord's Prayer, was almost invariable.

It is fitting that the glory of Christ should close this Epistle which has had so much to say about the ignominy of man. Peter displays that attitude of loving and reverent dependence on the ascended Lord which, throughout the Epistle, he had been seeking to inculcate in his readers as one of the great means of progress in the Christian life.

JUDE:
ANALYSIS

a. *The author and his readers* (1–2).
b. *The letter Jude did not write, and the letter he did* (3–4).
c. *Three warning reminders* (5–7).
d. *The analogies of judgment applied* (8–10).
e. *Three more Old Testament examples* (11–13).
f. *The prophecy of Enoch applies to them* (14–16).
g. *The words of the apostles apply to them* (17–19).
h. *Jude's exhortation to the faithful* (20–23).
i. *Doxology* (24–25).

JUDE:
COMMENTARY

A. THE AUTHOR AND HIS READERS (1–2)

1. We can learn a good deal about a man by listening to what he has to say about himself. Jude makes two significant claims. In the first place, he is a *servant of Jesus Christ*. The very recognition of Jesus as Christ or Messiah meant that the Christian saw himself as the devoted servant (lit. 'bondslave') of Jesus. Even apostles, like Paul (Rom. 1:1; Phil. 1:1) and Peter (2 Pet. 1:1), gloried in it, and both Jude and James (1:1), who were, it seems, brothers of Jesus, make a point of calling themselves his bondslaves! What a change from the days before the resurrection, when his brothers did not believe in him, but thought him deranged (Jn. 7:5; Mk. 3:21, 31). Now that he had become a believer, Jude's aim in life was to be utterly at the disposal of the Messiah Jesus.[1] One of the paradoxes of Christianity is that in such glad devotion a man finds perfect freedom.

Secondly, Jude calls himself *a brother of James*. The unadorned name James meant one person, and one only, in the apostolic church – James, the Lord's brother, the leader of the church in Jerusalem.[2] Though others called Jude 'brother of the Lord' (1 Cor. 9:5), he preferred to style himself *brother of James* and *servant of Jesus Christ*. It is a further mark of his modesty that he was prepared to accept the position of playing second fiddle to

---

[1] Contrast this fulfilment of Jesus' command to his followers (Lk. 22:26 ff.) with the reluctance of Christian churches generally to make the extent of a man's service the criterion of his greatness. The true barometer of spiritual stature is the quality and the depth of a man's devotion to Jesus and to his fellows.
[2] See Introduction, p.49f.

James, his more celebrated brother. Barclay cites the parallel of Andrew, content to be known as Simon Peter's brother. 'Both Jude and Andrew might well have been jealous and resentful of their far greater brothers. Both must have had the gift of gladly taking second place.'

Jude does not tell us where his readers lived, but he does give three remarkable descriptions of what it means to be a Christian. This is the first of several such triads in this short Epistle. It is possible that all three adjectives derive from the Servant Songs in Isaiah where Israel is described as called, loved and kept by God. In line with early Christian practice Jude takes over these attributes of the historic Israel and applies them to the followers of Jesus.

First, they are *loved by God the Father*. The text is uncertain. Many later MSS read *hēgiasmenois, sanctified* (AV), which is easier, somewhat parallel to 1 Corinthians 1:2, but clearly secondary, and a fairly easy corruption of *ēgapēmenois*, 'beloved'. While Paul often speaks of the believer as being 'in Christ' or 'in the Lord', there is no place in the New Testament where Christians are said to be 'loved in God the Father'. The NEB offers the dubious paraphrase 'who live in the love of God the Father'; Westcott and Hort suggested that the 'in' is misplaced, and should be read before *Jesus Christ*. We could thus translate, 'loved by God the Father and kept safe in Jesus Christ.' Perhaps Jude originally left a gap after the 'in' for the appropriate place-name to be inserted, when the messenger brought his short letter round the various towns and villages where the incipient heresy had begun to spread.[1] We could then translate, 'to those in——, beloved by God the Father, *etc.*' It is scarcely possible to render, with Mayor, 'loved (by us) in the Father', because all three participles, 'loved', 'kept', 'called', clearly have the same divine Agent as their subject. No doubt Jude means to combine the two ideas that his readers are loved by God, and also are incorporated in the Beloved One,[2] and so in God.[3]

Second, they are *kept by Jesus Christ*. Jude refers to the continu-

---

[1] A similar sort of thing seems to have happened with the 'in Ephesus' of Eph. 1:1.

[2] *Cf.* Eph. 1:5 and Armitage Robinson's note in his *St. Paul's Epistle to the Ephesians*, 1903, pp.229–233.

[3] *Cf.* 'I am in the Father, and the Father is in me' (Jn. 14:10).

ous preservation with which Jesus keeps those who trust him (*cf.* 2 Tim. 1:12, 1 Pet. 1:5; 1 Jn. 5:18). He keeps what we commit to him. It is interesting to compare this emphasis on Christ's keeping power with its correlative in verse 21, 'keep yourselves in God's love'. It is God's part to keep man; but it is man's part to keep himself in the love of God. These are the two sides to Christian perseverance (*cf.* Phil. 2:12–13). The phrase could equally well be taken, as RSV has it, 'kept for Jesus Christ', and would then mean either kept safe for him at the second coming (*cf.* 1 Thes. 5:23), or, if a Gentile destination for this letter is favoured, it would mean that the believing recipients have been preserved as a people for God's own possession, inheriting the elect place of Israel (*cf.* Jas. 1:1; 1 Pet. 2:9–10).

Third (not first, as in NIV), they are *called*. This is no anti-climax. It is one of the great biblical descriptions of believers and is here the noun to which both 'loved' and 'kept' refer. The author of the Christian call is God, and its nature is holiness (Rom. 1:7; 1 Cor. 1:2; 1 Pet. 1:15), *i.e.* the working out in life and character of what God works in us (Phil. 2:12–13; 2 Pet. 1:10; Rev. 17:14). This calling, which originated in the secret purposes of God himself (Rom. 8:28) and is big enough to embrace heaven (Eph. 4:4; Heb. 3:1), can nevertheless be used to apply to a man's marital state and his daily work (1 Cor. 7:20). For there is nothing about us or our destiny which is irrelevant to the call of God. For that reason, God's call forms the fitting climax to this triad of descriptions of the privileged position of the Christian. God loves him; Christ keeps him; God calls him.[1]

2. Jude has another triad of qualities which he prays for his readers. (Incidentally, how often do we mention in our correspondence the things we are praying for our friends?) Jude wants *mercy, peace* and *love* to be theirs *in abundance*; in other words, he wants them to be 'filled to capacity' (the same word as in 1 Pet. 1:2 and 2 Pet. 1:2) with these three things.

---

[1] As Bauckham observes, these attributes have been carefully chosen. His readers are in danger of apostasizing from their calling and incurring God's judgment at the parousia. God's action in calling, loving and keeping safe must be matched by a faithful human response – hence the main body of the letter. But at the end Jude returns to the note on

Why *mercy*? It is rare in a greeting (*cf.* 1 Tim. 1:2; 2 Tim. 1:2, 2 Jn. 3) but singularly important in these four places where it occurs, always against a background of false teaching. It is a reminder that not only at his regeneration (*cf.* 1 Pet. 1:3), not only at the judgment (2 Tim. 1:16, 18), but every day of his life the Christian stands in need of the mercy of God. Nothing but unmerited mercy can meet the constant needs of habitual sinners.

When a man knows himself to be accepted with God, undeserving though he is, this gives him a deep *peace* in his life. And so this old Hebrew greeting of 'peace' (*šālôm*) is filled out by Jude with deeper meaning.

Nor does this lead to quietism. For the gracious mercy of God not only transforms the life of the recipient, but reaches out through him to others. God's own love is poured out to overflowing in our hearts by the Holy Spirit (Rom. 5:5). Mercy from God, peace within, love for men – all in fullest measure (*plēthuntheiē*). Could one imagine a more comprehensive prayer of Christian greeting?

B. THE LETTER JUDE DID NOT WRITE, AND THE LETTER HE DID (3–4)

3. Jude does not merely talk about love; he displays it, both in the repeated affectionate address of *dear friends* (3, 17, 20, *cf.* 2 Pet. 3:1, 8, 14, 17) and also in the serious warning and stern rebuke he administers throughout the Epistle. Christian love is no sentimental acquiescence in what others are doing; it is no substitute for conviction. Rather, it springs from conviction, and as fire consumes dross, it must destroy all impurities in the loved one.

Jude never intended to write this letter! Proposing *to write* (does the present infinitive *graphein* suggest 'in a leisurely style'?) about *the salvation we share* he was driven to snatch up his pen (aorist infinitive *grapsai*) by the news of a dangerous heresy. Instead of a pastoral letter, he found himself writing a broadsheet. The phrasing here suggests it was a somewhat unwelcome task, but *I felt I had to write.* The true pastor is also

---

which he began, his confidence that God, their Saviour through Christ, will preserve them for his eternal Kingdom.

watchman (Ezk. 3:17–19; Acts 20:28–30), though this part of his duty is widely neglected in our generation, under the plea of tolerance. Whether or not Jude ever wrote his intended treatise, we do not know.[1] His eagerness (*spoudē*) to write about the faith recalls 2 Peter 1:5, where the readers are to display equal zeal in growing in the faith.

In this verse Christian experience is summarized by the one word, *salvation*, and Christian belief as *the faith*. Salvation, to Jude, meant not only past deliverance (v. 5), but present experience (vv. 23f.) and future enjoyment of the glory of God (v. 25). It is shared by author and readers, Jewish and Gentile Christians alike. 'The faith' is here a body of belief, *fides quae creditur*, (*cf.* Gal. 1:23), as opposed to the more usual meaning of *pistis* as 'trust', *fides qua creditur*. It is sometimes thought a mark of lateness that 'the faith' should be thought of in this rather static way.[2]

What is this body of belief? Jude does not expand, but he designates it as *the faith that was once for all entrusted to the saints*. By *saints* he means the people of God (as frequently in the Old Testament). By *the faith . . . entrusted* he means the apostolic teaching and preaching which was regulative upon the church (Acts 2:42). Indeed, in this verse, he comes very near to asserting propositional revelation, a concept widely denied today. God, he implies, has handed over to his people a recognizable body of teaching about his Son, in feeding on which they are nourished, and in rejecting which they fall. *Paradidonai*,[3] 'to entrust', is the word used for handing down authorized tradition in Israel (*cf.* 1 Cor. 15:1–3; 2 Thes. 3:6), and Jude is therefore saying that the Christian apostolic tradition is normative for the

---

[1] Some scholars translate the participle *pasan spoudēn poioumenos graphein* 'because' rather than 'although': Jude, on this view *is* writing the letter he intended to write. This is highly unlikely: our present Jude is not a letter about 'the salvation we share'. Moreover such a view neglects the distinction between the present (*graphein*) and aorist (*grapsai*) infinitives used in counterpoint, and makes the whole sentence very repetitive, which is not like Jude. More intriguing is Robinson's view that Jude did (later) fulfil his intention of writing about 'the salvation we share' in the Second Epistle of Peter, of which he was the amanuensis and agent. However, there are great difficulties in attributing both letters to the same author. See further the Introduction.

[2] See, however, Introduction, pp.53 f.

[3] On the Christian *paradosis*, as opposed to the traditions of men, see O. Cullmann, 'The Tradition' in *The Early Church*, 1956, pp.59 ff. and *Christianity Divided*, 1962, pp.7 ff.

people of God. Apostolic teaching, not whatever be the current theological fashion, is the hallmark of authentic Christianity. The once-for-allness of the apostolic 'faith' is inescapably bound up with the particularity of the incarnation, in which God spoke to men through Jesus once and for all. And simply because Christianity is a historical religion, the witness of the original hearers and their circle, the apostles, is determinative of what we can know about Jesus. We cannot get behind the New Testament teaching, nor can we get beyond it, though we must interpret it to each successive generation. Jude would agree with 2 John 9–10 that the man whose doctrine outruns the New Testament witness is to be rejected. The test of progress is, for him, faithfulness to the apostolic teaching about Christ (*cf.* 1 Tim. 6:20; 2 Tim. 1:13–14).[1]

There is no need therefore, with Windisch and Schelkle, to postulate a late date for Jude and see here a mark of 'early Catholicism'. Jude is simply displaying the same concern that his readers should adhere to the primitive apostolic faith as Paul does so frequently in his letters (2 Cor. 11:3–4; Gal. 1:8–9; Col. 2:6–8; 1 Thes. 2:13; 2 Thes. 3:6). Jude here attacks antinomianism with the same passion as Paul in Galatians attacks legalism. Both are perversions of the gospel of Jesus Christ to which disciples should adhere.

Jude uses the word *epagōnizesthai*,[2] *contend*, in order to emphasize that the defence of this faith will be continuous, costly and agonizing; the cost of being unfashionable, the agony of seeking to express the faith in a way that is really comprehensible to contemporary man. For, granted the once-for-allness of the Christian faith, we must not neglect Dietrich Bonhoeffer's passionate plea in *The Cost of Discipleship* against the cheapening of Christianity until it becomes a set of propositions assented to, of acts performed, of shibboleths observed, rather than the vibrant, vital personal relationship with Jesus which inflames, invigorates and permeates every aspect of political, social and personal life. Contending for the faith is spelt out in verses 20–23. Verses 5–19 explain why it is so necessary.

[1]See Introduction, pp. 30 f., 54 f.
[2]Paul uses *agōnizesthai* for the hardship, the costly difficulty of building up mature Christians, of sustained prayer, of self-discipline, of maintaining Christian faith, and of the whole contest of the Christian life (1 Cor. 9:25; Col. 1:29; 4:12; 1 Tim. 6:12; 2 Tim. 4:7).

4. Here is the peril which caused Jude to rush off this sudden, short letter. He heard of certain men who had *secretly slipped in* or 'wormed their way in' (NEB). The rare word *pareisduō* is similar to the *pareisagō* ('smuggle in secretly') of Galatians 2:4; 2 Peter 2:1). It is a sinister and secretive world. Diogenes Laertius[1] used it of a secret return to a country; Plutarch[2] of the insidious decline of good laws and the stealthy substitution of inferior ones. Such an incursion by *godless men* was serious just because it was subtle (*cf.* Gal. 2:4; 2 Tim. 3:6). It is always more serious when the danger comes from within the church. But it ought not to have been surprising. The Old Testament,[3] the teaching of Jesus[4] and that of the apostles[5] all contain ample warnings against the advent of false teachers. There will always be those within the sheepfold who have not passed through the door, but have climbed up some other way; and they will always be a menace to the sheep (Jn. 10:1). Probably the trouble makers were itinerant teachers – a common problem in the early church (see 2 Cor. 10 and 11; 2 Jn. 10; *Didache* 11–12; Ignatius *Eph.* 9).

The condemnation of these men *was written about long ago: progegrammenoi* simply means 'foretold in writing'. But what condemnation and where was it written? Can he mean the condemnation he is about to describe so eloquently? If Jude is dependent on 2 Peter, Bigg may well be right in supposing him to refer to the condemnation made more explicit in 2 Peter 2:3. The obscurity arises from his having written in haste, with 2 Peter fresh in his mind. *Palai, long ago,* has been thought to prove that Jude could not have been thinking of 2 Peter, but if the word means 'already' as in Mark 6:47; 15:44, it would make excellent sense. Peter had already marked them down for this judgment of which Jude goes on to write.

Alternatively, it may be that he is alluding to the condemnation of the Old Testament precursors of the false teachers (see vv. 5–7, 11) or to a phrase in *1 Enoch*, to which he certainly has recourse in verse 14. For details of this possibility see Mayor

---

[1]ii. 142.   [2]*Moral.* 216 B.   [3]Dt. 13:2–11; Is. 28:7; Je. 23:14; Ezk. 13:9.
[4]*E.g.* Mt. 7:15; Mk. 13:22.
[5]Acts 20:29–30; 1 Tim. 4:1 ff.; 2 Tim. 3:1 ff.; 2 Pet. 2:2–3.

in loc. More attractive is the suggestion of Bo Reicke. 'While he speaks of "this judgment" he fails to specify which judgment or provide fresh details. He is apparently drawing on a source in which the judgment was described in more detail (as in 2 Peter 2:3). An example of this kind of material is to be found in 1 QS iv. 9–14 where the spirits of iniquity are rebuked in terms reminiscent of the accusations of Jude, thus suggesting the existence of a certain tradition behind Jude's allusions.' There is a lot to be said for this view, which would explain both the similarities and differences between Peter's and Jude's treatments of the false teachers. The existence of similar material at Qumran heightens the probability that the early Christian leaders would have needed to agree on some 'pattern of sound words' for condemning heresy.

At all events, 'some who long ago were designated for this condemnation' (RSV) have been described in prophecy which also predicted that God would judge them. This is precisely what he now goes on to substantiate in the section verses 5–19 by a series of examples. *This condemnation* therefore, refers forward to verses 5–19 where Jude will both describe them and their sins from various prophetic examples, and will also point out the judgment to be meted out to them. Note the verbal links between *krima* (v. 4) and *krisin* in both verses 6 and 15. So, effectively, *this condemnation* points to the parousia 'which is prophesied typologically in vv. 5–7 and directly in vv. 14–15' (Bauckham).

These subtle intruders are described further. They are *asebeis, godless.* This seems to have been a favourite word of Jude's. It refers here to their attitude of irreverence to God, in verse 15 to their shameless deeds, and in verse 18 to their illicit desires; comprehensive *asebeia* indeed!

Furthermore, they are treating the fact that God graciously accepts sinners as an excuse for flagrant, shameless sin, *Aselgeia, a licence for immorality*, means in Greek literature, and particularly in Aristotle's *Ethics*, 'unrestrained vice'. Thus it comes fittingly as the climax of the foul catalogue in Galatians 5:19. Libertinism was to be found both in Pauline and Petrine churches (Rom. 13:13; 2 Cor. 12:21; Gal. 5:19; Eph. 4:19; 1 Pet. 4:3; 2 Pet. 2:2, 7, 18) and also in John's circle in Asia (Rev.

2:20–24). It is hardly surprising that men accepted the indicative of pardon and forgot the imperative of holiness. It was an inherent risk in the proclamation of the gospel of free grace, and it has always been so since then. The conclusion many preachers have drawn is to stop preaching free grace; the apostolic conclusion was to attack lasciviousness, but to continue to preach the grace of God who accepts the unacceptable.

By such unrestrained wickedness these men were *denying* Christ and his Father. 'They claim to know God, but by their actions they deny him' (Tit. 1:16). There are many ways of denying Christ apart from the obvious one of apostasy. These false teachers were certainly guilty of a practical denial of their faith by the way they lived, and possibly also of a theoretical denial of Christ's deity and Lordship by the form of incipient Gnosticism which they followed. Thus, like later Gnostics, they may have cast a slur on the Father by urging that the creator god was not the only, or indeed, the highest, God, and on Jesus by maintaining that he was a mere man on whom the divine Spirit descended at his baptism but left before the crucifixion. However, this is speculative. There are no certain traces of Gnosticism in Jude's opponents. Reckless self-indulgence is the charge against them. 'They regard themselves, not Him, as their Lord' (Luther).

The phrase, *deny Jesus Christ our only Sovereign and Lord* is reminiscent of 2 Peter 2:1, and its form in Greek raises the question whether the Father as well as Jesus Christ is in view here. This is probably the case, since *despotēs*, 'Master', in the New Testament always refers to God the Father except in 2 Peter 2:1, and also since 'the only' is here added.[1] As in 1 John 2:22, rejection of the unique Sonship of Jesus involves also a denial of the Father who sent him, and who, apart from Jesus, must perforce remain the Unknown God.

Why does Jude go to such lengths to show that the libertines troubling his readers were prophesied long ago? Surely because the prophetic predictions which they fulfil show that they constitute a serious danger to the church. They must be earnestly

---

[1] If so, this is somewhat parallel to *Enoch* xlviii. 10, 'they have denied the Lord of Spirits and his Anointed.'

resisted as his readers contend for the purity of the apostolic gospel. Nothing less than the faith is at stake. Hence the writer's passion and urgency.

C. THREE WARNING REMINDERS (5–7)

5. Professor E. Earle Ellis, an expert on Jewish biblical exegesis, has drawn attention (in *Prophecy and Hermeneutic* pp. 220ff.) to a most important aspect of verses 5–19. He is able to show that far from being a piece of unrestrained denunciation it is in fact a careful piece of exegesis, which shows Jude to be a highly skilled practitioner of Jewish exegesis. Jude is using a midrashic technique, making five citations (vv. 5–7, 9, 11, 14f., 18) each of which is followed by a commentary section (vv. 8, 10, 12–13, 16, 19), and there are extensive parallels for this at Qumran. It is a powerful way of showing that the prophecies from of old are now being fulfilled. Not all five citations are from the Old Testament, for there are two apocryphal quotations (vv. 9, 14–15) and an apostolic prophecy (v. 18) together with another Christian prophecy (v. 11), but the prophecy–fulfilment theme is clear, and sheds light on Jude's background.

After introducing his opponents, Jude proceeds to state in no uncertain terms what will befall them. He does so by drawing upon three instances of divine judgment with which they had once been familiar but which they had, apparently, forgotten. Judgment, he reminds them, was meted out first to Israel, second to the angels which sinned, and third to the cities of the plain.

All this he says by way of reminder: *I want to remind you.* He has not, of course, mentioned these things earlier in his letter. Does he assume a general knowledge of biblical history? That would hardly extend to the fall of the angels. Rather, he appears to refer to some apostolic tradition denouncing false teaching in which they, like the recipients of 2 Peter, had been instructed.[1] Such tracts may even have been called *hypomnēmata,*

[1] See Introduction, p.58 ff.

'reminders'.[1] *Certainly both Jude (here and verse 17) and 2 Peter (1:12–13, 15; 3:1–2, etc.*) lay great emphasis on 'reminders'. They are crucial for a historical religion.

The text is in disarray in this verse. Among the variants, 'though ye once knew this' (AV), 'though you were once for all fully informed' (RSV), and 'though once you all had knowledge' (P 72, *cf.* 1 Jn. 2:20), the best attested is the second; 'you knew it all once' is his meaning. There is no justification for NIV rendering of *hapax* by *already* and *eidotas* by *know*. But who did the saving and the destroying? Was it God, the Lord, Jesus (possibly Joshua; the names are the same), or some combination of them? All these variants occur. Commentators generally are attracted to the reading 'Jesus' (i.e. Joshua), following Justin, Origen and Jerome. For the typological idea behind this reading, see 1 Corinthians 10:4. But this cannot be right; the one who destroyed the Israelites in verse 5 also banished the angels in verse 6, and this rules out Joshua. Probably *the Lord* was what Jude wrote, and the other readings are scribal glosses to add precision. It is God who acts as Judge in each of the three incidents Jude mentions. It is God who will judge the false teachers.

This allusion to Israel in the wilderness makes it very plain that Jude's opponents were once orthodox Christians who had gone wilfully astray into heresy. They had experienced the redeeming hand of God from *Egypt*, the heathen land of bondage and death. They had known the release, the new life involved in becoming the people of God. But in their hearts they returned to Egypt. Reicke suggests that the sin of the false teachers was collaboration with unrighteous heathen powers, and that Egypt is the symbol for heathendom. It is more probable, in view of Paul's use of the same incident in 1 Corinthians 10:1–11, that idolatry and immorality, rather than politics, were the attraction, and that it was these which brought in their train unbelief, tempting God, and finally apostasy and judgment (*cf.* Heb. 3:12–19). Jude's reference seems to be to Numbers, where the people failed to take their opportunity of entering the land of

---

[1]The word is used in this way by Thucydides iv. 126, and *cf.* Justin's allusion to 'memoirs' of the apostles, '*ta apomnēmoneumata tōn apostolōn*' (*Apol.* i. 67).

promise because of the difficulties which loomed so large in their way (Nu. 14:2f.; 32:10–13, and *cf.* also 11:4–34; 26:63–65). In this example of judgment, Jude gives us a terrible warning of what can befall the people of God. Even the redeemed can backslide to a fate like this. Did not Bunyan show a short cut to hell from the very gates of the celestial city? Jude's severe teaching here is very like Paul's in 1 Corinthians 10:11–12. He argues from the fate of apostate Israel to the fate which could overtake apostate Christians. God will save *his people* for himself, even if some perish in the process through unbelief. It was this close parallel between Israel and the church which led Jude to give this example first, out of chronological sequence. God's judgment on apostate Israelites precisely fitted his coming judgment on apostate Christians.

The word *deuteron*, translated *later*, is so strange in this sense that it has led, in some MSS, to the transposition of *hapax*, *once*, to the subsequent clause, in a misguided attempt to balance it. *To deuteron*, which literally means 'the second time', may have been chosen by Jude because he was thinking of God's first intervention to save the Israelites, and his second to judge. This would apply exactly to Christ's first coming to save and his second coming to judge apostasy and unbelief (*cf.* Heb. 9:28).

It is noteworthy that despite the close similarity between 2 Peter 2 and Jude in this section, Jude alone speaks of deliverance from Egypt, and Peter alone of Lot and his rescue. This would certainly be surprising if one copied from the other, and the explanations given by commentators are unconvincing.

6. Jude's second example concerns *the angels*. They, too, were intended to be 'a people for God's own possession'. They, too, had many privileges on which they might have relied. In both respects they were like the false teachers to whom Jude addresses himself.

Jude refers here to the sin and fate of the fallen angels. Jews were very interested in angels in the last few centuries BC, and 1 *Enoch* records some of their speculations on the subject. The Greek myth of the destruction of the Titans by Zeus, the Zoroastrian legend of the fall of Ahriman and his angels, and the rabbinic elaboration of Genesis 6:1[1] all show how wide-spread such a belief was in popular religion, as an attempt to rationalize the contradictions and the evil in the world. Jude does not necessarily endorse its truth; he does, however, like any shrewd preacher, use the current language and thought forms of his day in order to bring home to his readers, in terms highly significant to them, the perils of lust and pride.

For it was lust and pride that led to the downfall of these angels. Pride, because they were not content to keep *their positions of authority* (*archēn*) given them by God; the word *archēn* here probably means, as Wycliffe has it, 'princehood'. Each nation was thought to have its governing angel (see the LXX of Dt. 32:8). Pride in the angels caused civil war in heaven, and the evil angels were cast out (see Is. 14:12; 24:21f.) and sentenced by God to everlasting doom. Not only the subject matter, but the form of expression here is influenced by the second century BC. Thus 'until the judgment of the great day' comes frequently in *1 Enoch*, with associated expressions (*e.g.* x. 6, xvi. 1, xxii. 4, 10–11, xcvii. 5, ciii. 8), where we also read that the angels 'have deserted the lofty sky, and their holy everlasting station' (xii. 4), and the fate for Azazel, one of their principal offenders, is 'Cover him with darkness, and let him dwell there for ever' (x. 5). The other evil angels are to be bound with great chains until the day of their judgment (x. 15–16). Interestingly enough, this idea of a present punishment which will be finalized at the day of judgment is to be found also in the Qumran writings (1 QS iv. 9–14).

Pride, then, was one cause of their fall. But lust was another. That is the implication of the story in Genesis 6:1–4, and it is elaborated in *1 Enoch* (vii, ix. 8, x. 11, xii. 4, *etc.*) and in a whole gamut of intertestamental literature.[2] Justin comments, 'the angels who transgressed their command mingled with women, and thus fell' (*Apol.* ii. 5), and that this point is in Jude's mind is clear from the words that follow in the next verse, 'in a similar way'.

The fallen angels were consigned to the nether darkness, and

---

[1] For details see Plumptre's and Bauckham's notes *in loc.*

[2] *Jubilees* iv. 15, 22; v. 1–10; *Test. Reuben* v; *Test. Napht.* iii; the *Book of Tobit*, and *cf.* also Josephus, *Antiq.* i. 3. 1.

bound in eternal chains: *1 Enoch* is full of it! Imprisoned now, their fate will be sealed in Gehenna at the Day of Judgment. Let the false teachers take note.

Were the false teachers arrogant? Let them remember that arrogance had ruined the angels. Were they consumed by lust? This, too, caused the downfall of the angels. Privileged position and full knowledge had not saved the angels whose faith had grown dim, and whose selfishness had waxed hot; let the readers, therefore, not presume! Jude reinforces his lesson with a touch of savage irony. The evil angels had been too arrogant to *keep* their position – so God *has kept* them in punishment. Jude clearly means that the *lex talionis* cannot be extruded even from the heavenly places.

7. The third paradigm of judgment which Jude takes is the destruction of the cities of the plain. He leaves the flood and Lot on one side, unlike 2 Peter, and concentrates on the most graphic example of judgment to be found in the whole of the Old Testament. Indeed, its overtones are heard throughout the Bible.[1] The same two characteristics of lust and pride[2] are found here, as in the two earlier examples he has given. In addition, the unnaturalness of their conduct is stressed. The men of Sodom and Gomorrah engaged in homosexuality:[3] that was unnatural. But Jude may mean that just as the angels fell because of their lust for women, so the Sodomites fell because of their lust for angels (*sarkos heteras* indeed!) The two cases were shockingly unnatural. It was no less unnatural for the Israelites to rebel against the Lord who had redeemed them. Jude uses the unnaturalness, as well as the heinousness, of rebellion against God to urge his readers not to follow in the train of the false teachers. Sin, rejection of the commands of God, is a violation of the divinely established order of things: it must be punished.

The destruction of these cities made an indelible impression

---

[1]Dt. 29; 23; 32: 32; Is. 1:9; 3:9; 13:19; Je. 23:14; 49:18; 50:40; Ezk. 16:46 ff.; Am. 4:11; Mt. 10:15; 11:24; 25:41; Lk. 10:12; 17:29; 2 Pet. 2:6; Rev. 11:8; 20:10 and *passim*.

[2]On the arrogance of the men of Sodom see Gn. 19:4–6, 12.

[3]The rare compound *ekporneuō*, 'fornicate', may suggest by the *ek* 'against the course of nature'.

on antiquity. George Adam Smith[1] explains how it may well have happened, as the bituminous soil, exploded. 'In this bituminous soil took place one of those terrible explosions which have broken out in the similar geology of the oil districts of North America. In such soil, reservoirs of oil and gas are formed, and suddenly discharged by their own pressure or by earthquake. The gas explodes, carrying high into the air masses of oil, which fall back in fiery rain, and are so inextinguishable that they float afire on water.' Thus Sodom and Gomorrah (and the cities round them, Admah and Zeboim, see Dt. 29:23), 'paid the penalty in eternal fire, an example for all to see' (NEB).[2] Jude may mean that the Dead Sea, a mere thirty miles from Jerusalem, was a permanent attestation to the fire which destroyed them. But normally in Scripture, *eternal fire* means hell fire; so the meaning probably is that their fiery destruction was a foretaste of that eternal fire which awaits the devil and all his accomplices (see *Enoch* lxvii. 4ff.; Rev. 19:20; 20:10; 21:8).[3] It represented a lasting warning to posterity.[4] It was a standing reminder that the triumph of evil is not final. God's judgment, though it delay, will surely come.

D. THE ANALOGIES OF JUDGMENT APPLIED (8–9)

8. From the preceding three analogies Jude draws three clear points. His false teachers are arraigned for lust, for rebelliousness, and for irreverence. These men are *dreamers*; the participle, *enupniazomenoi*, applies to the three actions which Jude goes on to detail. By saying they *pollute their own bodies*, he may simply be referring to their voluptuous dreams (*cf.* Is. 56:10, LXX). Or he may mean that they are dead to decency, sunk in the torpor of sin; so Calvin. But as the word occurs elsewhere in the New Testament only in Acts 2:17, where it is used of prophetic

[1]*The Historical Geography of the Holy Land*, 1931, p.508. See also J. P. Harland, 'Sodom and Gomorrah' in *The Biblical Archaeologist Reader*, ed. Wright and Freedman, 1961, pp.41–74.

[2]The Dead Sea area used to be very fertile once. *Wisdom* x. 7 and Philo, *de Abrahamo* 140 say it continued to smoke and burn.

[3]In *Enoch* lxvii. 4 ff. the evil spirits are imprisoned in a sulphurous burning valley of great swelling waters beneath the earth – after the analogy of the Dead Sea.

[4]*Cf.* 3 *Macc.* ii. 5.

dreams (*cf.* Joel 2:28), it probably indicates that the false teachers supported their antinomianism by laying claim to divine revelations in their dreams. 'On the strength of their dreams they pollute the flesh, reject the Lord's authority, and slander the glorious ones.'

Second, they *reject* (NEB 'flout') *authority*, thus displaying the arrogance and pride which has run through all three of the examples Jude has quoted. The question is, what authority? Some have taken *kurioteta*, 'lordship', to be parallel to *doxas*, 'glorious beings', and refer both to angelic beings. Yet, whereas *kuriotes* is certainly so used in Ephesians 1:21; Colossians 1:16, and *doxai* in 2 Peter 2:10f., nevertheless the form of the sentence here (three clauses denoting what these dreamers do) suggests a distinction between 'lordship' and the 'glorious beings'. It is possible to apply *kurioteta* to human authority, either the civil power, the church leaders, or authority in general. Any would make excellent sense here, but in view of what Jude has to say about their denial of the Lordship of Jesus (v. 4), it seems best to take the word in the same sense here. The heretics, like the Israelites, the fallen angels, and the Sodomites, were essentially turning their back on (*atheteo, reject*, is a very deliberate word) the Lord, though this may have found expression in civil or ecclesiastical insubordination. These men were anti-law, a common state of affairs when people follow their own lusts and exult in their own knowledge.

Third, they *slander celestial beings* or 'the glorious ones' (*doxai*). This clearly means, as in 2 Peter 2:10, 'angelic beings'; the allusion of the subsequent verse confirms the fact. It is more difficult to decide whether good or bad angels are intended. It would be most natural to suppose the former; the angels would be called *doxai* (so Clement of Alexandria[1]), because they are, as it were, rays of the Glory which is God himself. The false teachers would thus be guilty of irreverence towards God's messengers, the angels, just as the men of Sodom had been towards the angels who visited them.[2] On the other hand, the parallel in content with verse 9 permits the view that evil angels

[1] *Adumbrations* 1008.
[2] Gn. 19:5; *cf. Test. Asher* vii, 'do not be like Sodom which set at nought the angels of the Lord, and perished'.

are meant; the point being that as Michael did not slander the prince of evil, though sorely provoked, so they should not gratuitously despise and denigrate the angelic powers of evil. Nevertheless it is hard to see how *doxai* (glorious ones) could be used of evil angels. Why, then, did they slander God's good angels? Perhaps the undue deference paid to angels in some sections of Judaism (see Col. 2:18) produced this revulsion among the headstrong errorists, who became disenchanted with the whole notion of angels, and regarded such enlightened Christians as themselves as emancipated from such primitive ideas. Perhaps they blasphemed the angels as agents of the Demiurge (the inferior god of creation) if they were at all far advanced along the road to developed Gnosticism. But Chaine gives the most probable reason. Judaism saw the angels as mediators of the Mosaic Law (Acts 7:38, 53; Heb. 2:2; *Jubilees* i:27–9) who watched over its observance. It is hardly surprising that libertines should speak slightingly of guardians of the Law.

9. Their presumption towards the angels stands in stark contrast to *the archangel Michael*. He did not presume to condemn the devil for slander, when he was disputing with him over the body of Moses. In what follows, Jude appears to be drawing illustrative material from the apocryphal *Assumption of Moses*. So we are assured by Clement, Origen and Didymus, though the details here given do not figure in what survives of the *Assumption*. It is a story which obviously had great currency in oral tradition, and derives from speculation about what happened to the body of Moses. Jude is using it as an effective *ad hominem* argument to men who were steeped in apocryphal literature. A scholiast[1] on Jude gives the details.[2] When Moses died, the archangel Michael was sent by God to bury him. But the devil disputed his right to do so, for Moses had been a murderer (Ex. 2:12), and therefore his body belonged, so to speak, to the devil. Furthermore, the devil claimed to have authority over all matter, and Moses' body, of course, fell under this category. But even under such provocation, the story goes, Michael was not disres-

---

[1]For the text of the scholiast, see Bigg, *in loc*. The date of this writer is unknown.

[2]The Slavonic *Wisdom of Moses* 16 gives a similar story to the scholiast's – with variations, so does the *Targum of Jonathan* (on Dt. 34:5–6).

pectful to the devil. *He did not dare to bring a slanderous accusation against him.*[1] He simply left the matter with God, saying, '*The Lord rebuke you.*'[2] The point of the story lies just here. If an angel was so careful in what he said, how much more should mortal men watch their words.[3]

Such is the normal explanation of this remarkable apocryphal story. But Bauckham has made a particular study of Jude 9 and the *Testament of Moses* and maintains that the contrast Jude draws is not between Michael's restrained speech, even to the devil, and the blasphemies of the errorists against the angels. No, the point is much sharper. The errorists wanted to be autonomous, to please their licentious selves and to have no truck with the Law and its angelic guardians. The story of Michael shows that even an archangel is not autonomous. The devil was certainly bringing a slanderous and malicious accusation against Moses, but the archangel did not take it on himself to repudiate it. Moses was indeed a murderer, so Michael did not attempt to dismiss his charge as unjustified on his own authority. He could only appeal to the Lord for judgment and say *The Lord rebuke you* (words drawn from Zc. 3:2). What a contrast to Jude's opponents who set themselves up over against the Law, and against God who gave it.

Michael appears only here and in Revelation 12:7 in the New Testament. The concept of archangels (only here and in 1 Thes. 4:16) came late into Judaism. In Daniel 12:1 Michael is named as guardian of Israel (*cf.* Dn. 10:13, 21). *1 Enoch* has a developed hierarchy of seven archangels.

10. In contrast to the archangel who, out of respect for the Law surrenders himself and his case to God, 'these people speak abusively against whatever they do not understand'. Their attacks on the angels who mediated the Law shows that they have no proper understanding of angels as the ministers of

---

[1]The Greek could also be translated, 'to charge him with blasphemy', but this meaning is ruled out by the context. For that is precisely what Michael did, in appealing to God for judgment.

[2]This is itself a quotation of Zc. 3:2, apparently inserted into the *Assumption* because of its appropriateness.

[3]On Jude's use of apocryphal material, see Introduction, pp.57f.

God who is both Lawgiver and Judge (*cf.* Heb. ch. 1). These dreamers (v. 8) no doubt claimed visionary insight into the world of angels, and yet their behaviour is the very opposite of the angels. They despise and reject the Law which the angels revere and guard. How little they understand! Like the men of Sodom, they are engrossed in lust – and fail to recognize the angels.

What things they do understand, by instinct, like unreasoning animals – these are the very things that destroy them. Such is NIV's neat rendering of Jude's anacoluthon. The point is clear. What they understand is the physical appetites they share with the animals which have no share in their rationality; they are *aloga zōa, unreasoning animals.* How ironical that when men should claim to be visionary, they should actually be ignorant; when they think themselves superior to the common man they should actually be on the same level as animals, and be corrupted by the very practices in which they seek liberty and self-expression. Jude is stating a profound truth in linking these two characteristics together. If a man is persistently blind to spiritual values, deaf to the call of God, and rates self-determination as the highest good, then a time will come when he cannot hear the call he has spurned, but is left to the mercy of the turbulent instincts to which he once turned in search of freedom.[1] And those instincts, given free reign, are merciless. Lust, when indulged, becomes a killer. For a modern commentary on this theme, see Albert Camus's play, *Caligula.*

With these three warnings of verses 5–7 before them, Jude's readers are urged to beware of the spiritual decadence of the false teachers. This pervaded their whole personalities. Physically, they became immoral. Intellectually, they became arrogant. Spiritually, they denied the Lord. 'Progressive morality' and 'progressive thinking' often go hand in hand with progressive deafness to the voice of God. To live like that is to inhabit a dream world. The judgment of God will catch up with them as surely as the slaughterhouse with the cattle. The whole thrust of Jude's letter constitutes a stirring call to awake to moral integrity, intellectual humility and spiritual sensitivity.

---

[1]On the destructive nature of lust, see also Eph. 4:22; Phil. 3:19; 2 Pet. 2:12; *etc.*

E. THREE MORE OLD TESTAMENT EXAMPLES (11–13)

11. Once again Bauckham shows himself more perceptive than many other commentators who regard verses 11–13 as a substantial repetition of the charges he has already made in his first three examples, apart from the fact that now he concentrates on three individuals, not, as before, on three groups. But Bauckham perceives that the real difference is that up until now the errorists have been impugned for their sinful lives; in the verses that follow he portrays them as *false teachers* who lead others astray. Hence the stringency of his condemnations.

Jude adds Cain and Korah to Peter's citation of Balaam, and prefaces this characteristic triad of his by a *Woe to them!* in the style of Jesus in the gospels.

First, they are compared with *Cain*. Cain was the first murderer, and Jude may mean that as Cain murdered Abel's body, so these men murder the souls of others. But, more subtly, Cain was the type of the unloving man who cared nothing for his brother,[1] and envied him because Abel's deeds were good and his own bad (Gn. 4:4, 5, 9; 1 Jn. 3:12). Moreover, according to Hebrews 11:4 he is represented as the very opposite of the man of faith, and this view of him reappears in Philo and in the *Targum* on Genesis 4:7 where he is made to say, 'there is no judgment, no judge, no future life; no good reward will be given to the righteous, nor will judgment be inflicted on the wicked.' He stands for the cynical, materialistic character who defies God and despises man. He is devoid of faith and love. As such, he is the prototype of the men with whom Jude has to deal. But Cain is chosen for another reason. He corrupted the race of men, according to the rabbis. 'He became their instructor in wicked practices' (Josephus *Ant.* i:61). That is precisely Jude's quarrel with the false teachers.

Secondly, they are compared with *Balaam*. Once again there

---

[1] Bo Reicke cites 1 *Clem.* iv. 1–7, where Cain is given as the prototype of those informers who through envy, anarchy and social dissatisfaction drove their Christian brethren to death. In this sense, whether or not they were actual informers, the false teachers were fratricides and walked in the ways of Cain, for by their antisocial behaviour they aroused Rome to take active measures against the church.

is the obvious point, that he was exceedingly avaricious. It stands out clearly from the narrative of Numbers 22–24. But, as with Cain, there is more to be said. He, like Jude's opponents, taught Israel to sin. It was Balaam who involved Israel in the immorality and idolatry at Baal-peor (Nu. 31:16). No doubt he told the Israelites, whom he had three times found himself unable to curse, that they were so firmly ensconced in the favour of the Almighty that nothing could affect their standing with him. They could sin with impunity. Thus he led them into the *error*[1] of fornication and the denial of Yahweh's sovereign claims through submission to other, inferior deities. This is what the false teachers seem to have done. They were, like Balaam, greedy for money. Like him, they practised and led others into immorality. Like him, they boasted of prophetic dreams and visions. Like him, they encouraged apostasy. Like him they would perish.[2]

Thirdly, they are compared with Korah, notorious for his *rebellion* against Moses and Aaron, the divinely appointed leaders of Israel (Nu. 16:1ff.). These men, like Korah,[3] had clearly defied the duly constituted leadership of the church, refusing to accept their authority and setting themselves up in opposition. The Targums specifically call Korah a 'schismatic'. Insubordination of this sort was not unknown in the early

[1]Westcott's note on *error, planē*, in 1 Jn. 1:8 is valuable. He writes: 'the idea of *planē* is always that of straying from the one way; not of misconception in itself but of misconduct (as in Rom. 1:27). Such going astray is essentially ruinous.'

[2]G. H. Boobyer (in *NTS* vol. 5, p.45) shows how in intertestamental literature both Cain and Balaam became representative leaders of wickedness, and how it is stressed that they met with ruin, and would be denied a place in the world to come (*Jubilees* iv. 31, *Test. Benjamin* vii. 3–5, *Sanhedrin* x. 2 f., *Aboth* v. 19). The *Testament of Benjamin* reference is particularly germane to our letter, 'for ever those who are like Cain shall be punished with the same judgment'. This may well have been in Jude's mind as he wrote, and would strengthen the conviction expressed in the Commentary that all three verbs in this verse are meant to express the doom of the false teachers. Boobyer translates, 'They go to death in the path of Cain; they are themselves cast away in the error of Balaam; and they perish in the insubordination of Korah.' The datives, he rightly points out, are instrumental, the aorists futuristic.

[3]There are other factors in the story of Korah that might have been in Jude's mind. The story in Numbers shows him to have gathered a mob around him in rebellion, to have assumed an unwarranted liberty, to have invented his own way of worshipping God, and to have taken to himself functions to which he had no right, while falsely claiming holiness for himself and his followers. In general, here was a man who delighted to kick over God's traces.

church. It lay behind the injunctions of 1 Timothy 1:20; 2 Timothy 3:1–9; Titus 1:10–11; 3:10–11. It was represented by the revolt of Diotrephes (3 Jn. 9–10) and by the malcontents to whom Clement of Rome wrote his letter. Korah is mentioned last because his fate was so graphic (Nu. 16:35f.)

So in these three pen-pictures from the Old Testament we see three leading characteristics of the false teachers. Like Cain, they were devoid of love. Like Balaam, they were prepared in return for money to teach others that sin did not matter. Like Korah, they were careless of the ordinances of God and insubordinate to church leaders. It is not without significance for Jude's purpose that each of three Old Testament characters taught others to sin, and each met with ruin. It is equally obvious that these are the three major characteristics of second-century Gnosticism; we may have here in Jude the early inklings of an evil which was later to plague the subapostolic church.[1] Claims to special 'knowledge' made men indifferent to the demands of morality (you were, after all, saved by *gnōsis*, not by behaviour), indifferent to the needs of their brethren (it was essentially personal illumination and this made you feel superior to the common herd), indifferent, too, to the dicta of church leaders (for, after all, it was you, not they, who had 'arrived'). Those who lay claim to direct, immediate knowledge of the Almighty's mind commonly fall into the same dangers today.

12–13. 'These men are like sunken rocks in your love feasts!', says Jude in a vehement and brilliant diatribe. *Agapais*, love feasts, is unquestionably the right reading here (*cf.* note on 2 Pet. 2:13). There may be particular point in *these men are*, for the same phrase recurs in verses 16 and 19. Jude is thinking of the prophecies of apostasy found in the Old Testament apocryphal literature, or early Christian prophecy, and saying that these men fulfil it. The love-feasts provided the setting for the Holy Communion in the early church and very soon they proved

---

[1]It is important to stress, however, that there is no trace of Gnosticism proper to be detected here. Jude's opponents practise and teach antinomianism: they cause schism. They are treacherous, selfish, dangerous, but not Gnostics. That would be an anachronism.

liable to abuse through greed, disorder and immorality (1 Cor.
11:20ff.). Immorality at the love-feast had broken out in the
community to which 2 Peter was addressed, and so it seems to
have done here.[1] These libertines in the love-feasts were like
sunken 'reefs' (RSV mg.) waiting to shipwreck the unwary.
Indeed, it was upon reefs like this that the Agape did in fact
founder in the second century. There is some doubt as to what
spilades means, since it is a rare word, occurring only here in the
New Testament. In secular Greek it means 'rocks' or 'sunken
rocks', but by the time of the fourth century it had come to mean
blemishes, as the NIV takes it here. This would make a close
parallel to 2 Peter's *spiloi*, 'spots' (2 Pet. 2:13), but the older
meaning is to be preferred in this passage which is full of
striking similes.[2]

If *without the slightest qualm* is taken with the clause which
precedes it, the meaning will be 'as they revel recklessly'; if with
the succeeding clause, 'as they brazenly look after – themselves'. Either makes good sense.

In 'sunken rocks' we see the danger of these folk; in *eating with
you without the slightest qualm*, their arrogance. The next phrase,
shepherds who feed only themselves, underlines their selfishness
and recalls 1 Corinthians 11:20–22, 33f. They 'act the shepherd
to themselves', and one recalls Ezekiel 34:8: 'the shepherds have
fed themselves, and have not fed my sheep' (RSV). Instead of
looking after others, they have led them astray. Instead of losing
their lives, and thus gaining them, they have tried to save their
lives – and so lost them (Mk. 8:35). It is plain that they have
aspired to positions of leadership, and have abused the trust
placed in them by selfish behaviour. 'Many elders will be lawless and violent shepherds to the sheep . . . since they have no
holy shepherds.' So we read in the *Ascension of Isaiah*, 3.24. It
was like this in Jude's community.

[1] It may be that the sheer presence of these people at the love-feasts, behaving in their
reckless, irreverent manner, constituted the 'blemishes' of which Jude warns. But we know
from Clement of Alexandria of dissolute behaviour in the love-feasts among the Carpocratians (*Strom*. 3.2) and this is probable here, especially in the light of 2 Peter 2:13–14, the
parallel passage.

[2] Bigg remarks on the masculine article being used with the feminine noun. It increases
the possibility that Jude is quoting from some document, which he sees fulfilled in the false
teachers.

Jude continues to pile on the invective in four striking metaphors. They are clouds, trees, waves, stars. 'Sky, land and sea are ransacked for illustrations of these men' (Moffatt).

In the first place, they are like *clouds* which bring promise of rain, but give not a drop to the thirsty ground; they merely serve to hide the sun. These clouds are carried past by the wind, and the land beneath gets no benefit (see Pr. 25:14). Here is a graphic example of the uselessness of teaching which is supposedly 'advanced' and 'enlightened' but has nothing to offer the ordinary Christian for the nourishment of his spiritual life. I find this a solemn warning to those who, like myself, are professional theologians. We must constantly ask ourselves if our studies and knowledge are benefiting anybody at all.

Secondly, they are like barren fruit *trees*. There is much discussion over the precise meaning of *phthinopōrinos*. The AV, wrongly, takes it as 'whose fruit withereth'. Bigg favours 'autumnal' (*cf.* NIV, *autumn trees*), the literal meaning of the components of the word being 'end of the fruiting'; the season when growth has stopped and the branches are bare. Mayor complains that if this were the case, how could the trees be blamed for not fruiting? He thinks it means 'autumn-fruiting'. It may, indeed, simply mean this,[1] and the blame may all be concentrated in the word *akarpa* (which NIV construes with what follows) – they carry no fruit; though it is also possible that the word means they blight their fruit before bringing it to maturity. At all events, these teachers had barren lives, when they should have been fruitful. They were like the barren fig tree of Jesus' parable (Lk. 13:6–9).[2] They had forgotten Jesus' words 'by their fruit you will recognise them' (Mt. 7:20). Peter had a similar complaint to make about his readers. They had ceased to grow (2 Pet. 1:8; 3:18). They are called *twice dead*[3] and *uprooted* because they had once been 'dead in transgressions and sins' (Eph. 2:1) and were now dead again, in the sense that they were cut off from their

[1]Pindar, *Pyth.* v. 161 is a case where it has this meaning.

[2]This image of the barren tree had wide circulation in the early church, and was variously applied. See 2 Pet. 3:4; 1 *Clem.* xxiii, 2 *Clem.* xi. In 1 *Clement* the vine shows signs of death, revives, and bears fruit. In Jude the trees show signs of death, do not revive, and do not bear fruit.

[3]Clement of Alexandria, in the *Adumbrations*, understood 'twice dead' to refer to future judgment after death. But Jude is speaking of a condition which already prevails.

life-giving root, Jesus Christ (contrast Col. 2:7). The content of what Jude is saying has outstripped the confines of the metaphor, it would seem; though at a pinch the tree could be thought of as once dead because barren, and twice dead because uprooted. The uprooting of trees is a favourite Old Testament metaphor of judgment (Ps. 52:5; Pr. 2:22).

Thirdly, they are *wild waves of the sea, foaming up their shame, i.e.* their shameful deeds. No doubt Isaiah 57:20 lies behind this image, as it conjures up the restlessness of the wicked and their continual production of filthy scum, such as is found littered about the seashore when the tide recedes. The word *epaphrizō* ('foam out') is very rare. The poet Moschus uses it of the seaweed and other rubbish borne on the crest of the wave and then deposited on the beach.

Finally, they are like *wandering stars*, whose doom is to be imprisoned in darkness for ever. Jude is thinking not of planets, but of shooting stars which fall out of the sky and are engulfed in darkness — to the confusion of all who watch them. For this metaphor he goes to *1 Enoch* once more[1] (xviii. 14ff.) where the angel shows Enoch 'a prison for the stars of heaven'. Later, he see stars bound together, and is told, 'these are the stars which have transgressed . . . and this is the prison of the angels in which they are kept for ever' (xxi. 2, 6, 10). This suggests that Jude is thinking of the doom of the fallen angels (of which he had spoken in v. 6), when he talks of the doom reserved for wandering stars. This conclusion is strengthened by the fact that he goes on to quote *Enoch* in the next verse. They pretend to be lights, but have gone sadly astray and doom awaits them (there is probably a play on *planētai, wandering,* and the *planē, error* of v. 11). The allusion to Enoch is peculiarly fitting, as Irenaeus[2] pointed out. For whereas the wicked angels lost their heavenly home by disobeying God, and fell to destruction, Enoch gained heaven by obeying God, and was saved.

In these two verses, then, Jude has evoked a swift, bold

---

[1]He may be indebted to Enoch for three of his four images (1 *Enoch* lxxx. 2 rain withheld; lxxx. 3 fruit withheld; lxxx. 5 stars astray) and it is significant that they are drawn from all four quarters of the world (air, earth, sea, heavens), all out of joint. Such are the false teachers, however speciously impressive, who trouble the church.

[2]*A.H.* iv. 16. 2.

picture of the men he is castigating. They are as dangerous as sunken rocks, as selfish as perverted shepherds, as useless as rainless clouds, as dead as barren trees, as dirty as the foaming sea, and as certain of doom as the fallen angels.

F. THE PROPHECY OF ENOCH APPLIES TO THEM (14–16)

14–15. Jude now confirms this final analysis of his opponents with a prophecy of inescapable judgment, the judgment which will accompany the return of Christ. He quotes 1 *Enoch* (i. 9) to emphasize his point. Nowhere in the Old Testament, incidentally, is Enoch called *the seventh from Adam* (though this could be inferred from Gn. 5), but he is so called in 1 *Enoch* lx. 8, xciii. 3. *Seventh* is important, for seven is the perfect number in Hebrew thought, and emphasizes the stature of this man Enoch who walked with God (Gn. 5:24). A prophecy, for Jude, clinches the matter. There is nothing more to be said about the fate of the false teachers. It is interesting that Jude applies this prophecy from long ago to the situation of his own day, much as the men of Qumran (who also valued 1 *Enoch*) applied the writings of Habakkuk to their own time and situation. Although we have only a third of the text of 1 *Enoch* in Greek, we do possess this fragment, and Jude sticks very closely to his original. Whereas Enoch was thinking of *the Lord* as God coming in judgment, to Jude, of course, the *kurios* is the Lord Jesus and his coming is the parousia[1]; the *holy ones* who accompany him to judgment are the angels (*cf.* Mt. 25:31) and judgment is exercised on the wicked in respect of both their deeds and words. It is on their words that Jude will concentrate in verse 16, having already dealt fully with their deeds in verses 5–11. In 1 *Enoch* the harsh words are uttered against God. This may well be the thrust in verse 16.

On the whole question of Jude's explicit use of the Apocrypha, see the Introduction, pp. 57f. Whether or not he regarded 1 *Enoch* as inspired is perhaps beside the point, for he is quoting

---

[1] 'That early Christians expected the eschatological theophany to take the form of the parousia of the Lord Jesus has considerable importance for the study of the earliest Christological developments, for it was one route by which divine language came to be used of Christ' (Bauckham).

a book both he and his readers will know and respect. He speaks to them in language which they will readily understand, and that remains one of the most important elements in the communication of Christian truth.

16. Jude completes his picture of the heretics in terms which M. R. James thinks are taken from chapter 7 of the (Latin) *Assumption of Moses*, but which Chaine, with greater probability, sees as an application of the prophecy of 1 *Enoch*. Thus *grumblers* and *faultfinders* fill out the sins of word which they had committed (*'harsh words . . . spoken against him'*, v. 15); *they follow their own evil desires* refers to their sins of action (*'all the ungodly acts they have done in the ungodly way'* v. 15). Then, carried away by indignation, Jude adds one more phrase in each category to complete the verse.

For *grumblers,* Jude uses the delightfully onomatapoeic word, *gongustēs*; Paul had used it to reflect the smouldering discontent of the Israelites in the desert (1 Cor. 10:10), and this is Jude's reference, too. Whenever a man gets out of touch with God he is likely to begin complaining about something. To grumble and moan is one of the distinguishing marks of man without God (*cf.* Phil. 2:14). In their case, it was probably, like Israel in the desert, grumbling against God and perhaps the restrictions imposed by his Law. This grumbling extended, too, to their lot in life. They were always cursing their luck (that is the real meaning of *mempsimoiros, faultfinder*). The *mempsimoiros* was a standard Greek character, like Andy Capp in the *Daily Mirror.* 'You're satisfied by nothing that befalls you; you complain at everything. You don't want what you've got, you long for what you haven't got. In winter you wish it were summer, and in summer that it were winter. You are like the sick folk, hard to please, and *mempsimoiros!*' (Lucian, *Cynic* xvii). Unfortunately those words fit many a Christian. This whole spirit of grumbling is condemned roundly in James 1:13. It is to insult the God who gives us all things; it is to forget that whatever befalls us, nothing can separate us from his love, nor deprive us of that most priceless of all treasures, the Lord's presence in our lives (Rom. 8:34–39; Heb. 13:5–6).

Next, Jude reiterates his point, which one might be pardoned for feeling he had already overemphasized, that their behaviour is governed not by God's will but their own desires; *they follow their own evil desires.* Self-discipline and altruism are at a discount; self is all that matters. Such a philosophy of life is not at all uncommon today. It is given intellectual respectability by Nietzsche, Sartre, Camus and many of the modern playwrights, and it has affected the man in the street more than he cares to recognize, with his 'I'm all right, Jack' attitude of blatant self-centredness. 'We have only to think what the world would be like if all men were like that, to see what complete chaos would ensue' (Barclay). Of course, in reality, these false teachers were pitiful creatures. Look at Jude's final thrust: *they boast about themselves, and flatter others for their own advantage.* They are at the same time bombastic, noisy, full of themselves, among those they hope to impress; and also prepared to curry favour with those they deem important, so as to get some advantage out of it! On this question of toadying, Mayor says well, 'As the fear of God drives out the fear of man, so defiance of God tends to put man in His place, as the chief source of good or evil to his fellows.' At the end of all the thunderbolts which Jude has unleashed upon these folk from the armoury of God, we find them at the mercy of their own fears of what men will do to them. They are indeed cut down to size. Hitler, the bully, was a coward at the last.

Commentators try to find parallels for the unusual *thaumazein prosōpa, flatter others,* in the *Assumption of Moses* v. 5 ('*mirantes personas locupletum et accipientes munera*') but the idea was common in Judaism (Gn. 19:21 LXX; Dt. 10:17, *etc.*) where favouritism was hated (Lv. 19:15; Pr. 24:23; Am. 5:12). It is intersting that both Jude and James (2:1ff.) should find it necessary to echo this traditional Jewish hatred of the practice of currying favour.

G. THE WORDS OF THE APOSTLES APPLY TO THEM (17–19)

17. Jude has applied the words of *1 Enoch* to the situation; now he reminds his readers of the words of the apostles. The false teachers (*houtoi,* 'these men', v. 16) forget, *but . . . you* (RSV) (*humeis de*) must remember. Forgetfulness of the teaching and warnings of God in Scripture is a major cause of spiritual deterioration.

There is, in fact, a close parallel between verses 17–19 and verses 5–16 which precede them. In each case there is an exhortation to remember; in each case Jude begins by addressing himself to the faithful in warning and ends by addressing the heretics in condemnation.

Remember! It is the first imperative that Jude has used, and it heads a whole cluster of them in this concluding section. On 'remember' see on verse 5 and 2 Peter 1:12–13; 3:1. Jude points out that there is nothing in the current apostasy which could not have been expected. The apostles had foretold it. The use of the word *proeirēmenōn, foretold,* does not mean that the apostles all belonged to a previous generation, whereas Jude thought of himself as living 'in the last time', *ep' eschatou tou chronou* (v. 18). It simply means that they foretold it before it came to pass. Indeed, the apostles said it *to you* – palpable evidence that we are dealing with historical contemporaries of the first apostles (v. 18). The apostles themselves were conscious of living 'in the last time';[1] the coming of Jesus into the world had ushered in the last chapter of the world's history, which would continue until the parousia made an end of all things. Appeal to apostolic teaching would be very right and proper in one, like Jude, who was not an apostle, and seems to have been a very modest man (see on v. 1). It is noteworthy that he does not say, like 2 Peter, 'your apostles', which could well include the writer, but *the apostles,* which could hardly do so. The whole sentiment is simpler in Jude than in 2 Peter; the latter's 'prophets' are dropped and his 'commands' become 'predictions'. For the bearing of this phrase on the question of authorship, see Introduction pp. 48ff., 54f. By *the apostles* Jude means those apostles who had brought the gospel to his recipients.

18. The imperfect tense of *They said to you* stresses the repeated nature of the apostolic warnings. Clearly, warnings like Acts 20:29–30; 2 Thessalonians 2:5; 1 Timothy 4:1–3; 2 Timothy 3:1ff. are meant, though whether Jude's readers had

---

[1]*Cf.* 2 Tim. 3:1–2; Heb. 1:2; 1 Jn. 2:18.

them in an oral form (as is suggested by *said*), or had them
written down, is not clear. The particular warning that follows,
substantially identical with 2 Peter 3:3, has not survived in any
independent form. Whether Peter borrowed from Jude, or Jude
from Peter, or both from a common source, cannot be determined with certainty, though the five verbal discrepancies
between this and 2 Peter 3:3 favour the last-mentioned hypothesis. It is certainly difficult, as Bigg shows,[1] to suppose that
Peter could possibly have taken this verse from Jude. The hypothesis of a common source, designed for general use against
false teachers, is supported by the different use the two writings
make of this quotation. Peter applies it to the mockers who were
making fun of the second coming. Jude gives no suggestion that
this was the butt of their ribaldry. It seems clear from the next
verse that they laughed at those who refused to go with them in
the path of their own lusts; men who still had scruples and
'old-fashioned' or 'puritanical' standards, unlike the superior,
spiritual Christians such as themselves, who were exploiting
their Christian freedom! The false teachers were claiming to be
so Spirit-filled that there was no room for law in their Christian
lives. They claimed that grace was so abundant that their sin (if
so it must be called) provided greater occasion for it (*cf.* v. 4).
They claimed that the salvation of the soul is what matters, and
that what a man does with his body is immaterial, for it is bound
to perish. Those who fussed about sexual purity seemed to them
astonishingly naïve.

The Greek word *empaiktai*, here translated *scoffers* is found
only here and in 2 Peter 3:3 in the whole New Testament, but
quite often in the LXX. Jude's emphasis on *ungodly* is remarkable
– the word is absent from the Petrine passage, and Jude had in
fact four times used the word in verse 15, once more than the
1 Enoch prophecy which he was quoting. It may be that he is
harking back to *1 Enoch* in this verse; it may be that this repeated
stress on *asebeia* (see on v. 4) shows the revulsion of a sensitive,
godly man to those who make pious pretensions but utterly
belie them in their behaviour. The word can either be taken as
an objective genitive after *epithumias*, 'desire for evil things', or

[1]Bigg, p. 338.

else as a descriptive genitive, *ungodly desires*, in which case it would be remarkably similar to the delayed genitive in James 2:1.

In the last times (lit. 'in the final age') is equivalent to 'in the last days' of 2 Timothy 3:1; James 5:3. In the Old Testament this phrase refers generally to God's future (Nu. 24:14; Jer. 23:20; Dan 10:14). In intertestamental – and Christian – sources it denotes the time of fulfilment of the Old Testament prophecies (1QSa 111, *Apoc. Bar.* 6.8, 78.5). 'Early Christian writers, with their sense of living in the time of fulfilment, can use it with reference to the coming of Christ in the past (Heb. 1:2; 1 Pet. 1:20) and to their own present (1 Jn. 2:18; *Barn.* 4:9; Ignatius, *Eph.* 11:1) as well as to the outstanding future (Jas. 5:3, 1 Pet. 1:5, *Did.* 16:2). The same writer can use it with reference both to the past and future (1 Pet. 1:5, 20). So writes Bauckham, in an illuminating note on the passage.

Just as Jude has quoted 1 *Enoch* to evoke the expectation that the false teachers will suffer God's judgment, so he cites the warnings given by apostles to the same effect. He may be quoting some written warning, used and adapted by 2 Peter, or he may simply be generalizing in his own words. The early missionaries, in founding churches, warned that in the final age there would be apostasy in the church from true religion and Christian morality. Jesus, in his eschatological discourse (Matthew 24; Mark 13) had done just that. Jude now sees this expectation being fulfilled by the false teachers.

19. For the third time (*cf.* v. 12, 16) Jude bursts out with a contemptuous *houtoi*, 'these fellows'. And as in verse 17 he contrasts it with 'but you, dear friends' so here he uses the same phrase in verse 20. For all its forthright denunciation there is a careful balance and interrelation between the different parts of this short Epistle, and a real depth of affection for the recipients.

What else can he have to say about the heretics? This verse reveals a lot. He uses a very rare word and calls them *the men who divide you*, or 'create divisions'. It may be used (as in Aristotle) to mean, 'the men that make distinctions' (*i.e.* invidious distinctions between themselves and the other people). The word, found only here in the Bible, denotes those superior

people who keep themselves to themselves – Christian Pharisees. Bigg suggests various ways in which this divisiveness
may have shown itself. They probably formed a clique of their
own at the Agape (v. 12). They certainly despised the simple
pastors set over the church (v. 8), and attached themselves to
the rich (v. 16). Now, on the whole, the rich would have been
the educated. 'It was out of this state of things that Gnosticism
arose. Gnosticism was the revolt of the well-to-do, half-
educated bourgeois class' (Bigg). It is probably with a prototype
of Gnosticism that we have to do here. These men were arrogant
because they had arrived, spiritually and intellectually. They
were the *élite*. That is why they kept themselves to themselves.

They were, indeed, very like the Pharisees, and Jude deals
with them much as Jesus had dealt with the Pharisees. The
derivation of the name Pharisee probably means 'separated',
and denotes the exclusive folk who divided themselves off. And
Jesus told them that they were indeed separated – from the God
they claimed to know! (Mk. 3:23–26, Gk.) Here Jude does the
same. They claim to be separated off. He agrees. They are!
Exclusiveness always hurts the exclusive man more than those
from whom he separates himself. It seems that they despised
the ordinary Christians, and called them *psuchikoi*, men governed by the natural life, not dominated by the Spirit. They,
themselves, claimed to be *pneumatikoi*, to have the fullness of the
Spirit, and not to be bound to the restrictions and inhibitions of
ordinary Christians.[1] They were spiritual aristocracy, immune
to the laws of conduct which bound the ordinary man. Very
well, Jude seems to say. You ask for distinctions to be made.
You shall have them. In fact it is *you* who are governed by the
natural life, the natural impulses. *You* are the *psuchikoi*! And so
far from being filled with the Spirit, it is clear that you have not
got the Spirit at all. You are apostate, or perhaps even counter-
feit Christians.[2]

[1] Paul uses this same distinction between unspiritual and spiritual men in 1 Cor. 2:14 ff. in
just as polemical a way as does Jude here. James also makes the distinction (3:15). It is
noteworthy that 2 Peter, like 1 Peter, does not use this language. To Peter, *psuchē* stands for
'person'.

[2] Irenaeus attacks men like this who regard themselves as alone 'spiritual' in the sense of
1 Cor. 2:14 and other church members as natural (*psuchikoi*) and incapable of knowing God
(*A.H.* i. 6. 2–4).

The mystery cults, which for a time constituted a serious rival to Christianity, used language like this. Reitzenstein[1] cites a prayer of the Mithras cult in which 'natural human (*psuchikē*) ability' is contrasted with the 'holy spirit' conferred in the mystery. It is not impossible that the false teachers borrowed their invidious distinctions (and the language to go with them) from the mystery cults. They are then adroitly hoist with their own petard by Jude, who exploits the same language for orthodox ends.

H. JUDE'S EXHORTATION TO THE FAITHFUL (20–23)

20. Jude has had his say about the ungodly, and now turns to more positive teaching. For the second time he calls them *dear friends* (*cf.* v. 17), and on each occasion it is in contrast to the false teachers. And now he launches out on some highly compressed Christian instruction, which, if followed, would preserve his readers from contamination by the false teachers. This is, in fact, the main purpose of his letter: to equip his readers for Christian living in a context of false teaching.

Four injunctions follow, all in the participial form. They refer to faith, hope, love and prayer. In all probability the use of the participle is a Hebrew or Aramaic idiom and has an imperatival sense, as in catechetical sections of Romans and 1 Peter. See E. G. Selwyn's great *Commentary on 1 Peter*, (1946) pp. 467ff. This suggests that we have to do with an early code of Christian conduct, reflecting the usage of rabbinic Hebrew, and therefore likely to go back to the earliest days of the church. There is another formula in these verses, a trinitarian one (20–21).

Their *most holy faith* is the Christian revelation, handed down by the apostles (as in v. 3). In this they are to build themselves up. From other New Testament references it is clear that this required study of the apostolic teaching (*cf.* Acts 2:42; 20:32).[2] The Christian must study the Scriptures if he is to grow in the faith and be of any use to others (2 Tim. 2:15; Heb. 5:12). The

---

[1] *Die Hellenistischen Mysterienreligionen*, 1910, p.109.

[2] Polycarp wrote to the Philippians, 'If you study the Epistles of the blessed apostle Paul you can be built up in the faith given to you' (*Ep.* iii).

faith is *most holy*, because it is 'utterly different', entirely set apart from all others. It is unique in the message it teaches and in the moral transformation it produces.

Secondly, they must *pray in the Holy Spirit*. For the battle against false teaching is not won by argument. See 2 Corinthians 10:3–5 for the most apt commentary on this phrase. It is likely that the false teachers had given up prayer. Many 'advanced' Christians have done so today, on their own admission. But to outrun the apostolic scriptures and prayer is to outrun Christianity altogether.

By 'prayer in the Holy Spirit' it is sometimes suggested that prayer in 'tongues' is indicated. If so, it is hinted at very obscurely. The man who has the Spirit of God within him (that is to say, every Christian, Rom 8:9), the man who is led by the Holy Spirit in his prayers as in all else (Gal. 5:18), will certainly pray in the Spirit. It is he who utters within us the distinctive Christian address to God as 'Abba' or 'Father' (Rom. 8:15). Prayer in the Spirit may well include, but is not confined to, prayer in tongues.

21. Thirdly, they must remain within the sphere of God's love. It was his love which first drew them to himself (v. 1), but, as the false teachers have shown, it is possible to turn one's back on the love of God. They must cultivate that love relationship with him. It is interesting that in verse 1 he addresses them as men who have been found by the love of God, and in the next verse he prays that divine love, along with God's mercy and peace, may fill them; but here he urges them to fulfil their side of the covenant of love with God. The emphasis is here placed upon their contribution to that relationship, whether or not *God's love* means 'God's love for them' or 'their love for God'. The language recalls Jesus' words, 'I have loved you; abide in my love' (Jn. 15:9, RSV). And Jude would certainly have echoed Jesus' next words, 'If you keep my commandments, you will abide in my love' (Jn. 15:10, RSV). It was by flagrant disobedience that the false teachers had fallen out of love with him, and thus, inevitably, with men as well.

Fourthly, they must keep alive the fire of Christian hope. If too great attention is paid to the future hope, the Christian tends to become so other-worldly that he is not much use in this world. If, however, as is the greater danger today, the future element is soft-pedalled, Christianity becomes a mere religious adjunct to the social services. True Christianity is 'world-affirming' in the sense that it rejoices in God's world as made by him, redeemed by him, to be enjoyed with him. But Christianity is 'world-denying' in the sense that living as though this world were all there is is utter delusion. In these two verses Jude gathers up the three Christian virtues of faith (including prayer), hope and love – a balanced pattern for Christian living. Today the Christian hope is often forgotten and the content of Christian belief is widely doubted. Separated thus both from history and from eschatology, Christianity is presented to us in terms of love. But this love, on inspection, turns out to be the description of an attitude not, as one might have thought, towards God, but towards men. It degenerates easily into mawkish sentimentality or energetic do-goodism and is far removed from what the early Christians meant by *agapē*, 'love'.

Note the need for the *mercy* of God, not only initially but daily; not only daily but at the last (*cf.* 2 Tim. 1:18). It is of God's mercy that we are not consumed. It is of his mercy that we are given *eternal life*. Even 'man come of age' cannot afford to do without the mercy of God. It is interesting that it is the *mercy of our Lord Jesus Christ* to which Jude particularly refers – an allusion to the atonement he wrought upon the cross. Mercy is possible for sinful man only because of what he there achieved. By *eternal life* Jude means the unrealized part of that 'life of the (new) age' which has already begun in believers. It means the resurrection life of the age to come, given to believers at the return of Jesus Christ.

22–23. Salvation is not merely to be defined in the terms already given: faith, prayer, love, and hope. It involves service, and to this Jude now turns (as does 2 Pet. 3:11–15). Men are indeed saved to serve, and one of the best ways of discovering the true value of any new theology is to test it in active Christian evangelism and pastoral care.

Unfortunately, although the general drift of these verses is clear, the text has been preserved in different forms, and it is no longer possible to be certain which is the original. The possibilities are complicated, but are roughly as follows.

The main division lies between the majority of MSS, which read three clauses, and the excellent uncial, B, which omits the words *hous de*, 'and some' at the beginning of verse 23 and thus reduces Jude's injunction to two clauses. The NEB accepts this latter reading and renders 'There are some doubting souls who need your pity; snatch them from the flames and save them'. There are, on this view, 'two groups of people in question, both of which are to be treated with pity, though in the second instance pity is to be "mixed with fear".'[1] Among the MSS supporting the shorter reading is papyrus 72 which may provide the original reading, according to Dr J. N. Birdsall.[2] He thinks that the two senses in which *diakrinomai* could be taken (*i.e.* 'to be judged' or 'to doubt': there is a third possibility 'those who dispute') account for the origin of the three clause version of the text. This is possible, but not only flies in the face of the majority of MSS attestation but forgets the strong liking Jude has for triads. Accordingly, I think it most probable that the RV, RSV and NIV are right in sticking to three clauses, not two.

But we are still far from being out of the wood. There is a good deal of variety among the MSS which do retain the three clauses. There are three main variants for the first clause, *eleate diakrinomenous* ('show pity on the waverers'), *eleate diakrinomenoi* ('show pity with discernment') and *elenchete diakrinomenous* ('confute the waverers'). Of these the second is the worst attested, and looks like a correction to parallel the nominatives *harpazontes* ('pulling') and *misountes* ('hating') in the subsequent clause. The first, though well attested, looks suspicious in view of the *eleate*[3] below. The third gives excellent sense and has wide attestation, 'Argue some out of their error while they are still in two minds.' *Elenchō* means to overcome error by truth. When men are beginning to waver (as Jude's readers were under the blandishments of the false teachers) that is the time for a well-

---

[1] *The Greek New Testament, being the text translated in the New English Bible*, ed. R. V. G. Tasker, 1964, p.443.

[2] *JTS*, October 1963, pp.396–399. This MS reads *hous men ek puros harpasate diakrinomenous de eleeite en phobō*, which could mean either 'save some from the fire, and have pity on others who are judged in fear' or 'save some from the fire, and have pity on other doubting souls in fear'. See also C. D. Osburn 'The Text of Jude 22–23' in *ZNW* 63 (1972), p. 139–44.

[3] Unless the view is taken that only two clauses are original. In that case the repeated *eleate* (or *eleeite* – a mere matter of morphology) is clearly right.

taught Christian to come alongside them and help. A man who is flirting with false teaching is not to be 'sent to Coventry' by his Christian friends; they must have him in to coffee and chat it over with him in love. And they must know the faith so well that they can convince him while he is still hesitating. A loving approach, a sense of the right occasion and a carefully-thought-out Christian position – these are the qualities required by this first clause.

The second group are those who need to be saved from the fire. They need a direct frontal approach. They are on the wrong path and need to be told as much, and then rescued. God gives to his servants the privilege of co-operating with him in his saving work (*cf.* Jas. 5:20). Calvin presents this bouquet to the 'fire and brimstone' evangelist: 'When there is a danger of fire, we hesitate not to snatch away violently whom we desire to save; for it would not be enough to beckon with the finger, or kindly to stretch forth the hand.' Some MSS add, in various positions, *with fear*. This is an important point, even if it was not in the original text. Such rescue work can never be done in any spirit of sanctimoniousness or superiority. It must be done in fear, in recognition that 'there, but for the grace of God, go I'. Christian workers must have a sense of awe before the God who deigns to use us as his ambassadors. The phrase *snatch others from the fire* reminds us of the brand plucked from the burning in Zechariah 3:2, where Joshua is given this remarkable title. Incidentally, this phrase in Zechariah immediately follows 'the Lord rebuke you', cited in Jude 9. But Jude may also have in mind Amos 4:11, "I overthrew some of you as I overthrew Sodom and Gomorrah. You were like a burning stick snatched from the fire, yet you have not returned to me," declares the Lord.' This verse was in Jude's mind in verse 7, and may indicate that he meant by the plucking from the burning their conversion to Christianity; but despite this rescue when they became Christians, they, like Amos's Israelites, did not return to the Lord, but apostasized. More probably by the 'fire' he means either the passion of sensual indulgence to which the false teachers had given way (so Clement of Alexandria) or the fire of judgment to which they will be liable if they are not brought to a better mind.[1] This group differs

[1] Thus Chaine takes the 'fire' as judgment (*cf.* Mt. 13:42, 50) and understands *diakrinomenous* to mean 'while hesitating'. The waverers must be rescued from the fire to which they are heading along with the false teachers.

from the first in that they no longer hesitate; they have given way to the false teachers.

The case with the third group, assuming we are right in reading three clauses, is more subtle. Jude's readers are invited to *show mercy, mixed with fear*, (reading *eleate* with the vast majority of good MSS) *hating even the clothing stained by corrupted flesh*. That is to say, they are to have pity upon even the most abandoned heretic, but to exercise great care while getting alongside him lest they themselves become defiled. They are to retain their hatred of sin even as they love the sinner. 2 Corinthians 7:1 provides something of a parallel. The *fear* may be fear of being influenced by these heretics: more probably it is fear of God, knowing that he will judge.

What does he mean by *the clothing stained by corrupted flesh? Chitōn* means the inner garment, worn next to the skin. The idea seems to be that they are so corrupt that their very clothes are defiled. This is, of course, a hyperbole, but one with plenty of scriptural background; indeed instructions are given in Leviticus 13:47–52 that the garment worn by a leper should be burnt because it is unclean. Isaiah 64:6 says, 'All of us have become like one who is unclean, and all our righteous acts are like filthy rags', while Jude's favourite passage in Zechariah continues, 'Now Joshua was dressed in filthy clothes as he stood before the angel. The angel said to those who were standing before him, "Take off his filthy clothes." Then he said to Joshua, "See, I have taken away your sin, and I will put rich garments on you" ' (Zc. 3:3f.). The Christian worker has the wonderful offer of a change of raiment for the defiled, a robe of righteousness for the man clothed in filthy rags (*cf.* Is. 61:10), and he must proffer it in love and mercy. But once he begins to revel in the filthy garment, once he tolerates it and toys with it, he ceases to be a useful servant of Christ at all. Once he treats sin as normal and commonplace, he is on the way to betraying the gospel. For Jude insists, as strongly as John in the Apocalypse, that the man accepted before God is he who has not soiled his garments (Rev. 3:4); and these garments are looked upon both as the standing which God confers on the penitent sinners who 'have washed their robes, and made them white in the blood of the Lamb' (7:14), and also as that rightness of character which follows in the lives of those who have truly been justified (19:8).

Jude uses *sarx, the flesh*, in precisely the same way as Paul: it means human nature made by God and for God, but which has fallen grievously out of harmony with God, and become an active agency of evil. This principle of evil must be resolutely opposed and rejected, just as, in baptism, the candidate disrobed entirely in order to receive a new garment when he emerged from the water to the new life. Compromise with evil will inevitably lead to defeat.

I. DOXOLOGY (24–25)

24. It is a dangerous thing to live for Christ in an atmosphere of false teaching and seductive morals. It is a hazardous thing to try to rescue men for the gospel out of such an environment. If you get too near the fire, it will burn you; if you get too near the garment stained by the flesh, it will defile you. Is withdrawal the answer, then? No. Advance against the forces of evil, face the dangers involved, so long as you are strong in the Lord's might. Such is the thrust, and the context, of Jude's final verses.

This thrilling doxology reminds us of the power of God. Twice Paul had been driven to his knees in praise as he considered the might of his Lord. In Romans 16:25 he ascribes glory 'to him who is able to establish you by my gospel'. In Ephesians 3:20 he glories in the one who 'is able to do immeasurably more than all we ask or imagine, according to his power (the Holy Spirit) that is at work within us'. Here, too, Jude ends his letter with heartfelt adoration to the one who *is able to keep you* (not 'them', as in some MSS) *from falling*. True, he has told them they must keep themselves in the love of God (v. 21), but he uses a different word for 'keep' here. There *tēreō* is used; it means 'watch'. Here *phulassō* is used; it means 'guard'. There is a difference. We must watch that we stay close to the Lord, but only he can guard us so that we do not stumble. *Aptaistous, from falling*, does not occur elsewhere in the New Testament. It is used by Xenophon of a horse which is surefooted and does not stumble, by Plutarch of the steady falling of the snow, and by

Epictetus of a good man who does not make moral lapses. In the midst of difficult company, turbulent thinking and the questioning of moral standards, it is only the Lord who can preserve us.

But God can do even more than that. He will set us up, or make us to stand before his *glorious presence* in heaven. And we shall exult, because no fault will be found in us. The Christian is in Christ, and therefore *amōmos, faultless* or 'without blame'; he is incorporated into the Blameless One (*cf.* 1 Pet. 1:19). *Amōmos*[1] is a sacrificial word; only the spotless was fit for God. What a profound conception of heaven! What an amazing thing that in Christ we can be *amōmoi*, and constitute an utterly acceptable offering to the Lord! God is able to make us stand, though in ourselves we should shrink from his presence. God sets us before him (*katenōpion, his glorious presence,* is a strong word), and what deeper conception of bliss could there be than for the redeemed to be face to face with their God? God has no charge to prefer against those who are accepted in his spotless Son; and if God be for us, who can be against us?[2] This is indeed great cause for *agalliasis, great joy,* a word particularly used of exultation at the heavenly banquet, and its foretaste in the Eucharist. It is essentially a word that belongs to heaven.

This doxology is truly magnificent in its conception and scope. It probably owes something to traditional liturgical material which was circulating even as early as the fifties of the first century: see the close parallels in Ephesians 1:4; 5:27; Colossians 1:22; 1 Thessalonians 3:13. But the picture sketched is Jude's own. It sees the faithful Christians among his readers, after all the pressures of contending for the faith in a licentious age and permissive church, standing before God like perfect sacrifices in his heavenly sanctuary, in self-offering to the glory of God amidst the joyous jubilation of the redeemed.

25. To *God* alone be the glory! This is the final note of Jude's Epistle. There is but one God ('wise', AV, is an interpolation

---

[1]See 2 Pet. 2:14 and the note there, and 1 Cor. 1:7–8 for the same idea. Indeed, some MSS noting the parallel with 2 Peter have imported *aspilous kai,* 'spotless and' into the text here before *amōmous* from 2 Pet. 2:14.

[2]Rom 8:31.

from Rom. 16:27) and he is a *Saviour*. In the Old Testament it is emphasized that God is the Saviour of his people; there is none else (Is. 45:15). The Christian doctrine of salvation goes hand in hand with the unity of God. The one, personal, holy, loving God made the world, maintains it (*sōzō*, to 'save', is often used in this sense), redeemed it through Jesus Christ, and will be glorified in it. Far from setting the supreme God against the Demiurge (as some Gnostic systems were soon to do), this verse insists that there is only one God. Far from setting the attitude of the Father against the Son in redemption (as some Christians have done in their atonement doctrine), this verse gives glory to the one Saviour God through Jesus Christ. For God as *Saviour*, see 1 Timothy 1:1; 2:3; Titus 1:3; 2:10; 3:4, *etc*. Perhaps the closest analogy to this verse, urging the unity and saving activity of God, is 1 Timothy 2:5–6. Christ is sixteen times called Saviour in the New Testament, compared with eight times for the Father. In the Old Testament God delivers his people Israel if and when they call upon him. In the New Testament he delivers those who have no claim on him whatever, Gentiles on the road to perdition.

Through Jesus Christ our Lord (a phrase wrongly omitted by the AV) may refer either to the fact that it is through Christ that God saves man, or to the fact that glory can only properly be given to God through Jesus (*cf.* 1 Pet. 4:11). The former is preferable, for although there is a sense in which Jesus was 'the Lamb that was slain from the creation of the world' (Rev. 13:8), there seems to be no ground for saying that glory was given to God only through Christ *before all ages, pro pantos tou aiōnos*, another phrase which the AV curiously omits. His meaning is, surely, that the ascription of *glory, majesty, power and authority* belongs to God: it is a statement of fact, not a prayer (as in AV, RSV, NEB)[1] that these things may be ascribed to the Almighty. They do belong to him through the eternal achievement of the incarnate Jesus. They always have done. They do now. They always will – hence the certainty of the final 'Amen'.

Amen regularly closes doxologies (*cf.* Rom. 1:25; 9:5; 1 Pet.

---

[1] To make this into a prayer makes nonsense of 'before all time', and spoils the whole confident climax of the Epistle.

4:11), and sets a seal on this confident attribution of glory to the One to whom it belongs – the God who is able!

Of the four words here used to denote God's greatness, *doxa* means splendour, *glory*, like the radiance of light; *megalōsunē* denotes kingly *majesty*. It comes in the doxology in 1 Chronicles 29:11, and is twice used (in both cases of God) in the New Testament outside this passage (Heb. 1:3; 8:1). *Kratos, power,* suggests the control which God has over the world; it is his world, and reposes in his mighty hands; while *exousia, authority,* expresses his total sovereignty. God's eternal radiance was crystallized in Jesus Christ (Jn. 1:14; Heb. 1:3); so was his majesty, the kingly greatness which suffers without complaint; so was his control, in the Lordship of Jesus; so was his authority over men, nature and the demonic. Such is our God, such are his eternal qualities, unveiled in Christ. To him we must come one day, and must render our account. He himself will bring us thither if we let him, and will present us faultless before his presence. To him belongs the glory, and the majesty, and the power, and the authority for ever! *Amen.*